CANARY

By Tony Cohan

CANARY
NINE SHIPS
OUTLAW VISIONS (ed.)

CANARY

TONY COHAN

DOUBLEDAY & COMPANY, INC.   1981
Garden City, New York

Permission to quote from the following sources is gratefully acknowledged:

"T.B. Sheets." Words and music by John Lee Hooker, © copyright 1972 by Duchess Music Corporation, New York, N.Y. Used by permission. All Rights Reserved.

"Fool Killer." Words and music by Mose Allison, © copyright 1961 by Audre Mae Music. Used by permission. All Rights Reserved.

"Mannish Boy." Words and music by McKinley Morganfield, Mel London, and Ellas McDaniel, © copyright 1955, 1978 by Arc Music Corp., New York. Used by permission.

"Rock It Baby." Words and music by Bob Marley, © copyright 1975 by Cayman Music Inc., New York, N.Y. Used by permission. All Rights Reserved.

Library of Congress Catalog Card Number: 80-2045
ISBN: 0-385-170866
Copyright © 1981 by Tony Cohan

For Masako

The man that hath no music in himself,
Nor is not mov'd with concord of sweet sounds,
Is fit for treasons, stratagems, and spoils

WM. SHAKESPEARE,
playwright

My needle has got rusty
It will not play at all

ROBT. JOHNSON,
Delta blues singer

CANARY

Dead Wagon

Every day
I see
The Dead Wagon

JOHN LEE HOOKER

Part 1

1

Abdel Idriss Mohammed, a Moroccan, sat alone at a table on the porch of the Café de France on an early June evening, overlooking the Djmaa el Fnaa, the great square of Marrakesh. His hand gripped a steaming glass of mint tea as he watched dusk transform the milling, hooded crowd into wraiths, and mute the chattering hubbub into a whisper. His tongue still tasted of jet fumes from the airport as he lit another Gauloise, gazed into the darkening scene, and thought again about what had happened that day, the woman who had come, and the incident of the canary . . .

Dawn had broken hard. Up from the east she came, splitting the high, snow-peaked Atlas and rolling across the red plain like a desert horde. She lit the tip of the ancient Koutoubia mosque; and as the tower burned downward, the *muezzin's* dry cry spread across the quarter, and the first light stole in like an assassin.

Abdel opened his eyes. The call to prayer wound through the open doors of the balcony into the green, spacious room. He gazed at a large armoire against a wall opposite the bed. Next to it was a writing desk, above that a mirror. Abdel could see part of his face in reflection—dark, lean, sculpted, sleepy. In the corner was a suitcase and a guitar that belonged to the woman next to him.

He turned and looked through the open doors that led to the balcony. A pair of tiny, sunlit sparrows chirped on the wooden railing. He could see the tips of the orange trees, and beyond them the rich, orderly olive groves that bordered the hotel garden. And in the distance, the snowy Atlas where he had been born thirty-two years ago.

His eyes returned to the room, and fixed upon a flower ornament carved into the green door of the armoire. It was a motif he had seen repeated throughout the hotel, detailed in Chinese red and bordered by gold filigree. It was not unlike the folds of the woman's parts, he thought: concentrically wrought, sensual.

The sheet had fallen off her during the night. She was tall, like him, with long narrow legs, pale like sand. Tangled yellow hair spread across the pillow. Her lips dreamed; her breasts trembled. He thought how frail she looked, empty of the force that flowed through her waking eyes. That body: he had known it once a long time ago, and he had never forgotten.

Abdel reached over and touched her shoulder. He ran his hand to her neck, and down across her breasts. She stirred; the birds on the porch chirped; the muezzin fell silent. Her hand reached up and touched his cheek. Her mouth was like the desert sun, hot and dry. His loins swelled, and her legs cradled him and drew him in.

Outside, the garden opened its dripping branches to the

sky. Fountains gurgled, and flocks of tiny birds dropped to the trees.

Afterwards, they rose silently and slipped on gray hooded summer caftans. A waiter came with breakfast on a tray, placed it on a table on the balcony, and left.

"Why did you come?" he asked her, after she had poured coffee.

"To rest," she said. "To renew." Then she shrugged helplessly, and smiled. "To find you."

Abdel looked down at the garden. At the far end rose a wall, separating the hotel grounds from the scrambled, unruly quarter, and the great square.

"In Paris you sang in the streets," he said. "Now look at you."

"And you, the serious student. Did you graduate?"

"Yes." The *medina* wheezed and bayed in the distance, like a broken concertina. "I came back," he said, as if to explain. "I never felt at home in Europe. I belong here." He said it with a certain melancholy.

"And now," she said, "you are becoming the grand poet of the Maghreb."

"Who knows?" he replied quietly.

Just beyond the walls, a sleeping beggar, huddled against a mud wall, stirred inside the folds of his wretched robes. Only his hand stuck out, frozen, even in sleep, in the supplicant's eternal gesture.

"The mustache becomes you," she said. She had lit a cigarette and was gazing at him. He felt the heat of her curious, intelligent blue eyes, eyes that seemed to swallow everything they fell upon.

"Your work, your life," she said. "It's good." She fed a piece of croissant to a starling with long, pale fingers.

"You are romantic."

"Why do you say that?"

"Perhaps I wish a little more of what you have."

Tears welled in her eyes, and she laughed.

"What is it?"

"Being with you is like it was in Paris," she said.

Overhead, the sky was hard and blue, like a lacquer. A distant throbbing, a thunder, rose from beyond the walls. She turned toward it.

"The trance drummers," Abdel said. "They play all day in the square."

"We must see them," she said intently.

"Then we should go before it gets too hot."

She stood up and went inside.

Abdel watched her from the porch as she took off her caftan, put on jeans and a silk shirt, brushed her hair before a mirror. He was full of admiration for her, this strong, intelligent artist woman with the consuming eyes, Lisa Wilde, and he felt again the austere power that had haunted the years with her memory. Now she had arrived suddenly, as if in a dream. Or perhaps, the thought flickered, it was the interruption of a dream. Something was pushing hard against her, something she found difficult to throw off. It was almost as if he could hear a clock ticking.

He quelled his feelings and stood up.

Inside the room Lisa Wilde reached up to him, and her lips were soft and dry, like the padded feet of a puppy. Then she drew away.

"In America," he said. "You have a lover? A husband?"

"No."

"But you are famous. You should be able to have anyone you want."

"Then it is you," she said, "who are romantic." And there was a hardness in her voice that had not been there before.

The long, carpeted hallway blurred their eyes, and in the tiled stairs to the lobby their reflections rippled. He saw her breath gather as she gazed at the painted tiles and carved inlay that ran through the vaulted interiors of this vast, exhausted monument to colonial splendor.

Near the entrance a desk clerk called to her in English

that sounded more like French. Urgent calls from Los Angeles, he said, brandishing pieces of paper. Abdel felt her tighten. She smiled at the clerk, shook her head and walked on. "Come," she said to Abdel, and her laughter, as they passed outside, was without joy.

The wide, palm-lined boulevard was warm and still. A wizened, robed guide with a prophet's face moved to accost them, then drew away. They turned and began walking south, toward the drums.

"In Paris," he said, "we used to call you 'la grive.' The thrush."

The wide boulevard narrowed to a winding street, and then the street became a dusty alley, crowded with men in *djellabas* coursing toward the square. Lisa Wilde held Abdel's arm and allowed him to guide her through the press of swirling bodies that latticed the light pouring into their eyes. Red dust rose around their feet. The earth smelled of dogs and urine.

Then suddenly they burst into the square: Djmaa el Fnaa, great hub of the northwest Sahara—a pulsing sea of people, animals, vehicles, stretching as far as they could see in every direction. The smell of food, *kif* and incense, thick and sweet, threaded the air.

"What does it mean, 'Djmaa el Fnaa'?" she shouted.

"The Assembly of the Dead." Lisa Wilde looked at him, her eyes wide. "They used to have public executions here every day."

Turbaned porters bore food, skins, baskets of coins toward the *souks*. Leering merchants proffered leather, fezes, pipes, sandals. A cobra danced on a carpet to a reed pipe, sour and imploring. A circle of men gazed at a toothless mendicant, turban wrapped madly around his sun-furrowed head, reciting the Koran from memory. And Lisa Wilde gazed at it all, enraptured.

They saw a man thrust a pair of pliers into the mouth of another and, with a single jerk, extract a tooth. Blood

spurted from the man's lips and down his chin. He rolled his
eyes and grinned happily at them as they passed, and the
dentist flung the tooth into the dust. Lisa Wilde's eyes
brimmed with wonder. "The trance drummers," she whispered. And Abdel steered her toward the source of the
thunder that wobbled the air.

At the center of a large circle, a dozen men in loose white
robes of cotton flailed large drums, hung about their necks,
with curved wooden sticks. Faces black and gleaming, eyes
red-rimmed with kif, they danced a hopping dance, bare
feet pounding the dust into a cloud. A rumbling, recurrent
trance rhythm rose in an endless crescendo that rolled across
the city, swallowing the sky itself, a sound that left nothing
outside it.

As they edged toward the front of the circle, Lisa Wilde
became rapturous, her eyes shining, transported by the
magic of the trance. And for the first time, Abdel began to
feel a peculiar, welling sense of danger, which he could not
explain, and whose source was hidden from him.

An old grizzled man, dressed like the others, sat crosslegged in the dust to one side of the circle, brewing mint tea
in a tiny brazier and filling the kif pipes. The ancient looked
up, his eyes red and warm, and saw her. He smiled and
reached back into his bag. From somewhere in its depths he
extracted a crinkled, shiny date and handed it to a small
black boy, who brought it to her. Lisa Wilde ate it, smiling
her thanks. And when the boy ran around the circle with a
knitted cap outstretched, she gave him too many coins.
"They play for the gods," she said breathlessly.

The sun poured down on them, unremitting, a kiln, whit-
ing vision and furring their mouths. Abdel leaned close to
her ear. "Let us go to the souks," he said, "where it is cool."

Then, as he led her away from the circle, a hawker, holding three live chickens by the neck, waved them in their
faces.

When he turned to speak to her, she was gone.

He pushed through a crowd of gawking country berbers in robes and slippers, eyes entranced and distant. He scanned the dense mosaic of the square, seeking her among the throng.

He found her, a short distance away, gazing intently into a small circle of men. "Look," she said, with absorption, pointing.

A canary sat in a wooden cage in the dust, its feathers soiled and ruffled. A piece of its beak was chipped away. A thin, ragged man in a loincloth and knitted cap stood before the cage with a stick in one hand, the other hand closed into a fist. He held his fist up to the cage, and the canary pecked at it.

Then the bird lifted its head, and sang, beautifully.

"What is he feeding it?" she asked.

"I little seed of kif."

Extending from the mouth of the cage was a small incline, a ramp, fashioned of sticks. At its end, several feet away, was a pole made of a branch, with a looped string hanging from it. Affixed to the bottom of the string was a tiny Moroccan flag made of paper.

The bird's keeper grinned, and reached down and opened the door of the cage. Abdel felt an agitation take hold of Lisa Wilde.

The canary jumped gingerly onto the little walkway and hesitated. The man gave it a prod with his stick, and the bird began to hop across the ramp. When it had reached the end, the keeper held his fist to the bird's beak, and the bird took another peck. It raised its head and sang again, sweetly.

He felt her hand tighten around his arm.

"What is it?" he said.

"Don't you see?" Lisa Wilde said, shaking her head. "The master, how sympathetic he is. He speaks to the bird so softly, like a friend, feeding it kif, letting it in and out of the cage to perform. But the price he extracts for his confidence . . ."

The canary, at its master's coaxing, took the little string in its beak and, in a series of short motions, raised the tiny flag to the top of the pole. When it was aloft, the circle of men shouted and cheered. The keeper turned away from the bird, flashed a yellow smile, and bowed. Then he held his fist again to the canary's beak.

Abdel looked at Lisa Wilde. Her face had become a mask of grief.

The keeper cajoled the canary back across the wooden walkway toward its cage, talking soothingly, nursing it with the stick, offering the promise of the seeds in his fist. When the bird reached the entrance to the cage, it stopped and looked around.

"Abdel," Lisa Wilde whispered. *"Why doesn't it fly away?"*

The force of her question surprised him. "Perhaps," he answered, "it has lost all memory of freedom."

"And if it did remember? If one day it flew away?"

"I suppose then," he said, carefully, "the keeper would simply get another bird."

Lisa Wilde smiled bitterly at his answer. Words, Abdel thought. How can something which barely makes a breeze on the hand have so much power?

The bird's keeper tossed two kif seeds inside the cage. The canary stared at them, hesitant, unmoving. The keeper spoke softly, clucking, gesturing, inviting the soiled bird back into the safety of the cage. Abdel felt Lisa Wilde's fingers tearing into his arm.

The bird raised its head suddenly and sang a final time. Then it hopped back inside the cage. The keeper closed the door, bolted it with a wooden dowel, and whipped off his hat triumphantly.

Abdel felt her hand go limp and fall away. He put his hand on her back; it was rigid, cold. When the man came by

with his hat Abdel reached into his pocket for a coin. But
she grabbed his wrist and held. "No," she whispered. The
keeper rolled the whites of his eyes at her and passed on.
Abdel saw that small tears had rivered clots of dust on her
cheeks.

Suddenly a woman was pulling insistently at their sleeves.
Tattoos of blue divided her face, from her forehead to her
chin, and one milky eye stared heavenward. Lisa Wilde
looked at Abdel.

"She is of the Blue People. From Goulimine, by the desert. Ignore her. She is crazy."

"But she wants something," she said feverishly.

"She wants to tell your fortune."

"Then ask her," Lisa Wilde said, "why the canary doesn't
fly away."

Abdel addressed the Blue Woman quickly, in the glottal
clicks of the desert. She answered, her voice rising in a
screech. Abdel offered her a coin, but she refused it. Instead,
she removed a chain from her neck and pressed it into Lisa
Wilde's palm.

Then she was gone.

Lisa Wilde looked down at the chain. Hanging from it
was a small charm, a silver hand of Fatima.

"What did she say?"

"Nonsense. She is mad."

But her blue eyes bore in upon him, left him no escape;
once again, he was caught in the words.

"She said you are the canary. You must eat from the
master's hand, or you will die."

Abdel watched helplessly as she broke away, running
across the square.

He took off after her, stumbling into a startled crowd of
hooded pilgrims. A cart of chick-peas tumbled, and he
leaped their wake. He followed a trail of curses across the
square, losing her, then finding her again. His heart
pounded, his mouth clogged with dust. He stumbled into

the flanks of a donkey, then jumped away, catching the glancing kick on his shoulder. The spinning earth flew up and smashed his face. He scrambled to his feet and ran on.

And as he hunted her, time slowed to the speed of a dreaming stone; the Djmaa el Fnaa was a shifting, endless desert, coming apart at his feet.

At the end of the square he found her, huddled against a mud wall. Her face was streaked with red earth and the dried salt of tears. Her hair hung limply over her face. She clutched in her fist the hand of Fatima the Blue Woman had given her.

Abdel reached for her, but she gently stayed his hand. She looked at him strangely and smiled.

"The Arab," she said, "does not fear death."

"Why do you speak of it?"

But she simply shook her head.

She reached out and touched his cheek tenderly. Her eyes, which had been fearful, were now resolute, and gazed at something far distant, something Abdel could not see.

"I am sorry," she said. "I cannot stay here. I must go back."

And Abdel knew suddenly that he didn't understand her at all, this woman he had loved, Lisa Wilde, *la grive*. It was not like Paris, and never would be again.

He took the chain with the silver hand of Fatima from her fist and slipped it over her head. Then he led her down a cool, shaded path into the souks. And as they wandered there, the alleys of the quarter suddenly swollen with menace, Abdel no longer envied Lisa Wilde her fate or her fame.

Abdel's hand still clutched the glass of mint tea, though it was cold now. The Gauloise burned his knuckles. In the Djmaa el Fnaa the lanterns were lit against the black night. The hot, peppery smell of *tajin* stew drifted from the stalls.

Abdel took out his notebook. He wrote: *"The dream of*

innocence is the last dream of all. When it is gone, there is only darkness and night."

He rose, paid for his tea, and headed slowly across the dark square toward his home in the quarter.

2

On the sidewalk in front of The Maiden, a small, private Kensington hotel, a uniformed doorman grabbed a suitcase deposited by a cabbie, and cheerfully led its owner through the entrance's glass doors, trailing a delicious draught of unseasonably warm London summer air into the hotel's musty lobby.

As the new guest stepped to the desk, an elevator door opened at the far end of the lobby. An aged man in a worn uniform much like the doorman's pulled back the grating with frayed white gloves, and stepped aside to allow the elevator's three occupants to pass.

The first to emerge was an elderly, perfumed dowager clutching a mail purse in one gloved hand and a pink hankie in the other. She directed her ample body diagonally across the worn Persian carpet toward the small tearoom adjoining the lobby. Next out was a young Latin man with narrow, predatory eyes and a slight hunch. An inexpensive blue suit, crushed in the back as though it had been slept in, hung from his shoulders. His shoes were spitpolished. He looked nervous and hunted, as though he suspected he was being followed, when in fact it was he who was following the matron to the tearoom.

The third man out of the elevator also wore a blue suit. His, however, was well pressed and had cost considerably more when it was new. It was from Brooks Brothers, in the conservative style favored by American men some time ago. A striped tie fronted a pale-blue cotton shirt with collar buttons. His shoes were brown, polished and rounded at the toes. Small cuffs sat upon them. Hanging from one arm was a brown attaché case; draped over the other was a light tan topcoat and an umbrella, neither of which he would need on this sunny morning.

And beneath the jacket of his suit, there was the slight bulge of a shoulder holster and the small handgun it contained. He walked quickly across the lobby and arrived at the desk.

"Lovely morning, sir," the desk clerk said. "Will you be checking out?"

"Yes." And his tone was very pleasant.

As the desk clerk moved off to total the bill, the man turned and gazed across the lobby. An angular shaft of morning light, dancing with beads of dust, fell on his face, throwing it into relief. It was slightly pink, with a boyish smoothness that still did little to disguise his fifty-odd years. The impression of age came from something else not so easy to discern.

The eyes were gray and dull. They sat in a solid, aggressive body of good height. His silver hair was cut in what was once known as a crewcut, flattened off into bristle at the top, and short enough on the sides and back to expose some of the scalp in the light. It was an anomalous hairstyle, rarely seen any more except on certain older Americans, or Germans. It evoked Cold War, aerospace, or something not quite of the time—a certain monastic dedication to a national cause, perhaps, or some fading vision of a technocratic elite.

The face beneath it bore a peculiarly ambiguous quality of perspicacity and emptiness. Behind the drab gray eyes and crewcut there was intelligence without wit, a cheerfulness without the least trace of cheer. It is a quality one sees often in the faces of politicians. The expression, which could have passed for a smile, contained neither malice nor sympathy. It was a dogged, efficacious mask, utterly devoid of affect.

His eyes scanned the lobby, passing the dowager and her escort sitting quietly at the tea table as a waiter held a tray of French pastries for them to examine. The lady pointed daintily to a dripping éclair. The waiter grasped it in silver tongs and deposited it on her plate. Her companion jabbed hungrily with a silver fork at eggs on china. He looked up, and his doleful eyes met the eyes of the American standing by the desk, and passed onward—both theirs did—for there was really no point of contact. One was hot, textured, transparent; the other, smooth, cool, inscrutable.

"Your bill, sir."

The crewcut man turned and, without opening his jacket, took his wallet out of the inside pocket and removed an American Express credit card. The clerk banged it through the machine and handed it back to the man to sign. He wrote his name neatly, the way one learns in school: *Jennings Vaughan.*

"Thank you, Mr. Vaughan."

Vaughan smiled pleasantly as he put his card and his wallet back in his pocket, and picked up the valise, topcoat and umbrella. He passed the tea table where the gigolo now sat idly spooning his Lipton's and lemon. Next to him the woman bit greedily into her chocolate éclair, her bracelets gathering up around her chubby elbows, her powdered eyes pinched into black stitches of pleasure.

Vaughan stepped outside into the fresh London morning and took a deep breath.

"Taxi, sir?"

He nodded, and before the doorman could raise his arm a shiny black London taxi pulled up to the curb. Vaughan pressed a quid firmly into the doorman's palm and climbed into the back of the taxi.

"Thank you, sir. Lovely day, sir."

The door closed, and the taxi moved off.

"Good morning," Vaughan said, looking at the cabbie expectantly.

"It'll take us about ten minutes," the man said in a thick German accent. "Mr. Cross is expecting you."

At Marble Arch the driver turned right onto Oxford Street and slowed into traffic. Reaching New Bond Street, he pulled over.

"It's a few doors past Brown's, on the right, sir," he said, pointing. "Between a café and a ladies' millinery shop."

Vaughan got out of the cab without a word. The driver sped away.

Vaughan glanced at his watch, a Timex with a flexible silver band; it was ten-thirty. He walked down the center of the pedestrian street, moving among the early shoppers and browsers in the bright, innocent morning with a cultivated neutrality that neither added to nor took away from the activity of the street.

Passing Brown's, Vaughan veered right. He skirted a small outdoor café, came to a narrow, unmarked entrance, and stepped inside.

At the top of the landing he found a door on the left with a small brass plaque bearing the words: BRIGHTON PHARMACEUTICALS, LTD. A DIVISION OF THE HELLER GROUP. A dry, waspish-looking older woman answered his knock and gestured wordlessly for him to enter.

The office was old-fashioned, very British, with a clutter

of undistinguished antique lamps, furniture and carpets. The only visibly modern artifact was an IBM Selectric typewriter at the woman's desk. A tall, pale and rather professorial-looking man emerged from the inner office and stepped forward to greet Vaughan. He wore a Harris tweed and cardigan, and generally went well with the decor. When Vaughan had entered his office, he closed the door behind them.

Vaughan sat down in an overstuffed chair with doilies on the armrests and gazed across the desk at the gray, hawkish man. His name was Arthur Cross, he was sixty-nine, and he would soon be entering a most welcome retirement. It was impossible not to remark the vivid contrast Cross offered to the London outside the window behind him, in recognition of which he had closed the curtains. He lit his briar pipe slowly, then cleared his throat.

"It's been a long time, Vaughan," he said, with more weariness than warmth.

"Almost twenty-five years," Vaughan replied in a crisp monotone.

"Cairo, as I recall. Shepheard's Hotel," Cross said hoarsely. "Suez, and all."

Vaughan looked at Cross, who had now turned partway toward the window, and seemed to be drifting. The shimmering incongruity of a Bee Gees song drifted up through the closed windows into the dusty room. A poorly concealed file bearing Vaughan's name sat on the desk beneath a copy of *Punch*.

"What's the order of the day?" Vaughan said briskly, hoping to coax Cross back into the room from wherever he had gone.

Cross turned and gazed at Vaughan with a wary distaste. His pipe had gone out; slowly he relit it.

Vaughan, suppressing his exasperation, pulled back his sleeve and stared fixedly at his watch.

When finally Arthur Cross did look up again, his face broke out in a sudden expression of shock.

The object of his dismay was a small German handgun, a Walther PPK/S, its blue crosshatched grip sticking cheerily up out of Vaughan's shoulder holster, hanging just below his left ribs, exposed to view by Vaughan having loosed the button of his jacket.

"Button your bloody coat, Vaughan," Cross snapped, looking nervously past Vaughan at the closed door to the outer office. "This isn't bloody Burma, you know."

Vaughan, without expression, rebuttoned his coat.

Cross raised his hand to his face to conceal from Vaughan's cold, watchful eyes the slightest trace of a smile.

"You have an assignment for me?" Vaughan said.

Cross set about recomposing himself: he cleared his throat; he knocked his pipe out in the ashtray. Finally, he began to speak in a dry, deliberate voice.

"We're a small security office, Vaughan, for our parent organization. The Heller Group. A very large international corporation. Germans . . ." Cross's bitterness was scarcely concealed as the words left his lips. "Pharmaceuticals, originally. Now, God knows what. Electronics, munitions. In recent years they've gone quite heavily into communications and entertainment. Newspapers, film, television, publishing. That sort of thing. Now it seems they've got their eye on an American recording company. The deal has been agreed to in principle. Considerable amount of money involved, apparently. But there's been some sort of bother. A bit of underworld mixup, what have you. We need someone who knows the turf over there to go in—discreetly of course—and straighten it out. But Vaughan . . ." and here Arthur Cross pointedly took his pipe out of his mouth and gazed at the spot where Vaughan's Walther sat beneath his jacket. "This is strictly an insurance operation. Don't resort to the heavy hand. Do you get my meaning?"

Vaughan smiled tightly. "Of course."

For the next hour the two men spoke of details. When they had finished they rose and walked back through the outer office, past the dour secretary, to the door.

When Vaughan had left, Cross turned and stood ruminatively in the center of the room, puffing at his pipe and gazing at a faded coat of arms on the wall.

Cross looked down at the woman, and frowned suddenly. "Put in a call to my wife, would you?" he wheezed. "Tell her we'll go to the country this weekend if the weather holds up."

"Yes, Mr. Cross."

Arthur Cross wandered back into his office. He parted the curtain and peered down at New Bond Street. "Now it's the Arabs," he muttered aloud. "Janet says Harrod's looks like a bloody souk these days."

"Pardon me, sir?" Ratwick was placing a glass of water and two pills on his desk.

"Oh, nothing," Cross said. He turned and looked quizzically at her. "Ratwick," he said suddenly. "You'll have to call Zurich. Set up a numbered account. There's to be no trace on the company books. The first check will come from Frankfurt in a day or two. Just send it on."

"All right, sir. Could you give me his name again?"

"Bloke bothers me," he was muttering. "Hope I've done the right thing."

"His name, sir?"

"Oh. Vaughan. Jennings Vaughan."

When she had left the room, Arthur Cross wheeled in his chair and stared at the curtain that hung still against the summer heat. He felt a sodden weight upon him, a lingering uneasiness from the meeting. He had a terrible feeling no good would come of it.

But when the request from Frankfurt had come, he hadn't known who else to call but Vaughan. He was frightfully out of touch.

Ah well, he thought. One did what one could these days.

3

Michael Motta went up in the air, cocked, and released the ball. As he dropped back to his feet, there it was again: the old agony in the knee. A click, then a hot, jabbing pain. The ball hit the backboard and bounded harmlessly away.

Miffed, he turned and hobbled back down the court. He set up near the basket, his knee throbbing like a siren, to await the assault of the motley pickup team that congregated three times a week for a game of full-court at the Hollywood Y.

A short, springy guard—an A&R man from another record company—took a quick jumper from the top of the key that missed; Motta grabbed the rebound. He saw a tall, gaunt, shaggy figure at the other end of the floor waving wildly, calling out: "Mike! Mike!"

Motta threw the ball the full length of the floor.

Monk Purcell fielded it, took one dribble, went up for the

stuff . . . and blew it. The sound of his howl split the acoustic din of the gymnasium, and echoed all the way to the weight rooms.

The other team came back up on the attack. A lean young black kid came at Motta, faked him to the left, dribbled around him to the right, and went in for an easy layup. Motta stood, hands on hips, looking disgustedly up at the ceiling, as five waiting players poured past him onto the court.

Grabbing his teeshirt off a bench, he limped down the stairs to the showers, clutching the banister.

"I miss that dunk maybe one in twenty," Monk Purcell said grimly, coming down behind him.

They walked to their lockers through the heavy gymnasium air.

"Hear it's your birthday," Monk said. "What's the count?"

"Thirty-two."

"Well, cheers."

"Amanda's making dinner for me," Motta said. "Other than that, the sooner gone the better."

They left their gym clothes piled on the floor by their lockers and padded naked to the showers.

"June sixteenth, nineteen forty-seven," said Monk. "You missed the war."

"Which one?"

"The second."

"I've missed them all," Motta said. Steaming water spurted from the shower heads. "I've cleverly managed to dodge every major engagement of my time."

Their voices caromed off the walls; tiny pieces of pink soap whirled in the drains.

"How'd you slip Vietnam?" Monk said.

Motta pointed at his knee. It pulsed in affirmation. "The cartilage in there is like Silly Putty. They don't call it a trick knee for nothing."

The hiss of the showers swallowed Monk's loping laugh.

Motta bowed his head, locked his hands behind his back, and let the water pour over him, cauterize him. He wished it would burn away the smog, the torpor, the irresolution.

"They get worse as you get older," Monk was saying soberly. "Arthritis, calcium deposits . . ."

Motta looked across at tall, drooping, gifted Monk. Dark circles had settled under his eyes lately, and flecks of silver had sprouted from nowhere in his hair. Something was eating him. Monk claimed it was an ulcer. Motta wondered if it wasn't just art directors' dues: dope; drink; and the ingrained craziness of the record biz.

They sat on stools by their lockers, toweling off. Beads of water percolated on Monk's mustache. "I heard another rumor we're up for sale."

"Who'd want to buy a company with no hits?"

Motta tied up his tennis shoes, completing the ensemble—jeans, long-sleeved cotton shirt, a sleeveless sweater and the sneakers—he'd worn ever since Berkeley days.

"Music is megabucks, Michael. It's a four-billion-dollar-a-year business. Haven't you seen the *Wall Street Journal?* Every big corporation wants one. We're the largest independent left."

A mirror at the end of the row of lockers came into focus; Motta ran his hand through his damp brown hair.

"Latest I heard was an oil company," Monk was saying, climbing into his pants.

Motta shrugged. "Newspapers own forests. Vinyl comes from oil. I suppose you could consider music just another form of oil." He jammed his gym clothes inside his Adidas bag. "See you at work."

He threw his towel at the bin by the check-in counter, and couldn't hit that either.

Outside in the parking lot the air was hot and dry and sour with smog. The burning flanks of the hills steamed in the orange stillness. Favoring the knee, Motta slid into his 1965 Citroën DS, punched on the radio and waited for the car to make its hydraulic rise. The Disney effect, he called it. It always turned heads.

Motta's Citroën symbolized a particular memory of opulence—getting a ride in one once in a rainstorm, hitchhiking, outside Aix-en-Provence. When he had gotten to Hollywood the September before and found out his salary would be $3,000 a month, he had bought one, perhaps to provide himself as well with a certain insulation from the glossy world of gold, jewelry, brown Mercedes and white powder he was about to enter, some self-defined concept of class he could live with.

He pulled the car out onto Sunset, slipstreamed into the endless regatta of traffic, and let it carry him.

Cars: L.A. always revealed itself best to Motta when he was in his car. There was a particular spot, coming in from the beach on the Santa Monica Freeway, when it was unusually clear, and he felt, looking out across the basin at the buildings and the mountains at about 60 mph, that he knew the secret heart of the city. He had heard once about a family who lived on the freeways. The man worked a night shift at an airplane plant down the San Diego Freeway; she worked as a secretary downtown, and their kid went to school in Van Nuys. They used to live in the valley, but realized they were spending all their time driving anyway, so they bought a mobile home. Now they just lived on the freeways.

Motta fell out of the line to make a left turn. A few hundred yards south of the corner he pulled up to a guard gate fronting a large complex of elegant, gabled, one-story bungalow offices. It had been a movie lot in the Twenties. Now, significantly, it was a record company, proudly trumpeting a revolving logo above the entrance: RPM RECORDS, in the shape of a disc, turning slowly against the smog. A saucy, cookie-cutter Scavullo blonde in shorts, a halter top, and pert, airblown hair, about thirty feet high, smiled down at the street from a handpainted billboard. The words were:

CANDY SNOW. A REFRESHING DEBUT. ON RPM RECORDS AND TAPES. A refreshing debut, indeed. Motta cringed at his own handiwork.

"Hey, man!" Felipe called out of his guard box, waving his one good arm, the other permanently hung across his massive stomach in the gray uniform. His florid cheeks told Motta he'd been nipping at the Jose Cuervo stash that session-crashers replenished nightly as recording wore on into the late hours.

Motta floated the Citroën through the BMWs and Bentleys to his allotted diagonal slot in front of a bungalow on the north side. A sign in cool gray Futura lettering on Lucite hung against the wall: CREATIVE SERVICES. He hobbled around the side and down an eaved corridor to the entrance, ducking the hanging spider plants, ferns and begonias in redwood planters that Monk Purcell inevitably set swinging with his head.

The reception area was a hip clutter of antique wood desks, telephones, art files, rock posters in plastic frames, and piles of album cover slicks, ads, and artwork on the way in or out of the office. Cool, Swiss design bleeding into raw visual hallucination. Record biz graphics. Bosch, Bauhaus and Bugs Bunny, is how Motta liked to put it.

Dede, the secretary, was filing her nails at the desk, a Diet Pepsi in front of her, dressed in fashion. "For you," Dede said, handing him a thin stack of pink telephone messages; she went back to her nails. Motta had never known anyone called Dede in his life. Who were these people? What tribe were they? Why were telephone messages always pink? What was he doing here?

As he walked away toward his office, Dede called after him. Motta turned around. "Lisa Wilde called: She wanted to meet you this afternoon. I told her you had a meeting. But I mean she sounded real . . . *urgent* about it."

Motta's attention galvanized. "Call her back and tell her I'll meet her. Find out where."

"But you have a meeting with Rod to finish *Crossover.*"

"Lisa Wilde," said Motta, "is the only decent artist on the label. Call her and tell her I'll be there."

He walked down the narrow whitewalled corridor covered with more rock posters, Clio awards, rock-and-roll memorabilia, and Polaroids of the office staff, mugging, birthday cakes in the face, funny teeshirts. At the end were two offices: one said ART DIRECTOR; the other, EDITORIAL. Motta walked inside his and closed the door. He threw his bag on the couch, slumped down in the chair behind his desk, and rubbed his knee. Rock and roll played softly from a pair of Lansing speakers on the floor.

"Dinner at 6:30. Be there or be square," the pink message from Amanda said. The second invited him to a Candy Snow photo shoot on the sound stage—a TV spot he and Monk had storyboarded. The third was from a hokey stentorian actor who always called for voice-over work on radio spots, and sent him pens with his name on them: "A Voice You Can Believe." Motta never used him, never would, and the actor knew it; music, Motta would like to think, was not used cars or potato chips. But the guy called religiously every week, rain or shine.

He switched on the IBM Selectric that came with the job and spooled in a piece of paper. He had a copy line to finish for a trade ad—a rock group called Zone. The album's title was *Sun Spots.* He stared at the album cover artwork for a while, waiting for something to strike. They were easy to do, the lines, but hard to get into.

Motta's boundless fertility with these copy lines almost terrified him. At first he had written them a little too lyrical, too loose and discursive. But quickly he had caught on to the stark, crisp concrete poetry of record biz copy, the wordplay, the punning, and took a vicious delight in creating them.

Hypecraft, he called it.

Since he'd come to Los Angeles to join the vast army of

writers, photographers, illustrators, directors, actors and assorted creative freelancers who serviced the newly flush record industry, Motta had done copy for dozens of artists, on and off the label: words emblazoned on ads, teeshirts, posters, balloons, billboards, tucked into radio spots, TV spots, promotional records. He had heard there were collectors who actually saw fit to memorialize this stuff, the music business throwaways. There was a society in England, the Ephemerists, who collected all the passing artifacts of the age, the more transient the better—things like airsick bags from airplanes. The glutted river of words, images, *objets* that poured forth from the great culture mouth, flooding the world in a sea of snappy catchphrases and logos . . .

Motta typed out a few words, tried some lines; but they didn't work. He let his eyes idly scan his office, touching artifacts he didn't even see anymore. A few framed ads containing his deathless prose hung above the desk. One showed a nubile girl sucking her finger. The words were: *Goldenrod. So young, and so ripe.* Another showed a cowgirl firing bullets at an image of the Billboard Hot 100, bullets being the golden hieroglyphs that indicate a record is going up, not down the charts. The copy said: *Chart Attack.* That had been six months ago, when RPM was still hot.

But Motta's favorite was this one: *The hit single. From the hit album. From the hit movie . . . From the hit book.* Now *there* was a media parlay. An entrepreneur's dream. Everyone made money off that one. The ultimate: the product that crosses over.

Next to him, on the shelf with the tapes and the stereo tuner and the albums, was a bound volume of six years of articles and reviews he'd done for *The Rock.* On the glass coffee table in front of the sofa, among copies of *Billboard, Cash Box,* and *Record World,* was the last edition of *Crossover,* the chatty monthly booklet on RPM's artists that he and Monk put together. It was an innovation of Motta's—the title referring, in an industry sense, to the much-courted crossing over of a single or an album from one genre to another—country to rock, rock to soul, soul to rock. It meant more dollars.

Thirty-two? Don't be blue. Motta fingered birthday cards on his desk. Amanda's was a set of four pictures of her, mugging in the washed-out gloom of the photo booth on the Santa Monica pier, smooth stunning chocolate Caribbean skin, holding her Pentax up, taking a photo of the photo. And a kiss on her lips. Media licks; games; head trips. And somewhere in there, he supposed, a little love. Motta smiled.

There were a couple of cards from friends within the company, one from Momma in Mill Valley; and an official RPM company card dutifully signed by Marty's secretary in his absence: Martin E. Karp. And there was "To Daddy," from freckled son Jamie and Jamie's mother, Diane, still dabbing acrylics on canvas up in the Oakland ghetto, still living out her sixties dream. She still couldn't understand why, when *The Rock* had moved to New York, Motta had opted for Los Angeles.

But he had felt almost messianic about it, coming down to do battle with the material monster, rub up against the belly of the beast, feel the dragon's breath. At least L.A. wore its greed on its sleeve; a kind of Darwinian struggle of flash and filigree, a spiritually empty ooze, a tooth-and-nail jungle ethic among the inert palms. Perhaps, Motta mused, life itself had evolved out of some sort of primordial slime like Los Angeles.

And San Francisco had gone dead on him: unreal, a toy town, smug, going nowhere. His old friend seemed stuck somehow in the last decade, these overrefined progeny of the American seed. Motta had to get out. We can stay forever young, he would say, but we cannot stay young forever.

He stared at the *Sun Spots* album slick again, let his fingers run over the Selectric keys. The bands were coming up with worse names than ever. Had all the good ones been used up?

When Marty Karp had offered him the job he had thought what everyone else thought: it was a payoff, co-opt the enemy. After all, he had been in the middle of a piece for *The Rock* on RPM. But that seemed a bit paranoid. What were these guys? Gangsters? Just because Marty came from the Bronx and talked out of the side of his mouth. Come on . . . And the Senior Editor had already nixed the piece. Too hot, he had said, too provocative. Motta had failed again to fully appreciate the symbiotic, interfeeding dance of rock journal and record company. Ad revenues talked with greater eloquence than he.

Zone. *Sun Spots.* The artwork was a skinny model in a leopardskin outfit against an ersatz Rousseau background. Motta tried: *It's a jungle out there.* No; he couldn't live with that.

"Michael." Dede was standing at the door. "Lisa said to meet her at the corner of Beverly and Sunset at two-thirty. She said she really wants to see you."

"Why there?"

"She didn't say."

"Okay. Thanks." And Motta brightened as he gazed at Dede's silken flanks dancing down the hallway.

Then: *Expose yourself.*

Expose yourself to Sun Spots. That would go. He typed it out on a fresh sheet. Marty would think it was too esoteric. But it would do.

He stepped into Monk's office, dropped the sheet of copy on his drafting table, and headed across the lot to the sound stage.

In the old days silent men in baggy suits took pratfalls in front of bulbous black cameras on tripods and made the world laugh, where now arc and strobe lights illuminated a tall, very stoned woman wiggling awkwardly in a blue spandex outfit against a cardboard palm tree backdrop, every motion captured by three 16-millimeter cameras with zooms, two Sony porta-paks, a Nagra tape recorder and two still photographers with Nikons. A stereo blared Candy Snow's new single, "So Hot, So High." And the sounds that matched her glossy lips as she stretched the spandex around made Motta long for those old silent days.

Motta found her an artist of monumental poverty. That she could be on the same label with Lisa Wilde was an outrage. As he watched the filming, he recalled the afternoon at Marty Karp's house in Benedict Canyon when the deal was made. It was one of those incidents that as a journalist would have set him drooling; as a co-opted stoolie, as his old friends would put it, he had observed it with all the dumb fascination of an anthropologist watching a primitive tribal rite.

Marty had sat in a little rubber floating raft in his pool, in his trunks, with a telephone in it. At poolside, kneeling, was a man named Grossman, pleading with Marty, beseeching him. His belly hung out of a teeshirt, and he smoked joint after joint. An old street buddy of Marty's from New York days; he was broke, but he had a singer and wanted a deal. He evoked old dues, karma; he recited a litany of favors he had done Marty over the years, his voice keening across the oleanders. Before long, Marty relented. That was all there was to it; she was on the label. He called Kippel the lawyer, told him to draw up the papers and send the guy an advance of $100,000. Marty never listened to a demo tape, or saw what she looked like.

Motta had thought about the 300 tapes a week that poured into the offices of record companies from aspiring artists trying to get heard. And he had been awed at the depths of his own innocence.

The arc lights dimmed, the sound went off, and Motta, watching a makeup man regrease Candy Snow's face between takes, wondered again why rivers of money were being poured into her: TV spots, four-color posters on

Mylar, publicists, fancy photographers—the entire panoply of expensive devices usually reserved for a proven artist. Why? After a steady string of hits for a number of years, RPM had gone stone cold. Sales were thin, though nobody liked to talk of it. Marty Karp's heralded golden ears had turned to tin. Sometimes, Motta knew, acts were signed as a lure so managers or lawyers would bring over their other acts. But Grossman had nobody else. Was Marty Karp simply on a self-destruct?

Some stroking was going on. But who was stroking whom, and to what end, he could not ascertain. Motta had to admit he was unable to penetrate the fathomless mysteries of hype.

He and Monk Purcell had storyboarded the TV spot late one night in a mood of cynical perversity. The blue palm tree would sail away, shrinking into space, a $4,000 computerized video matte dissolve, and Candy Snow would spin off into oblivion with it. It was their private statement on the direction they were certain her career would take.

The arc lights went back on. "So Hot, So High" blasted forth from the twin Altec speakers on either side of the stage. Candy Snow began to jerk unsteadily to the music, out of sync. Motta saw by a cameraman's luminous dial watch that it was 2:15. With relief, he slipped off the sound stage and out into the white, empty glare of the sun.

He climbed into his Citroën, happy to have an excuse to get off the lot again, and eager to see Lisa Wilde.

At a stoplight on Sunset Strip Motta found himself sandwiched between two cars playing the same rock station: it gave him perfect stereo. Above him a $10,000 billboard with the handpainted heads of a rock group darkened the horizon. Blinking lights festooned the album cover. A real thermometer, thirty feet high, was built into the board. The words were: *Hot. And Getting Hotter.* Neither assertion tucked into the lines was true of the group. But it well de-

scribed the weather; and it wasn't a pleasant prospect to
Motta, the long polluted summer ahead. The light changed,
and he nursed the Citroën forward.

On the dashboard was a cassette of the interview he had
begun with Lisa Wilde a month earlier in the back room of
a Mexican restaurant in Hollywood, sipping margaritas. The
interview had taken an odd direction neither of them had
anticipated. Motta had thought about it many times since.
At Lisa's request he had never transcribed it; she had promised to meet him again and do another one. But he had
waited in vain for her to call. She left town, suddenly, in the
middle of an album. Morocco, he heard.

Now as he drove to meet her he popped the cassette into
the car player, spooled it to the beginning, and let it run.

*This is Michael Motta with Lisa Wilde. We were talking
about the early days, Berkeley, when you first performed
publicly.*

The old Steppenwolf, on San Pablo. Lifetimes ago.

Berkeley in the sixties: the formalism of the interview hid
a thousand references they shared. For they had both been
part of the interknit, emergent Bay Area scene—and brief
lovers, one long spring weekend among the purple wild-
flowers of Mount Tamalpais and the white winds of Stinson
Beach.

*You were working as a duo, Lewis and Wilde. Where is
Lewis now?*

In New Mexico.

Do you keep in touch?

*Not regularly. But we see each other if we're in the same
town.*

Motta had lost her to Lewis Adam, if indeed he had possessed her at all. Lewis was a tall, quiet blond genius in
leathers who played a battery of guitars, wore granny
glasses and a ponytail and drove a Harley. Later Lewis
faded, spun out, became a junkie; he blossomed early, as
Lisa put it discreetly on the tape.

What led to the split?

Lewis was the star. He got a record offer, I didn't. So he took it and went to New York without me.

Then you went into hiding for a while.

I was pretty broken up. I went down to Carmel to stay with an anthropologist friend, Maggie Hill. She had a little cabin in the Highlands, overlooking the sea.

That's when you wrote the songs.

Something clicked. They were good, and I knew it. We all did. I went to Cambridge and played for a while, then came back to Berkeley and worked at the Jabberwock. That fall I made my first record for that little folk label, Roundtable.

My first review.

Motta had submitted it to *Rag Mama Rag*, one of a dozen ephemeral underground publications that swept the area around 1967; to his surprise they accepted it. He wrote, poorly but passionately, of her "fleeting melodies, bitter-sweet verse and pure, sensual imagery." What he had not been able to sustain as her lover he did as an advocate of her art.

Marty Karp first discovered you, so the story goes, at the Jabberwock.

He was a song plugger from the Brill Building in New York who came west to see what was going on. He used to hang around the clubs. We called him The Rat. I think he was more interested in Janis Joplin. But he got me instead. One night he had me sign some papers. The next thing I knew he claimed he was representing me. To say I was naïve about those things would be to understate it. I handled the whole situation by running off to Europe for a year.

The tape hissed above the air conditioning as the Sunset Strip ended and the boulevard swept wide through the palmy mansions of Beverly Hills. Motta remembered how, while Lisa was in France, *The Rock* had emerged with a national following. He became one of their reviewers. Then, assigned to accompany the Stones crosscountry, he had writ-

ten a scathing pan of a concert that impressed some people.
He found himself on the masthead, with an expense account
and a chance to go for big interviews.

*You got back from France, and in the space of several
quick albums moved from cult figure to "the Muse of our
time," as* Newsweek *put it. Marty Karp bought a foundering
label with the profits and built RPM, so the story goes.*

A heady period, what I can recall of it.

*I tried many times during those years for an interview.
But it was difficult to get to you. You seemed distant, in-
accessible.*

It wasn't always my doing.

Though their lives had forked, he had never relinquished
an abiding sense of mythic liaison. He still dreamed of her
sometimes. Amanda even accused him once of forcing her
into an unspoken *ménage* with the spirit of Lisa Wilde.

The crackle of a tortilla chip broke free from the car
speakers.

*Some have portrayed Marty as the Svengali behind the
thrush, a guy who parlayed your success into a career of his
own, using you as a springboard to establish his own label.*

*That's a fiction. We have each attempted to do what we
do best.*

Is your business relationship amicable?

*Michael. I thought we were going to talk about music.
You're not a reporter anymore. You work for the company
. . . I'm sorry. I didn't mean that. It was supposed to be a
joke.*

Sun glinted off a Spanish wall outside the car window.
Motta swallowed; he had been hurt.

*Your career has seemingly cooled the last few years. Some
claim you've become too complex, too elitist, trading off your
acoustic guitar for symphony overdubs. Personally, I don't
agree. I feel you're challenging yourself.*

I'm glad to hear I have one fan left.

Indeed, Motta was her only champion at the label. She

seemed to be ignored, almost as if by decree, at the very company her success had built. Her sales had dropped dramatically.

At Beverly Drive he took a right and punched off the tape. Lisa's silver Jag was idling in the red zone. He pulled up behind, left his car running, and got out.

She reached for his hand out the window. He saw she was wearing a silk shirt and jeans, a hibiscus in her hair. Her face was chalk white; she seemed thinner than last time. Her eyes—those insatiable blue eyes—burned. He felt her hand trembling.

"Are you all right?"

"Yes. But I need to talk. It's important."

"Where are we going?"

"My place. It's up off Mulholland. Follow me. I'll explain later."

The streets began to wind, the trees to thicken: banks of oleander, flowering hibiscus, tall eucalyptus; and all along the roadside, like sentinels, the palms.

Motta looked at the image of Lisa through the back window of her car, speeding ahead. She had lit a cigarette. He found a certain literary curiosity in the exercise, listening to the tape of her while following her in a car. A street called Shadow Hill Lane, dark with pines, wound steeply away to the left. They plunged on up the canyon. Motta punched the cassette back on.

Do you remember that spring up on Mount Tam, Michael?

Very well.

We talked about art. T and B, we called it. Truth and Beauty. We thought it would carry the day, unleash a certain freedom, transform mundane conditions. Remember?

Yes.

It isn't that way. It's controlled.

What's controlled?

Culture. Art. What we get to see and hear and feel and think.

But who controls it?

You and I basically believe in the power of art. Most people are playing a different game. The art of power. These are two different philosophies. Do you understand?

I've never quite sorted that one out.

To someone who has been touched deeply by the power of art, it comes as a great shock that others are doing something else. The tendency is to pretend it isn't so. To those who pursue the art of power, art is a talisman, something they paint on their shields when they go off to war. It has a magical value. Sort of like getting the priest to bless you before battle. Art books on the coffee table, that sort of thing. The artist is vulnerable because he must market his work through people who pursue this other philosophy—lawyers, agents, managers, businessmen. Above them are men who play a much more blatant version of the same game. It's a war.

He raced up the canyon after her, listening to the intense, careful words on the tape, Lisa Wilde dissecting reality after her own fashion, with the same curious rigor that inflamed her lyrics. Whatever else had changed, her probing, restless mind had never deserted her.

As he passed wooded Cherokee Lane on his right, he recalled a party of entertainment executives Marty Karp had dragged him to that spring. The wealth had appalled him: the $60,000 cars in the driveway, the gold, the furs, the diamonds. Not a single artist had been present. Lisa slowed behind a truck that had faltered on the grade, and Motta, right on her bumper, waved. After a moment, she waved back.

Resources, and information. Those are the prized possessions. The war is raging all about us, Michael. Into this struggle comes the artist, with an entirely different message. To the extent that art is information, people contend for the rights to it. They'll even destroy the messenger who brings the information, but they don't notice. Because even the artist's death is information, and they can sell that too.

Now they were out of the canyon, and racing along Mulholland, a ribbon of road on the mountain crest. Motta found the tape disturbing; at the time it had seemed like a margarita-inspired speculation, a head rap. Now, alone in the car, the bare words alarmed him. He felt there was something she wanted him to know, and she had chosen him to tell it to.

Below, to the left, the city spread, hazy and indifferent. To the right the road tumbled off into brush and split-level homes. A car ahead of her slowed, then turned down a road that plummeted into the San Fernando Valley. A fire station slid by. Then Mulholland took a bend, and they were racing west, into the sun, just the two of them.

The more successful you get, the more extreme the tension is between these two philosophies. To yourself, you're making life-bringing visions. To them, you're just another digit in the power equation. It's a very lonely position to be in. There's a sense of guilt, even though you have perhaps done nothing. You begin to feel like a sacrificial lamb . . .

Motta became aware of a car coming up very close behind him. He glanced in the rearview and saw a black Mercedes. Suddenly it burst alongside. Motta stole a sideways glance into tinted windows. He could just make out the silhouettes of two men. As they hit a turn, the car slipped in front of him. Motta instinctively shied toward the shoulder, then drove on, more carefully. The Mercedes blocked his vision of Lisa's Jag.

You succeed into impotence. It's Faustian. The artist exchanges his kind of power for this other kind, which destroys him.

Motta came around a hairpin turn and onto a short straightaway. The road fell off steeply down to the valleys on either side. He saw that the Mercedes had pulled up

close behind Lisa's car and was honking madly. He waited
for Lisa to slow and let the car pass.

How do you defend yourself?

You can exercise the art of power on your own behalf.

What do you mean?

The Mercedes was still honking. He saw Lisa angle the
Jag toward a narrow shoulder.

The rest he watched with a blind horror: The Mercedes
gave Lisa's bumper a strong tap. The Jag wobbled, skidded
onto the shoulder, and turned its wheels back toward the
road. Motta could see Lisa inside, frantically spinning the
steering wheel, but to no effect. The car tottered on the
dusty rim of the shoulder, then tumbled out of view, over
the side of the mountain.

Motta watched, unbelieving, as the Mercedes sped up
and disappeared around a turn. In the frozen shock of the
moment, he registered that it had no license plate.

Dazed, he pulled up to the spot where Lisa's car had gone
over. He jumped out and gazed over the edge down into the
valley. It was a brushy, 150-foot drop. The steaming Jag was
on its side, jammed into a brace of eucalyptus trees, its
wheels turning slowly. The radio was playing; the sound of
a cheery FM announcer giving the weather drifted up from
below.

Motta scrambled down the dusty embankment. He tumbled and fell among the sage and the beer cans and ice
plant and poison oak, fell and rolled, cut himself and bled.
He hit his head on an oak stump he didn't see, fell away, got
up, rolled some more.

A front door, sprung open, gave off its maddening whine.
The engine hissed and steamed, and smelled of burnt water.
Motta chinned himself up into the driver's seat.

Her body was crumpled limply against the other door.
The limbs hung together unnaturally, askew, like a broken
bird's. Her face was gray, her eyes open and empty, staring
right at him. He saw blood on her blouse, but couldn't see

where it had come from. She was breathing; but it was a guttural, shattered sound. He reached over and turned off the radio.

"Lisa," he said. He reached over and took her hand. "Can you hear me? Move your fingers if you can." He imagined she responded. "I'll go get help." Her breathing was clotted, irregular. He said, commanded: "*Stay alive.*"

He thought he felt her fingers move.

Swallowing his panic, he climbed out of the car and started back up the hill. It was steep, silent, endless. A jay called at him from a pine tree, over and over, all the way up the hill. His limbs kept giving way. A couple of times he shouted back: "Stay alive!"

The second car that passed stopped. A corpulent man in a blue polyester leisure suit climbed out and looked at Michael warily. "Accident?" he said. Motta realized his hands and face were bloody.

"Down there," he wheezed. "Go get an ambulance."

"Anybody killed?" the man said.

"*Please go get an ambulance.*"

"There's a fire station back . . ." the man said, pointing. Motta nodded. The man got back in his car, turned around, and sped off.

Motta sat in the dirt, unable to move. A fire truck came. Somehow he got back down the hill with the two firemen and the stretcher.

A fireman got there first and crawled up inside the car. After a minute he called out.

"She's gone."

Motta gazed down at his hands. He noticed for the first time that there was a small silver hand inside his own, on a chain. Dazed, he sat down on the ground.

He stayed there a long time, allowing a terrible and mute emptiness to spread through him.

Then, clutching the chain, he began to crawl slowly back up the mountain.

4

Late-afternoon sun drained through muggy clouds onto a drab block in a drab section of New York's borough of Queens. Stone housing projects loomed stark and lonely against a pearl sky. Airplanes from both airports, LaGuardia and Kennedy, found the section on their flight routes, and shattered the air with their passing. Two bent rabbis in black overcoats and hats moved slowly along the dank cement. An old woman in a print dress struggled with an aluminum walker.

As a young boy in shorts and a yarmulke stood on a desolate curb, waiting to cross, Eddie Malone gazed at him from the back of the limousine, moving long and slow and black up the street. His ears still hurt from the flight in from the Coast. He popped a stick of gum in his mouth and worked his jaws, but nothing happened. The limo pulled up to a project in the middle of the block, and the chauffeur came around and let them out. Eddie stood up, brushed off his great beefy stomach beneath the yellow cardigan and polo shirt, and ran his hands through his graying straw hair. Somehow he could never get himself to look neat. Not like Marty, the little hatchet-faced man beside him, with his shiny loafers, checkered slacks, silk sport shirt and blue blazer.

They entered the building, Eddie and Marty, and crossed the hollow stone lobby to the elevator. Inside it smelled of medicine, sauerkraut, and the unnameable effluvium of old age, and death. In the reflection of the button panel, Marty Karp smoothed his coiffed silver hair with the heel of his hand.

"Eddie," Marty said. "Get rid of your gum." Eddie took the wad out of his mouth, but couldn't decide where to put it. When they stepped out onto the fifth floor, he reached behind him and stuck it on the retracting elevator door.

The green, peeling hallway came to an end, and Marty knocked at the last door. A series of bolt locks turned. A young woman's face peered through a crack over the lock chain.

"Is Mrs. Karp awake?" Marty said.

Wordlessly the eyes gazed at him from behind the chain.

"Look. I'm her son. I pay for this place. I pay your salary. Let me in." The meaty syllables of a Bronx childhood, unrectified by thirty-five years in the greater world, leaped salty and hard from his mouth.

The woman opened the door. She was dressed in a nurse's uniform, her hair severely short, her eyes dark and bottomlessly sad. Eddie Malone followed Marty into the apartment and across a dark, sour, curtained room into a small sitting room overlooking the street. The nurse stepped in front of them and turned the wheelchair around until it faced the old, doilied sofa against the wall.

The face of the old woman was frozen. The hands clutched the wheelchair's arm in an unbroken spasm, veins purple and spotted, knuckles white and stretched. A flannel nightgown draped her gaunt body. A plaid blanket lay over her knees.

"Hello, Momma," Marty said. He leaned down and kissed the old woman on the forehead. "I brought you some chocolates." He placed them on a table. Then he gestured at Eddie, who stood big and awkward on the carpet. "You remember Eddie Malone, Momma? From the block?"

The woman gazed back at her son, her face immobile, her expression set in permanent disapproval.

"Sit down, Eddie," Marty said. And Eddie Malone lowered himself next to Marty on the couch.

"Jeez, Marty," Eddie whispered. "Can she hear you?"

"Yeah. She can hear fine. She just can't talk, that's all." An airplane roared overhead, rustling the chintz curtains at the window and drowning Marty's last words. When it had passed, he spoke again.

"How are you, Momma?"

The old face looked back, frozen. The eyes flicked to the side once, then back again.

"I'm doing fine, Momma," Marty said. "Business is good. The kids are fine, they send love." The room was silent. The old woman stared at her son. "Are you okay, Momma? You don't want to go to the home?"

"She should go, Marty," Eddie Malone said under his breath. He picked at his sweater, wiped sweat from his forehead.

"No she likes the neighborhood. I tried to get her to go once, and she didn't want to."

"How could you tell?"

"She wouldn't eat."

Marty turned back to his mother. "Momma, we just flew in from L.A. We got business in New York. I wanted to stop by and say hello, and bring you some chocolates. We gotta go now. We got meetings."

Her eyes didn't change.

The scream of another airplane overhead trembled the floor. Its shadow crossed the curtains. Marty stood up, and Eddie Malone followed suit. Marty kissed his mother on the forehead again perfunctorily, and turned her wheelchair back to the window.

"Goodbye, Momma," he said. He nodded to Eddie.

At the door Marty handed the nurse a fifty-dollar bill. "Buy her a new blanket, would you? And feed her the candy."

Wordlessly the nurse took the money and let them out of the apartment. Eddie could hear the bolts fasten behind them, one after the other.

Then they were across the sidewalk, and the cool, dark interior of the limousine swallowed them. Eddie Malone dropped back against the leather seat, drenched in perspiration. Like a dark ship the limo glided forward, slowly, through and out of the empty, steaming project.

"Eddie," Marty said, "we gotta talk." He leaned forward and closed the sliding glass panel separating them from the driver. Then he reached down and took a bottle of scotch from the little bar built into the limo's floor. He poured out two glasses.

Eddie looked over at Marty. He knew that whenever Marty wanted to talk serious, he poured the scotch.

"Here, Eddie," Marty said, smiling. Eddie took the glass, and settled into the soft black leather. Beyond the tinted window, the shadowed traffic of the parkway drifted by.

"Remember, Eddie, when we were kids in the Bronx? We used to sneak on the bus downtown. We'd pick up coin running sheet music for the song pluggers. Remember?"

"Yeah. Sure, Marty. Sure I do." Eddie felt a little nervous. Marty had a way of springing things on him. A pool of sweat under his chin turned cold from the air conditioning.

"Remember the Brill Building? Miller's band? Artie Shaw? He was slick, wasn't he?"

"Yeah, Marty. He was slick." Eddie's face crinkled into a

soft, wheezy laugh. His stomach shifted beneath the yellow sweater Marty had given him for Christmas. "I remember running up Fifth Avenue in the rain with a new song for Dick Haymes at the Plaza. He tipped me big."

"You and me, Eddie," Marty said. His razor voice had softened into a soothing chant. "We go way back. You realize we're both going to be fifty next year?"

"Ain't that something, Marty."

"A big mick kid and a little kikey. We didn't do bad, did we?"

Eddie Malone nodded and sipped his scotch. "Yeah," he said softly. It was Marty Karp, not Eddie Malone, RPM Records' Assistant General Manager, who had made it big. But Eddie let it pass, as he always did. Wherever Marty had gone, whatever his fortunes, he had always found a place for Eddie Malone. That was the way it worked.

"You know how much we grossed last year, Eddie?"

Eddie knew, but he played. "How much?"

"Two hundred and fifty million dollars."

"That's real good, Marty." Then he said quietly, "Course, that's what we shipped. You know we got all those returns coming back this year. Millions. And we got no hits. You know I'm worried, Marty."

"I know, Eddie," Marty said softly. "That's what I want to talk to you about." Outside, the traffic slowed on the Triborough Bridge approach. Darkening clouds clogged the horizon. Marty refilled their glasses and moved a little closer.

"Eddie," Marty began, "I'm going to tell you something in the strictest confidence." Marty was sitting back in his seat, his eyes closed, facing forward. He looked almost serene, Eddie thought. "Eddie, we're going to sell the company."

Eddie Malone sat up and stared at Marty. "Marty. You gotta be kidding. Sell it now? With the shape we're in?"

"An offer has been made," Marty said quietly. "I'm going to take it."

"You're puttin' me on, Marty. You ain't serious."

"Last fall I got an inquiry from a German conglomerate. Heller. Very big. They own Multigram."

"Somebody owns *Multigram?*"

"Yeah. They did thirty billion dollars worldwide last year. Just in entertainment alone. Early this year they made the approach again, and I stalled them. I didn't think it was for real. Then, when we cooled, I thought I wouldn't hear from them. But they came back last month with a hard offer. I accepted in principle. It's already in the works."

"How much?"

"Fifty million."

"Unreal, Marty. Absolutely fuckin' unreal." His voice was a whisper. "Do we stay on?"

"If we want to."

"Do we want to?"

"Maybe."

"How come they want to buy when we're cold? Do they know about the returns and the stiffs?"

"Some. They know about the first quarter of this year. But I guess they want a record label. Who else is there? We're the only big independent left."

"When's the deal going down?"

"July tenth, at the Sherry. Their guys are flying in from Germany, our guys from L.A. That's in a month. If everything goes right."

Eddie felt his stomach tighten. The figures left him faint. Marty was reaching for the scotch again.

"Eddie," he said, "I have to go into that meeting with a second quarter statement. As of June thirtieth. That's in a few weeks, Eddie, June thirtieth. The first quarter was bad enough. This one's a horror show. We have to show a better statement for this quarter. It has to reflect a turnaround. Otherwise, I'm afraid they'll pull."

"It's too late, Marty. We got nothing. I looked at the print-outs on the plane." Eddie said it with a certain relief. The company was his life. He wasn't sure he wanted to see it sold. And if it meant leaving, he didn't look forward to the street again. Not at fifty.

"We can't doctor the books on these guys," Marty said. "They're not some artist, or some rack jobber from Pittsburgh. These guys have lawyers like you wouldn't believe."

"So what're we gonna do, Marty?" Outside, the sun shot its dying plumes through the troubled clouds. Eddie saw Marty's hard, glittering eyes in the dim of the car.

"Eddie," Marty said. "You remember back in the early fifties? Before the payola scandals? Before we moved out to the Coast? When you used to be able to buy a hit?"

Eddie Malone's mouth cracked open in a smile. "Sure. Those was good times. You could buy a disc jockey with a broad. You could fly up to Buffalo with a case of Jim Beam. Remember Artie Fox? He'd do it for some weed."

"Eddie," Marty said. "We're gonna buy a hit."

Eddie Malone sat up. The color fled from his face.

"Marty. You can't do that these days. The government's investigating this business. The program directors, the jocks, they're lilywhite. I mean maybe a little cocaine here and there, maybe a little black station down south or something. But look what happened to Frankie Cramer. He's in the pen. Jeez, Marty. Jeez. Talk serious."

"I'm not talking about a little airplay. I'm talking about buying a hit at retail, in the trades, across the boards. I'm talking about four million units shipped."

"Marty. Come on. We come too far to get into this." Outside, the struts of the Triborough Bridge clattering past made Eddie Malone dizzy.

"How do you think we got this far?" Marty was saying. "Are your hands so clean, Eddie?" Marty's voice was hard, spitting. Then it softened again: "There's money in it for you, Eddie. Lots. You'll never have to know the street again." Eddie listened, but he didn't exactly melt. He'd heard that one before.

"Marty. The business has done fine without these guys. What do they know about music? Germans. Shit. You know where their music's at? Polka." Eddie's face reddened with indignation.

Marty spoke patiently, as if to a child. "Listen, Eddie. Things are changing. We can't compete with the majors anymore. When Warner's needs more money for development, they just go upstairs. We have to go to the bank. We don't even own the lot we're on. All we have are a few receivables. And a lot of returns. There's already talk in the trades. Either we sell now, or we go down the tubes."

"I don't know, Marty. You scare me with this stuff about buying a hit."

"To build up a company and sell it is a legit thing. A success. It's something I want in life."

Eddie held the glass of scotch to his cheek and gazed glumly out the window as they swept down off the bridge into Manhattan. He knew that when Marty got something in his head, he didn't back off easy.

"Anyway, I did it already."

"Did what, Marty?"

"I bought the hit."

Eddie Malone hit his forehead with his open palm. Sweat burst out on his cheeks. "Jeez."

"We're buying a big hit for Candy Snow."

Eddie Malone's mouth fell open. "Candy Snow? But the broad's terrible. She got no pipes, no rhythm, she can't carry a tune. You only signed her as a favor to Grossman. What about the music, Marty? The music?"

"Don't you see, Eddie? It doesn't matter anymore. It doesn't matter . . ." He repeated the words, over and over, like a litany, and Eddie was confused and afraid as Marty went on, talking fast now, his hands going. "The album will hit the charts this week bulleted at forty-two. Next week it'll be twenty-five. The single will go right to eight. On Friday, June thirtieth, when the trades come out, it'll be number one. We're going to ship six million units. Fifteen million extra dollars in billing on our second-quarter statement. It's not great, but it'll carry the meeting."

Eddie Malone groaned. "Who did you buy?"

"The radio stations, the rack jobbers, the retailers, the trades, the consumer publications. And foreign."

"But how? Who?"

"Remember Lucchessi? Martoni? The guys from Cleveland? Chicago? Used to have the jukeboxes?" Eddie nodded weakly. "They're out in Vegas. They're stinking rich. They can do anything. I went up and saw them."

"I can't believe what I'm hearing, Marty. You're talking about the Mob. Don't you remember? Little Epstein's body in the gutter over in Brooklyn? They're killers. How you gonna pay them?"

"I offered something up as collateral."

"But what? We don't got nothing."

Marty's eyes bored right into Eddie. "Don't worry about it, Eddie. I got it. It's done. Okay?"

"Oh, Marty." Eddie looked like he was going to cry. "You're playin' with fire. You sure you want to give stuff to those guys?"

"I'm not giving them anything, Eddie. I'm putting it up on a six-month guarantee. By then it'll be over, and we'll buy it back."

"What if something happens?"

"That's where I need your help, Eddie."

"No, Marty. No more scotch. Please." Marty smiled, and replaced the bottle.

"Now listen up, Eddie. I need you to do something for me. Lisa. She's been getting interested in what she owns lately. She's got a hair up her ass, some crazy idea she wants all her rights back, including her publishing. There's been lawyers nosing around. Personally, I don't care. But not right now. It comes at a bad time. Understand?" Marty pressed in on Eddie. "I need you to help me duck her until this is over. Maybe stroke her a little, you know what I'm saying? Get her attention off it. Maybe put together a little tour for her, get her on the road. And I'll need you to run up to Vegas for me. I can't be seen up there again."

Eddie gazed disconsolately out the window as the darkening canyon of Fifty-ninth Street closed over them. Marty took the glasses and put them back on the limo bar.

"Buy a hit," Eddie Malone muttered, "in these times. Jeez."

"Fifty million bucks, Eddie," Marty whispered. And his teeth flashed in the twilight.

The bellboy opened the door into the Sherry Netherland's eighth-floor corner suite with the gold floral wallpaper and the view of the Plaza and the park. Marty Karp tipped him a five, and he left. "So what else? Keep going," Marty said. He ripped off his tie and slumped down on the couch.

Eddie Malone stood in the middle of the carpet, reading off a fistful of telephone messages. "Kippel called. One of the groups is bitching about their royalties. They want to come in and do an audit . . ." Then suddenly Eddie Malone's face went chalk white. He stared down at the phone message. His brow squeezed up, and his hand began to shake.

"Marty . . ."

"What? What is it?"

"It says here . . . Lisa's dead."

"What? Give me the goddamn message." Marty snatched it out of Eddie's hand. He ran for the phone. But it rang before he could get there. Eddie, watching Marty listen to the call, could tell by the expression that it was true.

Marty got off and sat down on the edge of the bed. He looked up at Eddie. "They say her car went off the road on Mulholland. She was killed."

Eddie Malone's face filled with pain and confusion. "Lisa," he whispered. He sat down slowly in a chair.

The two of them were silent for a while. Then Eddie said, "Was it an accident, Marty?"

"They don't know. The police are looking into it." He looked up at Eddie. "Somebody says they saw her bumped off the road."

"Who says?" Eddie whispered.

"Mike Motta." Marty stared down at the expensive, worn gold carpet, opening and closing his hands.

"Was it an accident, Marty?"

"I told you, Eddie. They're checking it out."

"No," Eddie said softly. "I'm asking *you*, Was it an accident?"

Marty looked up and his eyes flashed hard. "Look, Eddie. You thinking this has some connection to what I told you in the car? Is that what you're thinking?"

Eddie Malone got up and walked to the window. Across the street the Plaza Hotel loomed in the night, with its great facade and green roofs in the evening summer mist that had settled over the city. It glowed, like some great temple, with an inner light.

"Lisa's dead, Marty," Eddie said quietly, gazing out the window. "That gives you a clear road."

"What are you saying, Eddie?"

"I'm not saying nothing, Marty. I'm just saying the way it is. There'll be a big boost in her album sales. Remember all the money everybody made off those Jimi Hendrix tapes when he went? You know how that works, Marty. There's your second-quarter statement. Her, and the Candy Snow hit you're gonna buy. There's your deal. There's your fifty-million-dollar sale."

"Shut the fuck up, Eddie."

"You're home free, Marty."

Marty jumped up and pulled the phone out of the wall. He heaved it. It hit the wall next to Eddie Malone.

"*You sonofabitch*," he yelled.

Eddie Malone stopped talking and just stared out the window. A soft rain had begun to fall. The slick sound of traffic rose up, and the lights wavered. Eddie didn't want Marty to see him crying. Mute thoughts rose and drifted through his mind. He'd never told Marty how much he loved Lisa. She had always been kind to him; few were. He didn't want to see her hurt, but he had watched it happen over the years—maybe more than anybody else.

He looked back at Marty, who was sitting on the edge of the bed, staring down at his hands. He had always been loyal to Marty, always done what he said. But he had never loved him; Marty Karp wasn't someone you loved. With Lisa it was different. Once, after a concert, when he brought her some coffee, she had taken his hand and looked into his eyes and said, "Eddie, you're a real guy, with real feelings. And I appreciate that."

Tears streamed down his face. He didn't know how to deal with the thoughts and the feelings that pushed and pulled at him now. He was all torn up inside. He wondered how things had ever gotten this far.

5

"Happy birthday!"

Amanda, standing in the open doorway, dressed to kill, hand outstretched with her gift in it, became a freeze frame. Her ebony face dropped into bewilderment, and finally a kind of horror. Her hand, clutching the wrapped package whose shiny sides now seemed foolishly festive, fell to her side.

"God, Michael."

She reached out her other hand and led him into the apartment. At the kitchenette Motta pulled away, stumbled to the refrigerator, gazed around inside. He walked off, leaving it open, turned on the sink tap, turned it off. Then he wandered to the window at the end of the flat where the dying sun gilded the glassy water and the sand. He turned to Amanda once again, and gazed at her with a dark sorrow that scared the hell out of her.

He sat down in a chair by the window. Amanda took a blanket off the bed and put it around him. She turned the oven off the dinner, put the candled carrot cake back in the fridge, and the champagne too. Then she sat down at the table in the middle of the room and waited.

Outside, the sun was a fat woman squatting on the horizon as harpy gulls wheeled and cawed against her, and the old pier, rickety and crumbling, jutted out into the mirrored waters like a broken, accusing finger. Motta was his body, and his body was a thick, clotted thing, gorged with shock. Only the sea reached it, with its waves of sound matching his body and his pain—and they faced each other, the pain and the ocean, mindless, insistent occurrences without thought or explanation.

When it was dark and the sea was only a silvery sound, Amanda lit a candle on the table. She sat by the candle, watching its glow in the window, and waited some more. She knew how to wait on a man; Momma had taught her that, night after night, in the projects.

At some point, Motta found he was watching whatever he had been inside of, watching it from up behind himself somewhere. It was like a tiny lighthouse high on a hill, his consciousness, and his body the sea below. And the light became the reflection of the candle in the window; and as the sea rolled over and over, Motta was out of it, looking at it.

Into the picture came the flickering shape of Amanda's face, her dark eyes, waiting, in the glass.

He stood up, slowly, stiffly, and went to the table and sat down.

Amanda got up and took the salad out of the refrigerator. Vegetables cascaded onto a white plate; the colors were blinding. Motta held the food on the end of his fork for a long time. When he took a bite, the chewing was like the tumbling of granite cliffs. His jaws grew tired, and he put the fork down.

He looked at Amanda. "Sorry, baby," he whispered. The words detonated in the air, foolish little puffs of smoke.

And Motta knew now that he had come to the end of them.

"Let's go out," he said.

Amanda, happy to escape the ruins of the dinner, put on her coat. They walked down the stairs to the lobby of the old building, and stepped out onto the boardwalk. Amanda put her arm in his.

The fog rolled in, seeped into their throats and moistened the lids of their eyes and left beaded pricks of light on Amanda's wool coat. As they passed the merry-go-round they were able to discern the shadowy horses, suspended at various heights, like the great mastodons in the Russian steppes with grass still in their mouths, frozen in the middle of a bite.

That's when it comes, Motta thought; in the middle of a bite. The meal half-chewed. The ride never ends. Simply at some point the current is shut off. And in the frozen image of the horses, poised at different heights, he saw Lisa Wilde, a colorful, painted horse, frozen high on the silver pole, waiting for the music to start up again to the warm nudge of a child's buttocks.

Hank's Fish and Chips was still open, and a wizened waitress, skin folded by the sun, offered them Lethe in ceramic cups. They huddled in a booth, and Motta found that now he could talk a little.

"Lisa Wilde was murdered today," he said. "I saw it."

She looked at him, horrified.

He told her, elliptically, what had happened on Mulholland. He described going afterwards to the police station, delivering a statement. An investigation would occur. Motta wondered. Then, not knowing who else to call, he had phoned Marty Karp's office and told his secretary. Marty had left for New York, and as soon as he checked into the Sherry she would let him know.

Then, somehow, he had driven to the beach. He must
have, because he was here.

"But why?" she said.

Motta shook his head. "I don't know."

"Poor Lisa," Amanda said. Then: "Poor Michael."

Motta looked over at her, and for the first time since he
had gotten home he saw her, this tall, beautiful black
woman he lived with. She could feel it, and her eyes softened.

"You did your hair in cornrows," he said.

"Took me all day. Missed acting class to do it."

"I fucked up your party," he said.

"Forget it," she said softly, looking away. "Wasn't your
doing."

An old bum with fried hair and a wall eye, clothes so
shiny they were silver, stumbled into Hank's and asked for a
beer. The waitress told him they didn't serve beer. He ricocheted over to Motta and asked for a quarter. Motta gave
him one. Then the fog sucked him away.

"Michael," Amanda said carefully. "I've got an album
cover shoot tonight. At the airport."

He nodded. "That's good." Then he realized that she
wanted to know if it was all right for her to go. "Fine. Go,"
he said gently.

"Sure?"

"Sure." He reached across the table and took her hand.
She frowned.

"I'm sick of modeling," she said. "Being everybody's
pretty black face."

"You'll get a movie soon."

They walked back a different way, through the parking
lot behind the arcades and the shops, down the stairs and
along surf's edge. The tide was in, the angle of the sand
steep. The effort of walking made Motta feel better. They
passed another couple, kissing, and Amanda put her arm

around his waist and looked up. But it wasn't right, and her arm fell away.

"Funny," she said. "I always had the feeling you might just run off with that girl someday. But now . . ." She smiled sadly, "I guess that ain't gonna happen." She dug her toes into the sand. "I'm not sure if that's good," she said, "or bad."

They reached the point on the sand parallel with the building, and walked back up to the boardwalk. The old structure glowed through the fog, her fluted cornices like crusted barnacles in the mist.

"My stuff's in the car," Amanda said. Motta walked her downstairs into the basement garage, and saw her into her Fiat.

"Gas?"

"Yeah," she said. She smiled sadly up at him. "You okay, Michael?"

He nodded, reached down, and gave her a stiff parody of a kiss.

"Give 'em that smile," he said.

Exhaust filled the stone basement. A cockroach sat poised over a scrap at Motta's feet in the headlights, its antennae dancing slowly back and forth. Motta flattened it into a dark stain on the cement.

Walking back out onto the boardwalk, he heard the Fiat gear off into the night, heading south toward L.A. International.

He walked back out on the beach and sat on the cold sand. Things rose up inside him, jabbing, forming into shards of thought.

He knew nothing, had experienced nothing. The level on which he lived life was not where it was played. His inability to accommodate Lisa's murder into his own sense of reality terrified him. He had no resources with which to even begin to understand it. Motta looked at a shifting shadow on the sand, and realized that a flock of gulls had settled all around him. To them, he was dead.

You succeed into impotence. It's Faustian . . .

In the night's blind fog, ingestion and elimination, systole and diastole, movement and stasis, merged. He heard the burble of the gulls around him, watched the moon trying to burst through the steaming, boiling sky. He sat, and he waited.

You can exercise the art of power on your own behalf, to a certain degree.

What do you mean?

Dawn was dripping yellow through the fog when Motta got up, wet and stiff, and headed back toward the flat. The gulls were busy at the shoreline, and the first joggers had taken to the beach.

He opened the door to the room slowly, slipped in, and closed it. Amanda was asleep on top of the covers, still in her modeling clothes, her face streaked with tears. He lay down next to her, pulled the spread up over the both of them, and gazed up at the flocked ceiling. Outside, the ocean ran quiet, at ebb, slapping and slurping and whispering.

Amanda stirred, and nuzzled against him.

"You cool?" she whispered.

He kissed her until she fell back to sleep.

Then Motta stared up at the ceiling, his eyes swimming like larvae, physically exhausted but in some other sense fully awake; and for the first time in this particular existence of his, he knew that, finally and forever, without an inkling of what it meant, or any concern about it anymore, he had crossed over.

Mannish Boy

I'm a man
I'm a full-grown man

MUDDY WATERS

Part 2

6

"*Lisa Wilde's Greatest Tits.*"

A green light glowed on the silver face of a tuner. Spinning silently on a turntable, untouched by the needle still in its cradle, was a shiny black test pressing. A cassette tape recorder, and a small library of records—some in bright covers, some simply black acetates in yellow unmarked sleeves—completed the objects on the shelf. In the upper corners of the room, two large speakers hung, quietly hissing.

Along the same windowless west wall was a large green blackboard on wheels, on which were written, by month, RPM's projected release schedule. Standing by the blackboard, chalk in hand, was a frizzy blond girl with great tits of her own who, blushing at the entendre that hung in the air, now leaned over and wrote, beneath a list of nine releases for the present month of June, *Lisa Wilde's Greatest Hits.*

The languid chuckles that followed Tiny Braun's, Promotion, pun might have been more inspired had the regulars at the cynical ritual of the Monday morning Product Meeting not heard it before from the same bearded lips. Now Joe Ruffino, Marketing, merely looked across the table, littered with pitchers of coffee, hardening strands of Danish, and stuffed ashtrays, and said, smiling and shaking his head, "Crude mother."

Pale sunlight drifted into the room through the slanted blinds of the bungalow's eastern windows facing the RPM lot. A different light oozed from recessed fluorescent bulbs in the ceiling, tinting the room with a sleepless, all-night cast, a waxen suspension of time. The walls, a brown thatched acoustic mesh, deadened sound against instances when the men in the room were actually forced to listen to music.

"I can't believe it," said Ruffino. "A Top Twenty album just drops in our laps. We must be living right." He turned his eyes heavenward, put his hand over his wide-striped purple silk shirt where his heart was, and said, "God Bless you, Lisa Wilde, wherever you are, for turning our second quarter around."

And even dry Darrell Johns, Sales, peering up over his bifocals, had to smile at that one.

An uneasy gallows humor prevailed around the long, rectangular polished oak table. Each of the regulars, sitting as far away from the others as possible, had crept out of his private fiefdom within the company, enclaves of male privilege—secretaries, expense accounts, tradeoffs and deals going on the side—to attend the obligatory meeting. And as their voices rose, each in turn, into the listless air, the light, the emptiness, there was, after six grim months of siege, a ray of hope. Elizabeth "Lisa" Wilde was clearly a candidate for imminent enshrinement as an angel, albeit a lesser one, in the starry firmament of rock heaven. And that meant sales. *If* they moved.

"You gotta hit the streets yesterday with this kind of thing, Jack," said Tiny Braun. "Run with the headlines. Unless maybe it's Elvis who died or something." He sat back, folded his hands over his massive belly, showed his teeth through his beard, and watched the blond secretary slip quietly out of the room.

Braun, who called everybody Jack, occupied a peculiar position among the men at the table, at once privileged and vulnerable. With his flower shirts, his jeans and leather, his long brown curly hair and earring, he was said to be a big favorite at the radio stations. This was important, radio being the record company's symbiotic sister, and airplay its lifeblood. A kind of dope-and-music Johnny Appleseed, Tiny Braun was dispatched from RPM Hollywood on a long leash, with Marty Karp's blessing, to spread a discretionary expense account among the radio stations' program directors and disc jockeys to keep them favorably inclined toward RPM. His was a job with intangible statistics; some said he was very effective at getting airplay, that he had "credibility." Still, he was a freak, and viewed with a certain benign suspicion. And though Marty scattered titles among his juniors like birdseed, Tiny Braun was the only one at the table, with the exception of Monk Purcell, who wasn't a Vice President. He would probably never know the pleasure of opening up the trades on Monday morning to read of his ascent to that meaty, if transient, echelon.

"What happened to her anyway?" said Ruffino, glancing toward the end of the table.

Jay Kippel, Legal, was sitting in front of the blackboard. He took his pipe out of his mouth and said in a soft but firm tone that made it clear that no further discussion would be entertained on the matter: "She ran off the road up on Mulholland."

"When?"

"Friday."

"I heard she was loaded," Tiny Braun said under his breath.

Kippel, though he heard the comment, said nothing.

"Was it in the papers?"

"Page three of the *Times*," Ruffino said.

"Picture?"

"No."

Kippel hunched over and relit his pipe. Gray and small and sepulchral, Jay Kippel had been with the label since its beginning. Nobody else signed checks, or tampered with fiscal affairs. Marty often used him to convey inside information down through the company, and to chair meetings in his absence. In this business Kippel passed, without much scrutiny, for a brain. His credentials consisted of the fact that before RPM he had worked fifteen years in the Seventh Avenue garment industry and, on the side, for a New Jersey bookmaker. He dealt with the others as if they were children. This morning he monitored the meeting with a particular interest, for Marty had sent him there on a very important mission.

Joe Ruffino, Marketing, spoke again. "The business loves a tragedy," he said. "Remember when Hendrix died? And that guy walked in peddling those old studio jams we bought? Then we found out he'd sold some to every company in town. So what? Everybody cleaned up." He shook with laughter, and fiddled with the gold chains that hung against his chest through his open striped shirt. This touch of flash, Ruffino firmly believed, made him better able to "relate to the artist." For a guy who used to play a little trumpet in a strip joint in Buffalo—his upper lip still bore the crease of an embouchure—he had done well, making it up through the branch system, and finally to The Lot, as the guys in the field called RPM Hollywood. In truth, Ruffino might just as easily have ended up in shoes, or plastics, or hardware. His concessions to the style of the business took on extreme, ridiculous forms: the loud clothes, outdated

street jargon, the graceless consumption of drugs at open-
ings, and a final grotesquerie: an ill-fitting brown toupee,
which he called a "toop," flecked with rust highlights, sitting atop his own black and gray sideburns. "Christ," he
said. "I love it. You know that guy still spends half of every
year in Bermuda living off those tapes? If Hendrix was alive
he'd be starving."

"So what do we do?" asked Tiny Braun, looking again
down the table at Kippel.

"Marty says milk it," said Kippel softly.

"Where is Marty?" said Ruffino.

"In mourning in his office, Jack," said Tiny Braun, chuckling. "With a line of coke." Nobody could get away with
comments like that but Braun.

Ruffino turned to Darrell Johns: "And he wonders why he
hasn't made Vice President."

"Darrell?" said Kippel.

Darrell Johns looked up from his computerized inventory
sheets and pushed his bifocals back on his nose. "I was just
going over how much of her earlier product we got out
there." He read off, in a monotone: "Fifty thousand units at
the Indiana warehouse. Thirty thousand out here. That's
total. Four albums. Her first album we can't find anywhere."

"That was a pickup from Roundtable, a little folk label,"
said Kippel. "When she used to sing with that kid Lewis
Adam. The junkie. Don't worry about it. It was a courtesy
deal. We don't make anything on it."

Darrell Johns gazed expressionlessly down at his figures.
He was among the few in the business who had never propi-
tiated to rock style. He still bought at Sears, splashed his
face with Old Spice, wore checkered wash-and-wear jackets.
For this, he was the butt of endless jokes. Perhaps he would
have gotten hip had he known how. But he remained the table's WASP, a fundamentalist Christian in fact, a cornfed
Iowa boy who had made his mark running a big national
distribution chain out of Minneapolis.

Finally out of his thin, hard lips came the words, slow and solid: "I'd say we press and ship two hundred thousand of *Greatest Hits*. See how we do. Say forty thousand for each major market, ten thousand each for the secondaries. And some extra for San Francisco. The branch up there tells me she's still got a local following."

"No, Darrell," Kippel said softly. "We press more like three million."

Darrell Johns looked up, and a kind of shock settled into his eyes. "I don't think we can move that kind of product, Jay," he said slowly, fearfully. "Even if we can get the stores to stock it, it'll just sit there. We'll have to eat the returns eventually. Just like the last two quarters."

"Three million," Kippel said. "That's straight from Marty. And it all has to be shipped before the end of this quarter. In addition," he said, "we're going to press and ship three million of Candy Snow."

Intakes of breath were audible around the table. Darrell Johns shook his head slowly, sadly, the creases in his pink neck bunching. "This overloading of product," he said, "is a dangerous game, Jay. If the stores decide to call in their credit, or the market goes soft for a couple of months, we're finished. These figures are making me a little nervous." His euphemism, normally a cue for a joke, this time fell unremarked into the silence.

"Jay," Ruffino said. "Candy Snow isn't even out yet. We got no single. We don't know how it's going to do."

"The broad's a stiff," said Tiny Braun. "Nobody's going to sit still for her."

"There'll be a single this week," Kippel said coolly. "It'll do fine. Just work it. Fast, and hard. We're going to have two hits this quarter. I want to see those numbers on the books."

The burgeoning sense of unreality that had blossomed within the company during six hitless months now settled once more over the table, in the shape of an inert gloom. Braun pulled at his earring. Ruffino scratched his "toop."

Down at the other end of the table, Monk Purcell, Creative, sat sallow and waxen, slumped in his chair, gazing silently, dolefully at the others as if they were madmen. Darrell Johns spun a yellow pencil between his fingers.

Finally Tiny Braun said, "That's two weeks, Jack. We gotta hump." He looked around the table, shrugging. "I mean it's not like my phone's ringing off the hook with job offers, you know?"

"If that's what Marty wants," said Ruffino, concurring, "I guess we get behind it. I mean what the hell. Live fast, die young."

The remark served to break the pall. For nobody knew better than the men at the table that Ruffino's cliché epitomized the business. It had always flown by the seat of its pants. Buoyed by the technology of the long-playing record, the business had ridden the crest of an extraordinary wave of fortune. Nobody understood it; nobody wanted to. It was pennies from heaven.

"We got artwork on Lisa?" Darrell Johns asked. He turned and looked down the table at Monk Purcell. Purcell, ailing and ulcerous, sat immobile, the ceiling lights hanging steep shadows over his cheekbones. From a pile of artwork in front of him, he gave a limp, vindictive toss. Four album covers spun to the middle of the table, and stopped.

All eyes went to them; and what they saw, in the silence, was a curious tableau of the passage of Lisa Wilde.

The first cover showed her early in her career, standing alone on a cliff overlooking the sea, an acoustic guitar over her shoulder, her back to the camera. Her hair was long and straight, and so was the madras dress she wore. The color separations were poor, the photo amateurish; but they couldn't restrain the soft, lyrical, unabashed innocence that flowed from the image.

In the second, she was posed against the marquee of a rock club in the snow, in the middle of some forgotten East Coast winter tour, with members of her band, looking a little harder. Her hair was shorter, the folk simplicity given way to a black leather miniskirt. The guitar, now electric, was in the hands of a band member.

"Shit," said Tiny Braun. "She was pretty."

The third was taken onstage at the Amphitheater. Lisa stood, in profile, before a microphone, dressed in bright silks, her mouth open in song, partially silhouetted by a spotlight. In the background, just visible, was the string section of a symphony orchestra. There was a strength, an urgency, a sense of her performing at the height of her public presence; and there was a swirling, desperate mania, too.

The fourth cover was a highly stylized black-and-white handtinted photo, shot with a strobe. It deeply contrasted the one before it. In a soft, simple black dress, wearing a hat, she sat at a table in the corner of a small restaurant, alone again, as in the beginning. She gazed directly up at the camera with frank, curious, open eyes—a regard of consuming intensity. It was a spare, haunting, beautiful image, suggestive of exile, awakening, thoughtfulness.

"This the one you won the Grammy for, Purcell?" Darrell Johns asked.

"Yes," said Monk Purcell quietly.

"So what do we use for the new one?"

"This is what she wanted for her next album," Purcell said. A large color transparency inside a plastic sleeve slid down the table.

It was a closeup of a small bird, a canary. There was a tiny birdcage to one side of the picture, a rope extending from it. The door was open, and the canary, its back to the cage, was rising in flight, its wings fluttering, out of focus. But the head of the bird was very clear. The eyes, intent with the effort of flight, stared into space. A ray of light glinted in the frozen eye. A reddish tinge from the dust, or soil, behind the bird, against which the bird's yellow colors were set, gave the print a brilliant, sensuous quality.

"I don't get it," said Ruffino.

"It's not right," said Darrell Johns, looking up. "You need a photo on a *Greatest Hits* album. The public wants to see the artist. Not a bird. Nobody wants to see a bird."

Monk Purcell reached his long arms forward and gathered in the artwork. "I don't have a recent picture of her," he said darkly.

"Somebody run down to the morgue and snap one off," said Ruffino. Tiny Braun was the only one who laughed.

"Purcell," said Kippel, from the other end of the table. "See what you can come up with."

"Posters?" said Braun.

"No," said Ruffino. "Not enough time. But we'll do a radio spot. Where is Motta, anyway?" When nobody answered, he just said, "Purcell, tell him we need a sixty-second radio spot. Something tasty, you know?"

"And a trade ad," said Kippel.

"Black borders? The whole bit?" Ruffino asked.

Kippel nodded.

"What should it say?" asked Monk Purcell.

Tiny Braun ventured: "In Memory of Lisa Wilde. For bailing us out of a shitty quarter, and getting us all bonuses. I hope." But this time he didn't get the laugh. The images on the album covers had chastened the room.

"Tell Motta to write something nice," Ruffino said to Monk Purcell.

The door had opened, and everyone turned to see an older, goateed man in a tweed jacket walk slowly into the room with a cane, breathing with some effort.

Len Woolf, Artists and Repertoire, sat down at the far end of the table. He leaned his cane against the table, and looked into the expectant silence, saw the covers of Lisa Wilde's albums piled in front of Monk Purcell. He was quite aware that his entrance had brought a shift in the air; it always did. He let it settle for a moment.

Len Woolf had been there longer than anyone else except Kippel. He was an increasing rarity, an A&R man who func-

tioned as in-house producer, not just a buyer of work done
on the outside. He had been, for the last few albums, Lisa
Wilde's nominal producer—her "producer of record," as he
liked to phrase it with self-effacing wit; for in fact she had
done most of it herself. Once a musician, he was accorded a
peculiar respect because of his knowledge and taste: the
aging hipster connoisseur. He was, as Ruffino once put it,
RPM's "Holy Ghost." It was common knowledge that
Marty had made him head of A&R partly because he could
be controlled, for he was not interested in power; partly because he knew that Len Woolf would slow him down, serve
as his brakes; but most of all because Marty's vaunted
"golden ears" actually hung on the gray, shaggy head of
Len Woolf.

It was known that he was soon to retire. For one, he was
ill. But there was more to it than his health. He was a throw-
back to a school of men who had built the industry with a
genuine passion for music, men who saw that things were
done for the artist they could not always do for themselves.
With the changing times he was something of an an-
tediluvian monster, an anomaly, a relic; and as such, a walking rebuke to the others who now sat waiting for him to
speak. Though he knew it would fall on deaf ears, Len
Woolf cleared his throat, with difficulty, and began. For it
was his place in the order of things.

"She was quite a good artist, you know. She wrote very
well, sang beautifully. She was a damn fine musician besides . . ." He looked up at the far wall, where the speakers
hung dark and silent.

Tiny Braun looked over at Ruffino, and pulled on his earring. Ruffino was pushing crumbs of Danish into a pile on
the table with his business card.

"Seems like we suck them dry," Len Woolf said, "then
spit them out when they falter, or deviate from some for-
mula. Then we begin to nurture lousy, inferior artists in our
own image. Like Candy Snow." He gazed around the table,

his face creased with fatigue, his shoulders heavy. "Sometimes I think if we could find a way to carry on our business without the artist, we would. With electronics, maybe we can. Shit. Maybe Muzak is what we wanted all along." He smiled ruefully. "We're like snakes nibbling our own tails. Pretty soon we'll just be talking to ourselves."

Len Woolf paused, clearly in the grip of some emotion. Then he turned and looked at Monk Purcell, sitting next to him. "Monk," he said, "put a goddamn tasteful cover on it. And let's not do the 'late, great Lisa Wilde' routine. Tonight I'll go into the studio and remaster some of her old things and program the cuts for the *Greatest Hits* album. There are a couple of new tunes I'd like to include. They're good. Let's make it a nice memorial to her. Oh, and there'll be no single. That's all I want to say. I'm done."

He smiled slightly, almost sheepishly, as if to make light of his own comments and ease the space in the room for the benefit of the others. For he harbored no rancor toward them.

"A quiet but effective campaign," Ruffino echoed, looking around the table. Everyone knew he said it for Len Woolf, and that the subject was now closed.

"Gentlemen," Jay Kippel said from the other end of the room. "There's something else I have to say." He laid his pipe down in an ashtray and waited until he had everyone's attention. Then he said, flatly, looking down at his own hands on the table, "The company is going to be sold."

Fear does indeed have an aroma. As it rose through the air, mixing with the sweat and the tobacco, the fundamental terror that lurked at the center of each of their lives became a vivid, palpable presence—instantaneous, sad, hopelessly transparent.

"Who'd we sell to?" asked Ruffino, his voice breaking.

"A German company. Heller. A very large conglomerate. You know them as Multigram."

"Multigram," whispered Tiny Braun. "Film company. Publishing. They're huge."

"Actually," said Kippel, "Heller owns a number of recording companies already, outside the U.S. York, in England. Berlin Grammaphone, the classical company. Multigram Tokyo."

"I always thought they were American, Multigram," said Darrell Johns, hoarsely, with a trace of disapproval.

"Let me say," said Kippel, "that we don't anticipate anybody being let go. Marty will stay on. I'll stay. Things will be pretty much as usual." A guarded feeling of relief swept around the table, and the settling of bodies made the chairs groan.

"When's this gonna happen?" asked Braun.

"July tenth," said Kippel. "Marty and I will fly to New York to meet with their people. As I said, you needn't worry. As long as we perform well this quarter. As we have discussed. It is very important that we do that." Kippel looked around the table, letting his words sink in.

"So that's why we overstock Lisa Wilde and Candy Snow," Ruffino said.

Kippel noddel. "Yes. We need to go into that meeting with big numbers."

"Even if it's all just hype?" said Tiny Braun.

Kippel didn't respond.

A bleak, dogged fear swept the table. The terms of their survival had suddenly been reduced to the simple task of working two albums: one by a dead artist, the other by a bad one. Events had spiraled far beyond their domain, or their ability to control them. They had fed long and well at the sweet nipple of the long-playing record. Now they had to perform, prove themselves again, or be cast out, back to the streets.

Only Monk Purcell, among them, felt nothing. He was cauterized, wounded, locked in a failure of will. For he, like Len Woolf, had loved the music, and lost.

"Nazis," Ruffino said. "You're a Jew, Kippel. Darrell, you fought in the war."

"It's just a business arrangement," Kippel said. "In fact, we'll have more money for artist development."

"We gonna change our name?"

"Multigram," said Braun. "It sounds more like a vitamin."

"Actually," said Kippel, "Heller is one of the biggest pharmaceutical firms in the world."

"Hey," said Tiny Braun, tapping his nose. "Now you're talking."

"I'll tell you what it means," Darrell Johns said. "I saw it happen at IRC. It means the lawyers and the accountants—nothing personal, Jay—move to the center. And there's a lot of talk in the corridors about 'blockbusters.'"

"We were the last major independent left," said Ruffino.

"Who's gonna stand up for the artist?" Tiny Braun said, suddenly taking up Len Woolf's cry.

"What do you think, Len?" Ruffino said, looking down the table with appeal in his eyes.

"I'd say it's time for me to retire," he said softly.

An uneasy mood locked in over the table, expressing itself in idle, flip chatter.

"*Sieg Heil!*" ventured Ruffino. But nobody thought it was funny.

"Hey, you know, Darrell?" Tiny Braun said. "It's just like Jonah and the whale. We're being swallowed up. Right into the belly of the beast." He looked over at Darrell Johns, baiting him. "It's just like becoming religious, isn't it, Darrell? From now on there's somebody upstairs."

Everyone turned and looked at Darrell Johns, Sales, anticipating the possibility of a rare show of feeling. But he just took a long, deep breath, and stared down at his white knuckles folded over the inventory reports.

7

Michael Motta sat on a couch in the reception room, un-shaven and sunk down inside himself, gazing at the closed door of Marty Karp's office. Muffled voices leaked through the walls behind him from the conference room where the Product Meeting was in progress. Marty's secretary, a tall black girl with lots of bracelets, sat typing at a glass desk before a gallery of gold records in frames on the wall.

"He'll be out in a minute." Motta turned, startled at the sound of her voice. "He's on the WATS to Philadelphia," she said, and smiled at him softly. He could smell her perfume all the way across the room.

Motta picked a copy of *Billboard* off the glass table and leafed mindlessly through the pages. A bird chirped in a hibiscus just outside the window. He stretched his feet along the pile carpet and waited.

He heard a song of Lisa's pulsing faintly through the

walls behind him. It evoked no particular emotion; it wasn't one he knew. Then the needle slipped across the grooves, making a zipping sound, and it was silent again. Somebody in the conference room laughed.

The door to Marty's office opened, and Motta looked up. Marty Karp stood there, small and thin and neat and tan, gazing at him expectantly. The solicitous expression on his face looked, it occurred to Motta, freshly composed on his behalf. Traces of the old one lingered somewhere in his visage, his stance. He was wearing gray slacks, shiny brown loafers, a sport shirt.

"Mike," he said, stepping forward and extending his hand. As Motta stood up and shook it, Marty's other hand closed over his, and his earnest eyes sought Motta's as if to confirm that they were both bearing up under a great strain together. "Come on in."

Motta took the step down into Marty's oak-paneled office. "Hold the calls, sugar," Marty called to the secretary. And then the door closed.

"Sit, sit," Marty said, gesturing toward the Eames chair in front of the desk. As Motta crossed the Persian rug and sat down, he watched Marty walk back around the desk on the balls of his feet—the way so many short men do—patting the side of his neat silver hair with his hand. "I know what we've both been going through," he said, his back still to Motta.

Watching him, Motta felt as he always did around Marty: fascinated, repelled, and finally, disarmed. Marty used behavior the way a conductor used a baton—for effect, to move things around. It was something utterly beyond any consideration of sincerity, and so foreign to Motta that he regarded it with inexhaustible awe. To him, Marty Karp was a pure creature of opportunity—unfathomable, vile, alluring. He symbolized all of Michael Motta's ambivalent feelings about Hollywood; for he had never been able to decide if Marty's way was entirely bad.

Marty turned and stood over his desk. "You look from hunger," he said. "You been sleeping? Eating?" He said it paternalistically, full of ersatz concern. "Christ. I've been depressed as hell. Couldn't sleep last night." He walked nervously over to a little wet bar next to his desk. "Everybody here is pretty torn up. Including me, as you can imagine."

He opened the door of the tiny fridge under the bar and gazed around inside. "You want something to drink? Juice?"

"No, thanks."

"Apple? Strawberry? It's organic."

"No, Marty." Motta clasped his hands in his lap and waited. He had called Marty when he had arrived at the company that morning, only to find that Marty had already called and wanted to see him.

Motta noticed, on his desk, a picture of Marty and Lisa from years ago; he didn't remember having seen it there before. There were pictures of his wife and kids, and an old woman who had to be his mother. A third picture showed Marty and the President on the White House lawn with a group of music business executives.

Marty came around the front of the desk with his drink, and leaned against it. "So what happened, Mike?" he asked.

"She was driving on Mulholland and a car bumped her off the road."

"You weren't hurt?"

"No."

"That's good. You saw it?"

"Yes," Motta said softly. "I saw it."

"I knew Lisa for twelve years, Mike. We came up together. This company was built on her early hits." He stirred his drink with his finger, then licked it off. "But then, why am I telling you? You know all about that. I mean this has really devastated me." He walked to the window at the other end of the room where the curtains were closed against the lot, and put his knee up on the window seat. "I'm thinking of selling."

"Selling what, Marty?"

"The company."

Motta turned in his chair and looked at him. Marty was poised dramatically at the curtain, one hand in the pocket of his expensive slacks, staring down at the floor, shoulders hunched. "I'm tired," he said. "Real tired. I don't know if I can go on after this."

Marty turned, looked up, and began to pace. Motta, watching his motions and his shiny eyes, realized he had snorted some coke just before he had come in. Marty was a legendary user, long before it became fashionable. "You get offers all the time," he was saying. "There is always interest. I tell them to go to hell. But I'm just very distressed right now." His Old Testament act, Motta thought. His deep, suffering ethnic routine. He'd seen him do it once before when an agent wanted too much money for an act.

Marty walked back to his desk and sat down. He leaned forward, elbows on the desk, and looked earnestly at Motta, his face a mask of glittering solicitude. "What were you doing up there, Mike? On Mulholland?"

"I was following her to her house to interview her for *Crossover*. I had asked her a couple of months ago. She called me Friday and said to meet her in front of the Beverly Hills Hotel."

"So you didn't get the interview?"

"No."

"She say anything to you before she died?"

"No. She was unconscious when I got down there."

"Did you tape anything?"

Motta felt a sensation in his stomach. "No. How could I have? We were in separate cars."

The uncharacteristic darkness of the room pressed in on them. Motta had the sudden feeling this meeting was not at all for the purpose of commiseration. Marty wanted something. Motta felt himself drawing inward. The room swelled with silence.

"What was your interview going to be about?"

"Just the usual. Music, career, and so on. Her next album." Motta suddenly didn't want to mention the earlier taped interview, the one he had been listening to at the time of the accident.

"You knew Lisa, didn't you? In Berkeley?"

"Years ago. Before the whole thing started. But we didn't stay in touch." Motta spoke guardedly now, fishing for position, trying to disguise what he was leaving out of his words.

"I suppose *The Rock* will want to do something on this," Marty said, looking away at the window behind Motta.

"Undoubtedly."

"I wish they wouldn't."

"Why not? It will certainly be laudatory. She was a big critical favorite there." And quite suddenly Motta felt depressed. He wished he were back at the beach, back in bed. He wasn't ready to be talking about Lisa in these terms yet.

Marty didn't answer for a moment. Then he said, "Out of respect for her memory."

Motta looked up at him. "What do you mean?"

But Marty didn't answer. He just looked at Motta, as if trying to read something in his face. "Mike," he said finally, "is there anything you want to tell me?"

"No, Marty," Motta said. "Nothing. I'm just very tired too."

"You told the police somebody pushed her off the road."

"They did."

"I can't believe that, Mike."

"A black Mercedes with no license plates, two guys inside, bumped her off the road. I was right behind her. I saw it."

"People don't go around doing that kind of stuff, Mike. With other people watching."

"I don't have an explanation either, Marty. But I saw what I saw."

"That just couldn't have happened, Mike."

Motta felt himself growing angry. His hands began to tremble. "I'm a journalist, Marty. I know my own powers of observation." He looked up at Marty, his eyes hot.

Marty took a breath, screwed up his face, and leaned forward over his desk, fingers spread, eyes jumping from the coke, and looked directly at Motta. "Look, Mike," he said. "I think there are some things maybe you don't know about that it's time you did."

Motta felt a bolt of fear, hot and gnawing, crawl up into his stomach and lodge there. "Like what?"

"A lot of things changed with Lisa after Berkeley, Mike. It's been a long road. The star thing put her through a lot. You understand?"

"What are you trying to tell me?" Motta heard the quaver in his voice.

"Drugs, Michael, drugs," Marty crooned. "Amphetamines. And horse, heroin."

Motta fought to keep his eyes locked into Marty's. "Go on," he said.

"I can personally tell you, in confidence, that Lisa was doing hard dope. We all knew about it. I mean the few of us here. Ask Eddie Malone. Ask Kippel."

Motta felt the walls waver, and Marty's face began to pulse in front of him. He gripped the leather arms of the chair.

"See, I think it went back to that kid she started out with. Lewis Adam. The junkie. Remember him? The tall blond kid with the granny glasses?"

Motta opened his mouth, but nothing came out.

"I mean if she was loaded, in that state," Marty was saying, "it probably freaked her out, this guy honking behind her. And she made a mistake."

"She wasn't stoned," Motta said. "I saw her in front of the

Beverly Hills Hotel. I know when somebody's loaded. She was nervous, but she wasn't stoned." His voice sounded hollow, like a tape echo.

Marty shook his head sadly, over and over. "It's all in here, Mike," he said. He was holding a sheaf of papers stapled together. With a show of great reluctance, he handed them to Motta. "The Police Report," he said. "The Coroner's Report is attached."

Motta took it. It was a standard police report form, with the information typed in. He turned to what Marty wanted him to see: "*Death at approximately 3:22 p.m. Acute heroin/morphine intoxication due to inhalation.*"

He closed the report and handed it back to Marty. "This is a setup," he whispered. "Somebody fixed this."

Marty looked back at him with an expression of great personal aggrievement. "What can I say, Mike? It's what's in here." He flicked the police report with the back of his hand.

"You're saying she wasn't killed. That she killed herself," Motta said weakly. "And that I didn't see what I saw."

Marty jumped up and began to pace behind his desk. "Okay, look, Mike. Here's the point. Suppose you did see what you say you did? Personally, I don't think Lisa Wilde had an enemy in the world. Except herself. But does it matter? Supposing it was some dealer she got involved with. Somebody burned somebody's connection. Under the circumstances . . ." Marty looked down at the police report. "I mean, for the sake of her reputation . . ."

"This is a whitewash," Motta said, fighting to control his voice. "I don't believe a word of it. Who fixed it, Marty? Was it you?"

"Look, Mike," Marty said softly. "I know you've been under a lot of pressure this year, coming to L.A. and all. I know you thought a lot of her. You always stuck up for her at the Product Meetings. You've been working hard here at the company and doing a great job. And now this thing . . ." Marty gazed down at Motta, and Motta saw that his little hatchet face was adamantine, resolute, committed to his stance.

"So that's how it is," Motta whispered. "You know you're lying, Marty. Or somebody is. Why?"

"Whaddya mean?" Marty threw his hands up in the air, wounded, full of injured innocence.

Even the artist's death is information, and they can sell that too . . .

Motta, in a bound, was up and across the room. He skirted the desk, and went straight for Marty in his chair. Marty had stood up, but was trapped behind his desk; he braced for the charge, his eyes wide with surprise. Motta met his arms, and they locked. He threw Marty down in his leather chair and fell on him.

"Mike! Mike!" Marty called out. But Motta was beyond orders. He had become possessed by rage.

He took a swing at Marty's face. It wasn't a good blow, but it connected. His retracting arm smashed into a gold record on the wall. It came shattering down around them. Marty fell against the desk, more surprised than wounded, sweeping a Grammy from the desk, and sending the glass of apple juice spraying across the room.

As Marty struggled up, Motta fell on him. He picked him up, turned him around, and backed him into the stereo system next to the desk. As it tumbled to the floor, howling protests shot from the speakers on the walls.

Motta turned Marty around again, and folded him back over his own desk. His arms slid up to his throat, and found it. He held him there, surprised at his own strength, his hands dripping blood from the glass. Amazed by his own violence, but far beyond any desire to control it, he watched Marty's face turn a bright red, and his tongue and his eyes pop out.

Just when he could squeeze no longer, he felt a pair of big, beefy arms grab his own. They pulled, until his grip on Marty broke away, and the arms enfolded him in a bearhug.

Motta fought frantically, lashing and kicking against the huge body. He jerked his head around wildly, and found himself staring into the sheepish, apologetic eyes of Eddie Malone.

"Ease off, Mike," he whispered. "Ease off."

Eddie held him very tightly; and slowly, Motta stopped resisting. Eddie half-carried him back over to the Eames chair and sat him down. He went around back, without letting go, and put his hands firmly on Motta's shoulders. "It's okay, Mike," he said. "We loved her too."

Motta sat in the chair, glazed and panting, his sweater torn, gazing with wonder upon what he had done. Marty was bent over his desk, holding his throat, coughing. Seeing the normal color return to his face, Motta was relieved. Marty sat down in his chair, closed his eyes, and occupied himself with breathing.

Motta looked down. His knuckles were torn, and blood dripped onto his jeans. A convulsion passed through him; he felt Eddie Malone's hands tighten on his shoulders. He could see the big red hamfist out of the corner of his eye. But all desire to struggle had left him.

Motta looked up. Marty was refilling his glass of apple juice. Turning away from the room, he drank it slowly, touching his face with the wetness, patting his hair with his hand, straightening his clothes.

When Marty turned back around, he looked practically as though nothing had happened. He gazed across the room, breathing heavily, and placed his fingertips on the desk in front of which he stood, among the broken glass and the spilled juice. Then he began to speak.

Motta sat, trapped, watching and listening. He could do nothing else.

"You know, Mike, when I hired you away from *The Rock*, it wasn't because you were doing an article on us. I know people said that. It wasn't because I wanted to buy you off. It's true I didn't want you to do the story. I admit it. But not

because of me. I got nothing to hide. It was for Lisa. I
thought it might make her feel more comfortable with you
here. It was crazy, I know, but that's what I thought. You
used to know her. You were a fan. I read some of your reviews. I thought you'd be her . . . *advocate* at the company.
I knew what was happening to her. And I was worried. I
didn't want her name dragged through the mud . . ."

Motta watched transfixed, unbelieving, as Marty wove his
story. He had the feeling Marty didn't care if Motta
believed him or not; he was simply reeling off a prepared
rap, reading it into the record, as if Motta were some kind of
dictaphone, or a mirror before which he was practicing. He
paced back and forth like some mad Queeg, commandeering
the deck of his shattered, bloody office.

"I was just a little song plugger from the East when I met
her. She was this *goy*, long blond hair, understand? She cast
a sun on my life. To her I was The Rat. But I didn't care. All
I wanted to do was see her make it. Then when it happened,
she seemed to resent me, as if I had put her in some sort of
trap. But I was just doing my thing, and making it so she
could do hers. When we got money, it made me happy. Not
her. The more successful we got, the less she liked me. I
don't think she ever wanted the fame, and the money, all
this . . ." Marty gestured around the office. "She felt cut off,
imprisoned. 'Lisa,' I would say, 'look. You can't go back to
Berkeley.' But it got worse. She hated me more and more.
She was talking of running her own company, or something.
Artists sometimes go through that."

As Marty glanced at him, it dawned on Motta that Marty
suspected he had talked to her, and wanted to cover anything that might have been said.

"You have to realize," Marty said, looking directly at him,
"an artist is a commodity. A package. It takes genius to put
them over to the public. That's where guys like me come in."
He could hear Eddie Malone's thick breathing behind him,
feel his fingers on his shoulders. "Let's face it. Talent is com-

mon. It's that extra something that does it. Lisa couldn't accept that. She was an idealist, an innocent. The pressures got to her, Michael. She was too beautiful to survive in this world." The phone buzzed, but Marty ignored it. "You see, Michael. There's a place for all of us in this life. Her place was to write and sing beautifully. What I know about is power. I devoted this power to her and others so that this beautiful sound could be heard all over the world. But she hated me for that. Why? Why? Something in her was very self-defeating. Finally it just exploded."

"You're full of shit, Marty," Motta said levelly.

Marty looked up, as if surprised to see Motta there.

"Look, Michael. You saw the report right there. You're going to have to accept what happened. If you don't you'll be in danger. From yourself, I mean." He had turned away again and was staring at the ruined stereo on the floor. "I want you to take a month off. Get your head back together. And then I want you to come back. I'm going to need you. We'll bump your salary. I think you're worth it." He turned and looked down at Motta with his best charade of warmth. "You know," he said, "I'm glad you came at me. I respect that. I feel it cleared the air. We understand each other better now. Eddie?"

"Yeah, Marty," Eddie wheezed.

"Go see Kippel and get him to draw a check for Michael for a month's salary, and a five-hundred-dollar bonus. Okay, Mike? You need anything else? Prescriptions? Something to get you through? Some Valium? I got some here. Any medical bills, just send them here. I have a shrink who's very good. I can send you over."

Motta closed his eyes, and a flood of nausea passed through him.

"Listen, Michael. Anything that comes up in your mind, let's talk. Okay? Keep close. Don't let it build up. You got my number, you know where my house is. Come up. Use the pool. Let Hedda cook you a meal. I care about you. So does

Eddie. We all care." He waved his hands in the air. "And come back after you're rested."

Before he realized what had happened, Motta was on his feet, and Eddie Malone was escorting him out of the office.

He stumbled out of the bungalow into the steaming noon sun of the RPM lot, where Eddie left him between two cars: one was a black Cadillac with a uniformed chauffeur inside reading a comic and eating a sandwich; the other was Marty's brown two-toned Bentley.

So that is what it feels like, Motta thought sickeningly, to get stroked.

8

The Grill was a little restaurant off Santa Monica Boulevard where Motta often met Amanda on evenings when they were both in town. It featured an old jukebox with vintage forties jazz, show tunes, a good house red, and such rare East Coast dishes as scungilli. The fat, boozy ex-actor who ran the place stood by the bar dismantling The Method while his fluttery wife concocted rich, toothsome desserts back in the kitchen. The walls were dotted with dusty framed photos of nothing in particular, hung in random arrangement over sagging, dark-lit booths, lending a feel of tacky intimacy. Sometimes a customer, or a waiter, walked over and played the tuneless upright in the corner. The Grill possessed, unarguably, a certain *atmosphere;* in a fast-food town, this was reason enough to exist.

From the door Motta saw her alone in a booth, wearing a funny hat with a plastic flower, drinking burgundy and nib-

bling at a plate of fried calamaries. Smiles and fretful frowns
seemed to play alternately off her dark, expressive face. As
he approached he saw that she had her portfolio of com-
posites on the table.

"Where've you been?" she chided. He slipped into the
booth beside her and planted a kiss on her cheek. Suddenly
she noticed his torn shirt. "My God, Michael." Motta
reached for her glass of wine. "And your knuckles are
bloody." Amanda looked at him, horrified. "You hit somebody."

"Marty," he said, downing her wine. "And some glass."

"Oh, no." Her hand went to her mouth. She searched
fearfully for his eyes.

He grinned darkly. "It felt good."

A waiter brought another glass of burgundy and left.
"They have a Coroner's Report," Motta said, "that says Lisa
was loaded. On heroin, or morphine. They're saying she was
a junkie." He quickly drank the wine.

Amanda twisted a red linen napkin in her lap. "I don't
understand, Michael."

"The message is for me to change my story. Say I didn't
see anyone bump her off the road. 'Out of respect for her
memory,' to quote Marty. I'm supposed to take some time
off. Come back for more pay. I don't know if it's Marty or
not. But somebody wants to cover it up."

Amanda gazed silently down at her hands, reluctant to
speak. After a moment, she said, carefully, "I mean it *is* a
possibility, isn't it?"

"What?"

"That she was loaded."

Motta looked at her with a flash of fury. "Not you, too,"
he said.

"But you hadn't seen her for years. She's gone through a
lot."

Motta slumped, and gazed into his wine glass.

"Is it possible you sentimentalize her?" Amanda contin-

ued. "Your first love, and all? I mean, what if someone really did kill her? For some reason you don't know about?"

"They're going to put her forward as a ravaged junkie. It's
a lie."

"Who's 'they'?"

"I don't *know*," he said agitatedly.

"*Your* life is not *her* life. Is it your battle? Does it matter
that much to you?"

Somebody walked to the jukebox, and Billie Holiday's
"Strange Fruit" wafted through the room, eerie and sad.
Amanda fell quiet, and tears welled in her eyes. She dabbed
at them with a napkin.

"I have something to tell you," she said.

"You're pregnant?" he ventured wanly.

"No. Nothing that bad. I got a movie part."

Motta tried to smile. "That's wonderful. That's great.
Speaking?"

"Two lines. Guess what I play?"

"A hooker?"

"Yup."

Motta shook his head. "They won't let you off the meat
rack, will they?"

"A *black hooker*, Michael," she said, upset.

"Would you feel better if they'd cast you as a *white*
hooker?"

"It was humiliating." She lowered her voice. "The director came on to me. Leers and smirks. The whole bit."

Motta reached over and took the last of her calamaries.
"I'm sorry," he said. "What does your agent think?"

"She says take it. Major studio, and all."

"When?"

"Day after tomorrow. In Nashville. For three days." She
smiled weakly. "I don't know whether to be happy or sad."

He put his arm around her and smiled wearily.

"You must feel very alone," she said.

"Sure," he said. "You too."

She nodded. "I don't want you hurt."

"I'm already hurt."

A waiter came, stood expectantly for a moment, then withdrew. Amanda gripped Motta's hand. It was cold, and the fingers twitched. Her dark round eyes searched his face. "My sweet honky baby," she whispered. "Couldn't we just both go away for a while? Jamaica, maybe. I could show you where I was born. We could swim, get some sun. Dance to some reggae. Forget about all this . . ."

"I'd like that," Motta whispered.

They sat without speaking for a while.

"Chinese chicken salad," Amanda said finally, holding up her open menu.

"I'm not hungry."

"You'll get drunk if you don't eat."

"Too late," Motta said. "How about you?"

She shook her head.

"What are we doing here, then?"

"I don't know."

Amanda's body began to shake. Motta took the menu out of her hand and put it down. "Oh, Michael," she blurted. "What about us?"

"I don't know," Motta said quietly. "I really don't."

The waiter, unable to get their attention, went to the upright and launched into a strident ragtime version of "I Can't Get Started."

"Sometimes I've thought that growing up meant becoming a little more like Marty Karp," Motta said. "Maybe that's why I came to Hollywood. Today I had him over the table with my hands on his throat, those hard little eyes bulging out at me. And it was as if he were another race of people, who would destroy me if allowed to. Before it was always abstract. Today I felt it in my hands."

"You're going to try and fight this," she whispered.

"No," he said. "I'm not."

She looked at him, struck with surprise. He had slumped dispiritedly against the tattered back of the booth.

"Maybe you're right," he said. "Her life is not mine." He started to look at her, then didn't. His eyes dropped instead to his lap. Their fingers, which had been locked tightly together on the seat of the booth, slowly loosened, untangled, and fell apart.

"I need the money," he muttered.

Amanda was unable to look at him.

"Can you live with that?" she asked.

Motta could feel her disappointment. "I'll have to," he replied.

Amanda didn't know what to do with her hands. Finally she reached forward and fingered the stem of her empty glass.

"So what about us?" she said flatly.

Motta didn't reply.

"You know, Michael," she said suddenly, lapsing into black street dialect, her voice hard, "we're both just working for The Man, aren't we?"

Motta could feel the sting of shame, and reddened.

"I'm going to take that part," Amanda said. "I'll fly to Nashville tomorrow."

Motta looked away, humiliated.

"What about you?"

"I'm going up to Berkeley tonight. For a little while."

"See your kid?"

He nodded.

"Yeah," she said, softening. "Maybe that's good."

"You got money?"

"The Art Director gave me an advance from the cover shoot at the airport." She was reaching for her jacket and her portfolio. "I'll be okay," she said, with defiance.

Motta watched her through broken, shifting eyes as she stood up. She turned and looked down at him, her jacket slung over her shoulder.

"Will you remember about Jamaica?"

"Yes," he said.

She reached down and kissed him on the cheek. Then helplessly he watched her sweep off toward the door.

9

Motta was drunk on the wine as he drove his Citroën east on Santa Monica Boulevard through a soft summer rain, unusual for June. Hunched over the wheel, he looked out at the street boys in their tight jeans, driven into doorways by the night drizzle, waiting for the chickenhawks to cruise by and beckon. At the corner of La Brea, a hooker in a blue dress and spiked heels sat on a bus bench, a newspaper over her head against the rain, unwilling to relinquish her station.

Los Angeles was a litmus, Motta had written in a letter to his ex-wife Diane. Its character lay precisely in the very absence of one; it offered no direction, no cues. The city took on whatever colors the viewer lent it, became as large or small as one's contemplation of it. It simply *was*. Motta had sometimes wondered if large souls like Stravinsky, Huxley, Thomas Mann had chosen it for just this reason—not for the weather as much as for the limitless, empty horizon line, the utter lack of focus. Los Angeles was the infinite nothing. The individual always stood against it as figure-to-ground. To try and derive content from the environment was like attempting the same thing at a bad movie. One worked too hard, and got nothing in return. Now as the brown eaves of the bungalows on the RPM lot loomed into view through the rain, Motta perceived, deep within the city's mute heart, a shuddering, unspeakable emptiness.

He pulled up to the guard gate and rolled his window down. Felipe was snoozing in his chair, his face swollen with tequila, his bad arm hanging dead in the air like a flag on a windless day. A hysterical Mexican station blared from his portable radio.

"Felipe," he called.

Felipe opened one eye slowly, then composed himself with remarkable speed, as people who commonly sleep on the job learn to do. "Hey, Miguel," he called, and waved his good arm and grinned.

"Felipe," Motta said. "I need your keys to get into my office."

Felipe fiddled with his belt and removed a ring of master keys. He picked one key and, dangling the ring by it, handed the whole ring to Motta through the window.

"Here you go, *hombre*. Bring them back, okay?"

"Thanks," Motta said, and waved. He pulled his car onto the lot, and parked it in his space in front of the Creative Services building.

When he got out of the car, he turned and looked back at the guard box. Felipe's chin was slumped back down on his chest. Motta walked quickly away from Creative Services toward the building at the center of the lot that housed the recording studio. He opened one of the tall wooden double doors and slipped inside.

He stood for a moment in the middle of the empty reception area's parquet floor, his head pulsing with the wine, listening to the hush. Recording studios, though silent, have in fact a strong undercurrent of sound, the accumulation of all the electricity that is *on*. It is about as silent as standing in the middle of a power station.

The walls, paneled with acoustic cork, bore a colorful gallery of RPM artists in glass frames. Avoiding a glance at the picture of Lisa, whose position on the wall he knew well, Motta walked down the long central corridor. Halfway down, where the doors to Studios A and B fed off to either side, a klatch of string players were gathered around the coffee machine between takes. It provided Motta with a black amusement to see these drab, sedate itinerant classical musicians, called in to "sweeten" pop recordings, hovering in rock's glittering corridors, looking vague, confused, guilty, dancing somewhere inside to a much different drummer. One bespectacled girl had brought her knitting.

Motta glanced through the tiny window in the door of Studio B. Craggy, goateed Len Woolf was huddled over the massive console with an engineer. His cane was propped against a 32-track Ampex tape machine. Pressing his ear to the glass, Motta could hear Lisa's voice, in rich, resonant stereo. He turned and plunged drunkenly down the hall, clutching Felipe's ring of keys.

At the end he turned right, and walked quickly past three darkened mixdown studios, a tape duplicating room, and the smaller Studio C. He came to a tall double door that led to the huge, darkened sound stage; to the right was a smaller door, the one he sought.

He tried the keys on the ring, each in turn. Halfway through, he found the one that worked. The door swung open. Motta walked inside, and let the door close behind him.

A soft light glowed from the Tiffany lamp on the desk. The curtains on the window overlooking the lot were still closed. Crossing the room, Motta could see that the broken stereo equipment from the morning's fight had been replaced. The gold record whose glass he had smashed was gone from the wall. The carpet was clean. All signs of struggle had been removed. His heart pounded as he walked behind Marty's desk and stood in the silence. He heard the sound of a car driving onto the lot; that would mean Felipe was awake. Hurriedly, he began to examine the papers on Marty's desk.

Marty always had his secretary arrange the papers into a neat pile to his right, just off the blotter, at the end of each day. Now, quickly, Motta leafed through them. Beneath a stack of the ubiquitous trade papers were a series of manila file folders. He found one handmarked "Wilde," and opened it. Right on top was what he had come for: the Coroner's Report. As he removed it from the file, he saw beneath it a letter from a Century City law firm, addressed to Marty. It was an inquiry about the status of certain of her publishing rights. It referred to the "early published works of Ms. Wilde, to which you allegedly hold certain administration rights, under the terms of a verbal agreement of dubious legal validity, dating back some twelve years." The letter went on to demand the return of revenues from these songs, estimated to be somewhere in the neighborhood of $1 million, along with legal acknowledgment of her full ownership of the rights, and her rights to administer them henceforward. It also requested permission to do an audit of all records pertaining to her publishing "at the earliest possible date."

There were several more letters from the same law firm. Motta read no more, but grabbed the entire folder and stuck it under his arm. Careening around the edge of the desk, he banged against it, spilling another file of papers on the floor. Bending down to pick them up, he saw that the file was marked "Heller." Inside were letters, addressed to Marty, from The Heller Group in Frankfurt. The topmost one, dated June 2, opened with an expression of delight over their anticipated imminent acquisition of RPM Records.

Motta stuffed the papers back in the folder and took it

with him. Quickly he let himself out the same side door through which he had entered, and hurried back down the empty hallway.

The string players were drifting back into session, leaving behind a strew of Styrofoam cups and candy wrappers. Motta reached the studio's darkened reception office by the front entrance, found which of Felipe's keys fit the door, and let himself in. He went directly to the Xerox machine and turned it on.

He was entirely visible through the glass that surrounded the office to anyone who might pass by. He heard voices outside Studio A, but nobody came. Waiting for the machine to warm up, he leafed rapidly through the files.

The legal correspondence in Lisa's file had all been written over the last two months, and had to do with her various publishing rights to which, the letters asserted, Marty Karp had no legitimate claim. The figures mentioned ran into several millions of dollars, and spanned twelve years. The most recent letters seemed to indicate that the earlier ones had gone unheeded or unanswered. In the margin of one, Marty had scrawled the word, "Pricks!"

The Heller file contained several letters expressing, with a formalized but unequivocal delight, the general terms of Heller's acquisition of RPM Records, and referred to the anticipated conclusion of negotiations on July 10 in New York City, at the Sherry Netherland Hotel. Each letter was signed, in a robust hand: *Klaus Heller*.

Motta began copying the papers, one of each. The originals he put back in their folders; the copies he folded twice and stuck in the back pocket of his jeans.

The last piece in the Heller folder was a paper from Marty's notepad. It bore nothing more than the words *Jennings Vaughan* scrawled in Marty's rough hand. Motta put it aside, assuming it was a piece of scrap he had inadvertently mixed in with the Heller file. Then, as an afterthought, he lifted the Xerox machine's flap and placed it against the glass.

Suddenly his eyes exploded with a blinding light. His arm went to his face; squinting, he waited until it passed. When he looked up he saw Felipe, the guard, standing outside the room, a high-powered flashlight in his hand. Tilting slightly, he looked straight into Motta's eyes, drunk, expressionless, like a store Indian. There was no time for Motta to compose his face or cover the papers. All he could do was gaze back at Felipe. Like two soldiers stumbling upon each other in the jungle night, forced to decide in the space of a frozen instant whether this was friend or foe, they faced each other.

Then Felipe's eyes flickered. He rocked slowly back on his heels, and his head bobbled a little on his fat neck. Neither smiling, nor changing his expression, he simply turned and walked back out of the building through the tall double doors.

And in that crystallized moment, Motta saw that, for the first time in his life, he had moved something, changed events outside himself, by the force of his own desire.

Trembling with relief, he pressed the button on the Xerox machine, stuffed the last copy in his pocket, and put the paper back in the folder. He took the manilas and slipped out of the office. Retracing his steps down the hallway to the rear door of Marty's office again, he let himself in. He replaced the file folders on the desk; then he let himself out of the office once more, and walked back down the studio's silent corridors.

Len Woolf was standing by the coffee machine, slowly stirring his coffee with a plastic stick, his cane propped against the wall.

"Hello, Michael."

"Len," Motta said, pausing.

Len Woolf gazed down into the steam rising off the coffee. "I always seem to be the guy they choose to bury

their dead, give the requiem. I don't know if I'm the priest,"
he said wearily, "or just the gravedigger." He looked up at
Motta and gave him a thin smile.

"I'm taking a little time off, Len," Motta said. "I just
came to pick up some things."

"Good," he said. "That's good." He gestured behind him,
at the door to Studio B. "I'm sitting there all night at that
two-hundred-dollar-an-hour computerized thirty-two-track
custom board. We've got quad. Digital. A million bucks'
equipment in that room. I can take somebody like Candy
Snow, who can't even sing in the shower, and make her
sound like a *diva*. Double-track her voice. Correct her pitch
on a variable speed oscillator. I can duplicate that entire
string section in Studio A with a little mellotron. I'm like a
makeup artist, a plastic surgeon. I can turn shit into roses."
He shook his head. "Except when I'm done, it doesn't have
any smell. It doesn't smell like shit, it doesn't smell like
roses. It's a plastic flower." He chuckled softly. "Sometimes
I look at that big console, glowing in the dark, and I talk to
it. But it never answers. If it has a soul, I can't find it."

They looked at each other. "Len," Motta said, "I'll see
you."

"So long, Michael," Len Woolf said, and shook his head.
As Motta was nearing the door, Len Woolf called out after
him. "Hey," he said.

Motta turned and looked at him.

"So long," he repeated, looking steadily at Motta.

Motta smiled, and waved goodbye.

Outside, the rain had softened to a mist. He crossed the
lot quickly to the Creative Services building. If Felipe saw
him from the guard booth at the gate, he didn't show it.
Motta let himself inside with the master key, and walked
down the dark corridor to his office.

Turning the light on, he stood for a moment in the center
of his office. His black portfolio leaned against the wall,
empty. He went over to it, opened it, and placed it on the

couch. Then he looked around the room, trying to decide
what to put in; and as he gazed at the glossy remains of a
year's work, hung in bright white frames on white walls,
bathed in light, Motta suddenly saw the room as a queer,
tiny museum of meaningless artifacts. At the center of the
glossy dance, the busy chatter of culture, Motta perceived a
profound, appalling deadness. The ads, the posters, the
copy, the booklets and brochures and slick award-winning
one-liners—even the bound copies of *The Rock*—he would
leave behind. Frozen in a flashbulb of urgency, Motta knew
that it was over. He would leave it all for the Ephemerists.

He turned and walked out.

In the darkness of the hallway, Motta saw a light on in
Monk Purcell's office.

"Monk?" he said softly, peering inside.

Monk Purcell was sitting slumped at his drafting table, a
half-empty bottle of Jim Beam on one side of him, a vial of
pills on the other. He turned as Motta entered, and looked
up.

"You gotta get out of here," he slurred. He gazed miserably up at Motta as he approached. "The hype is in. All the
way. The fuckers are selling the company to the Germans."

"Heller?"

"Yeah. Kippel ran it down at the meeting today. We're being colonized." The pills on his table were prescription
downers. "You know who they are, Heller?" He held up his
plastic vial so Motta could see the logo. "Isn't that perfect?
Full circle. The pushers are buying up the junkies. From
Heller all the way down to the kid on the street, at a rock
concert with his Quaaludes. The planet is a living laboratory.
So you want some?"

"No," Motta said softly. He looked around at the fluorescent room, hung with stunning graphics—the slick explosive
airbrushed touched-up beauty shots, all the dazzling, brilliant eclecticism of record biz images that so often outper-
formed the music between the covers. Monk Purcell sat in

the center of it all as if amid ruins. A half-finished acrylic painting of a cactus he had begun in New Mexico sat gathering dust in the corner.

Motta looked at Monk Purcell. Here, he thought, at the very heart of the culture, is where exile is the deepest.

Coming closer, he saw that Monk had been playing with several different C-prints of the same image on his drafting table.

"This is what she wanted for her next cover," he said.

"Who?"

"Lisa. But I'm not supposed to use it. They want cheesecake. It's the Candy Snow era, you know?"

Motta looked at the images of the canary and the cage for a long time. In the cooked, lucid intensity of his own leap into space, he absorbed its meaning perfectly; whatever realm of understanding he was about to enter, Lisa Wilde, he knew, had been there before him.

He turned to Monk Purcell. "Why don't you get out of here, Monk?" he said. "Go to New Mexico and paint. That's what you want to do. Everything is falling apart here. It's dying. It's the wrong kind of light."

Monk Purcell gazed slowly around the screaming, vivid room with deep, aching eyes. "Yeah," he whispered. He grew still again; his eyes dropped to the C-prints on his table, and locked onto them. "But I'm caught up in it."

Monk slowly wheeled his towering body around on his stool and stood up.

They embraced, awkwardly.

"Monk, I'll see you," Motta said.

Outside, there were very few stars. The smog simply dimmed them out, washing instead the city's own light back over itself. Motta got into the Citroën and started it up.

At the guard gate he handed Felipe his keys through the window. Their eyes met briefly. Then he was away, speeding south down La Brea.

Amanda's image rose up through the mist as he drove. He

wondered if he would ever have a chance to explain to her why he had said what he'd said in the restaurant, or the reasons for what he was about to do.

Halfway to the airport he thought he saw a dark car following him. He greeted its appearance not with fear, but with relief. He welcomed the arrival, at last, of an enemy.

10

A spectral summer mist hung over the valley of Kyoto in the early morning. A silver ribbon, the Kamogawa, wound through the center of the city, its canals rippling with silk dyes like thousands of iridescent carp. Along the eastern Higashiyama hills, the tips of the pines hovered like ghost heads.

A few blocks beyond the last noisy eastern boulevard, a stone street abruptly turned into an earthen path. The city din became a muted echo, wooded pine forests pressed in, and a temple gong pealed in the mist. The footpath ended at a tall, unvarnished wood *torii*, a gateway, behind which lay the ancient compounds of Daizen-ji.

On the grounds, a stillness ruled. A large wooden building, the central monastery, nestled among the pines. Several smaller structures ran behind it up the mountainside. The only sound was made by a shaven-headed monk in a brown robe, carefully combing the pebbled entrance to the building with a wood rake.

Inside the monastery there was the rustle of slippers along the burnished wood corridors, the splash of a bucket emptying, the hiss of a broom sweeping a floor, as the monks went about their chores. In a reception room near the entrance, facing onto a tiny, simple sand garden, the abbot, the *roshi*, sat observing the tea ceremony with two officials from the prefectural government.

In the long, rectangular *zen-do*, the meditation hall, the paper *shoji* doors were drawn against the garden; the monks sat crosslegged on cushions, in two rows, facing away from each other, eyes cast downward, unfocused. A lone monk, a monitor, stood quietly in shadow at one end of the room, a bamboo switch in his hand. The faintest sound of breathing was heard.

Among the north-facing monks sat one who differed from the others by his size, his imperfect posture, and his eyes: they were a pale, transparent blue. His face was lean, waxen, hollowed with austerity. He was the one the younger monks called *Gaijin-san*, "honorable foreigner." They did so in spite of the roshi's admonition not to differentiate, as this impeded their work. Here one had no name, no face but the Buddha's. And even that face must one day be annihilated. But the young monks called him Gaijin-san anyway; and sometimes, even *henna Gaijin-san*, "honorable crazy foreigner."

Gaijin-san sat, his attention centered in the *hara*, the pit of his stomach, counting his breaths. The polished wood floor upon which his empty gaze fell did not penetrate his mind or occupy his senses. It was not, however, because his mind was the still pool, the empty mirror, he would have desired.

Though he had long ago become comfortable with the act of sitting, this morning Gaijin-san's back hurt terribly. On two fingers of his right hand, an outbreak of the little heat

rash the Japanese call *mizumushi*, "waterbug," itched terribly, causing him to quiver with the effort of restraint. As
thoughts rose, he let them go; but others rushed in to replace them. The damp, oppressive summer heat that had
begun to burn through the morning mist seeped into the
hall, wetting his chest, his arms, his loins. He hoped—something he should not do—that this morning the roshi would
grant him an interview.

On days like this he felt as if all the years of sitting had
been in vain, nothing had been accomplished. This, too,
Gaijin-san knew, was an illusion. But still they came, the
thoughts, the images, the unruly, unwanted emotions, to tor-
ment his meditation, whip his mind into a stormy, agitated
sea.

He had known days of sitting when that same mind was
still, and he could skip an impulse across its surface like a
stone across a clear pool, or gaze into its bottomless depths
forever. On those days he became transformed, and all of
life, within and without, was seamless, vivid, perfectly without value: it simply *was*. He had had his victories. But the
dragons always returned. He would awaken suddenly in the
middle of the night, bathed in sweat; an inexplicable onrush
of weeping would shatter his meditations; for days he would
suffer a bleak, wracking emptiness, tinged with pain, regret,
guilt. For Gaijin-san was one of those who would carry his
past with him like a stone around his neck to the ends of the
earth: he was the eternal penitent.

Perhaps this morning was so difficult because he knew
that his callow, acquisitive adopted son had flown in from
Frankfurt, and awaited him at his *ryokan* a few blocks away
with papers to sign. His son's arrival always served to stir
the muddy swamp of memory.

He held on to the rhythm of his own breath like a drowning man. In, and out. The mizumushi screamed at him.
Sweat ran from his forehead. But nothing could stop it from
coming: the unreeling of the awful movie, the parade of im-

ages. It always came in the same sequence, pattern, chronology, wove itself around his head, a suffocating tapestry of circumstance.

It began with his wife and son's charred bodies in the rubble of Dresden: an imagined picture, for he had not been there to see it. He had been trapped in the Polish countryside, west of Warsaw, a young Waffen first lieutenant—much too young—part of the straggling remnants of a roving extermination squad, one of Kaltenbrunner's SD units, witnessing horrors of his own. He had not spoken out; did one dare?

In the clamping heat of the zen-do, sweat poured down his body, trickled over the blood group number still tattooed below his left armpit.

A tiny, damp basement laboratory in downtown Frankfurt: making penicillin and morphine for the war-wounded —a self-imposed penance, he had considered it then. He, and the scarred little urchin boy he had found wandering in the streets, taken in, given his own name; the boy who would grow up to despise him with cold, narrow eyes of hatred.

The fifteen years that followed: the horrible, ironic success; the basement laboratory swelling into a gleaming complex of glass and steel—the international pharmaceuticals corporation that bore his own name. Then: medical equipment, electronics, "wonder drugs," napalm, X-ray machines, telephones; and later, film, television, music, publishing companies. "Klaus Heller," *Stern* had said, "*is* the postwar German economic miracle."

Through it all, like a sickened river, ran his own monstrous, secret addiction—to the morphine he had once imagined to be the symbol of his atonement. The spiraling consumption, the attempted cures, apomorphine, clinics in Switzerland, the changing of his blood; mistresses, and prostitutes; fast cars, and hushed Autobahn crackups. And the nightmarish rise of the company, a black flower, pouring billions of dollars of drugs onto the black market; spawning

chemicals for warfare; engendering price-fixing scandals in
distant nations. The entire world, it seemed, rushed to follow him down the black tunnel of addiction and despair.

The numb years toppled forward, leaving him with the
terrible conviction that his was a *vie manqué*. Every note he
played seemed to bloom into a death song. A desperate,
abasing flight into Catholicism followed, and failed.

And then the rainy morning in Hamburg in 1959: the little bookshop by the Elbe; finding the tattered copy of *Der
Zen Weg*, Eugen Herrigel's brief volume describing his encounter with Zen Buddhism; his trembling hands as he read.
In the spare elucidation of the warrior's spirituality Heller
found a mirror for his heavy heart, an echo of the ideals of
his youth, and the distant image of a self-awakening that
made him tremble with longing.

Furious days followed. Then the first trip to Kyoto: the
rigorous two-week *sesshin* by the icy winds of the North
Sea; the gradual abandonment of his company, and his life
in Germany; the ever-longer stays in Kyoto. Sitting, sitting,
sitting. To what end? One should understand, said the roshi,
that sitting *is* enlightenment, *satori*. One did not sit to
achieve something; this was simply more illusion. "We are,"
the roshi said, "practitioners of the Soto, not the Rinzai,
school. Not for us the *koan*, the riddle to solve. Only sitting."

Sitting: But with it came solace, discipline, an ethic and
an esthetic; brief flashes of understanding; and the thin fila-
ment of hope that the source of the suffering which life in
this body had brought him could, as Buddha Sakyamuni
had preached, be known. It *could* be known . . .

The terrible movie in his mind softened, dimmed,
abated . . .

Gaijin-san's itching fingers had become anguish. Heat
choked the zen-do. It seemed he would have to wait yet another day to see the roshi. He stood up and walked slowly
out through the door, bowing first to the monitor, then to a
small statue of the Buddha. He padded along the *genkan*,

the walkway, toward the entrance. As he passed the roshi having tea, it occurred to him that another small contribution to the temple fund might expedite his meeting; he very much desired to have his spiritual progress examined. But then the thought shamed him.

At the entrance he slipped into his wooden clogs and his old straw hat, and clopped along the gravel, down the footpath, through the torii, and out of the compound of Daizen-ji.

As soon as he was out of sight of the monastery, he stopped. Then with all the errant passion of a guilty schoolboy, he began to scratch furiously at the mizumushi.

Two blocks later he crossed the busy boulevard that marked the edge of the city. Turning down a side street, he came to the plain wooden gate of a ryokan; entering, he crossed the garden and slipped inside the door. At the top of the stairs he found the shrunken old *obaa-san*, the housekeeper, running his bath. "Your son was here," she said. "He left papers for you to sign."

"Oh, good. Then maybe I won't have to see him."

"*Nani?*"

"Oh, nothing." Gaijin-san slid open the shoji and stepped into his room.

Inside was a simple low lacquer table, his bedding, and a few books piled on the *tatami* matting. A stack of papers sat on the table next to his lunch—a cup of *miso* soup, a small plate of dried fish and seaweed, a bowl of plain white rice, and a pot of tea.

Gaijin-san sat, and began to look through the papers he was supposed to sign. They were all new acquisitions: three more drug companies in South America; an electrical plant in Bulgaria; a film company in Holland—and a record company in America. Whenever he thought of relinquishing his right of signature—though it was a mere formality at this point—he thought of the young predator who bore his name, and he couldn't bring himself to do it.

A mischievous thought came: what if he didn't sign them? Would the world stop? What would young Klaus Heller do? He toyed with the idea until it lost its savor. Ah, well, he said aloud, in German. Let fools play.

He began to initial each of the documents. When he came to the last one, the American record company, he stopped and smiled faintly. He had once been a lover of music. Perhaps here was an acquisition that would do a little something to enhance life, further the culture. Could a young Beethoven lurk in the wings? Old, faint dreams flickered, sweet ones; he initialed the last page, authorizing the acquisition.

He put the pen down and picked up his chopsticks. He ate slowly, chewing each bite many times, as monks learn to do, gazing at the scroll that hung in the alcove in the corner: a simple, vigorous ink drawing of Boddhidharma, The First Patriarch, Who Came from the West.

When he was done, he rose and walked down the hallway to the *ofuro*, the bath. A cool soak might relieve his back. Even austerity, he thought, loosening his robes, has its limits. The Buddha himself had come to that conclusion twenty-five hundred years ago, had he not?

Feeling oddly happy about the record company signing, Gaijin-san lowered his pale, shrunken body into the bath, humming a line from the "Pathétique."

Motta rolled down the window of the co-op cab and let the air rush in off the bay as the cabbie steered the battered, listing Plymouth up University Avenue. He was an old Berkeley type, the cabbie, with a doughy gray face, rimless spectacles, stringy hair draping to his shoulders from a balding pate. Pale, white arms stuck out of a faded Grateful Dead teeshirt and gripped the wheel. Early into the drive from the heliport, he and Motta had decided that they'd known each other during the draft demonstrations at the Oakland Induction Center.

"Your dad still a lawyer with the ACLU?" asked the cabbie.

"He died. A couple of years ago."

"Drag. What happened?"

"He just fell down one day. He always ran too hard."

"I remember him way back, during the HUAC Investigations," the cabbie said, "with his big shaggy mustache and tweed coat, tie flying in the wind, out there with a bullhorn. Old fiery North Beach Italian liberal. A righteous man. Very hip. Ran for councilman in San Francisco. Right?"

"A couple of times. He never won."

At San Pablo Avenue Motta glanced down the street to where the old Steppenwolf Café used to be; it was a wash-and-dry now, gray and sagging.

"It's changed up here a lot, brother. I'll tell you that," the cabbie said. "I see it from my cab route. I'm a painter my-self. Collage. Doing some research with this physicist at Cal. He has some new vines from the Amazon he gives me. Mixes tracer molecules in with them to see where they go in my body when I paint. Weird. He runs the results through com-puters. Been doing some anti-nuke demonstrations at the Rad Lab. Got a house over in Canyon . . . My old lady does volunteer work for KPFA . . . Works at a day care center . . . We're still in the co-op . . . Between that and the wel-fare and the cab we do okay . . . We're into occult . . . I Ching . . . Hydroponics . . . Holistic health . . . Lamaze Method . . ."

Motta looked out the window, wondering if he was really hearing the cabbie's counterculture catechism or simply filling in the blanks himself. The taxi wheeled right on Shat-tuck Avenue, passed a building where he had once lived above a pet store. The street looked drab, quiet, suburban, empty of character. And smaller: everything looked much smaller.

The cabbie grinned at Motta through bad teeth in the rearview as he pulled the cab over at the corner of Dwight and Telegraph.

Motta got out and paid him through the window.

"What was your name again, brother?" the cabbie said.

"Michael."

"Right," he said, extending a soft, dry hand that seemed to have no bones in it. "Hey, Michael?"

"Yeah?"

"Stay high. Okay?"

Motta looked at him bleakly. The whole kit, the whole package, he thought: an entire symbol system, an archaeological wonder, perfectly preserved, *in situ*. Everything but the God's eye hanging from the mirror.

Walking north up Telegraph Avenue, Motta was surprised by its unfamiliarity. It lay in the summer warmth and quiet, The Avenue, sinister with straightness. Where once anarchy had reigned, now clean boutiques, restaurants and bookstores bloomed, looking suspiciously solvent. The street people had receded, disappeared, like maggots before the light. A young girl with long straight hair and earnest eyes asked him to sign a petition. Motta signed it, without reading, and walked on.

He found himself in front of the Café Mediterranean. Passing through the double glass doors, he saw, with some relief, that it, at least, was unchanged. Standing in line at the espresso bar, he searched the crowded, noisy room for the face of the man he had come to see, wondering if, after ten years, he would recognize him.

Old hardcore Berkeley street people and unreconstructed radicals hunched at the tables. Bearded Rasputins, shabby and archaic, sat packed in along the balcony like a New Delhi fourth-class railcar, gazing balefully down at the room below. A trio of leather bikers were descending on a stoned, vague blonde alone at a table with a copy of *Magister Ludi*. The women here, Motta realized, don't wear makeup; and in this sudden, inconsequential perception, he took his own pulse, registered his own changes of view, and *venue*. A black *rasta* with filthy braided hair pushed against him, asked for a cigarette. The boomy clashing of sound off the high pastel Greek mural walls provided the ultimate intimacy, the privacy that only intense convocation can bring.

It could have been Popov's in Paris, the Socco Chico in Tangiers. Almost any town but L.A., where people lived alone in their cars, gazed across at each other at stoplights, separated by galaxies.

NO SOLICITING OR DEALING said a sign on the wall behind the espresso machine.

Motta took his coffee to a small marble-topped table by the front window. Gazing out at the street, he felt the curious dislocation that accompanies return to an old haunt. Time cards shuffled; he got lost in them somewhere. If he waited long enough, he knew, the present would overtake the past; but for a while the two interpenetrated each other, memory and reality, like strobes, like a night at the old Fillmore. Lisa was in it; *The Rock* was in it; so were some old, lost friends.

"Hey, man," a voice whispered.

Motta looked up. The man who stood above him smiled down through stained, ragged teeth, one arm leaning on a hand-carved ivory cane. If Telegraph had changed, Bad Jack Horn, with the years, had simply hardened all the more into his essence: old black Carnaby Street double-breasted jacket with the sleeves too short over a striped pirate tee-shirt, black chinos, cycle boots, earring, and a black patch over his right eye. And that odd, rebuilt London Cockney hipster speech.

"I didn't see you come in," Motta said.

"That's because I was sitting up there," said Bad Jack, pointing at the balcony with his cane, "watching you."

"I didn't see you up there either."

"That's because I blend. It's an art," he said, sitting down, "to blend."

Cigarette makings jumped out of his pocket and landed on the table. Motta looked at him, fascinated: Bad Jack Horn was a very special piece of work. One imagined him having been born looking just that way—it was inconceivable that he had ever had a childhood. Like many junkies, he seemed immutable, changeless, outside of time, like a fetus in a jar—almost as if the junk served as a cryogenic preservative, an amniotic fluid in which his molecules eternally bathed. Mulling the peculiar endurance of some junkies, images of Lisa Wilde drifted disturbingly across his mind.

"I got your message," he said. "So what's happening?"

"I've been down in L.A."

"L.A.," he whispered, looking perplexed out of his one good eye. "What's down there?"

"Money," Motta said simply.

"You still a journalist?"

"No. I took a job at a record company."

"A little rock and roll, eh?" said Bad Jack. "So what brings you back?"

"I need something."

A gray laugh jumped from his face. "Everybody needs something. So what's yours? Dope?"

"I need a gun."

Bad Jack Horn's head went up and down in the street junkie's nod of chronic, empty affirmation. "Funny. I remember you ten years ago, man. A kid, trying to deal some hash around here. You were the worst criminal I ever seen. Scared shitless. You were a liability. You never blended." He scrutinized Motta's face. "Some guys are tourists," he said, spreading tobacco on a paper. "You were always a tourist. Tourists don't carry a piece." He licked the paper and lit it.

"Things change," Motta said.

Bad Jack held his handrolled up to his face through yellow fingers. "That's very heavy." He sat back and looked around the room. "I tell you, man. This place has changed a lot. The street ain't what it used to be. They let *anybody* out here these days. The *quality* has dropped off. It's not *exclusive* anymore. I mean there's still junkies. But they're not *creative* junkies. You know what I mean?"

Motta nodded, and drained the rest of his coffee.

"I'm thinking maybe China," he said softly. "Up in the Western Hills. There's a scene happening. Some refugee lamas passing out some good shit. But I got bad teeth too. I was thinking if I could get over to London and get them fixed free. I don't know, man. Things are a little tight."

"I need a gun, Jack. A handgun. Something small, that works well."

"For protection?"

"For protection," Motta echoed.

"Funny," he said, "you picking up a piece just when I'm laying mine down. See, I was going to sell it anyway. It just makes trouble. But it's very funny to me that it would be you I sell it to. The tourist." He stared at Motta, full of a kind of unabashed wonder, as if this were some occult, preordained moment, and should be appreciated. "You got a problem with somebody?"

Motta didn't answer.

"Okay, man. Give me about a half hour. Meet me back here, in front. It'll cost you two hundred dollars cash. It's a very good piece. I'll throw in some ammo."

"I'll be here," said Motta.

Bad Jack Horn grinned suddenly. "Hey. Remember that old shrink with the beard used to live across the street, up above Cody's? Used to come over here and get the little girls and take them up to his room for *therapy?* He's gone, man. You remember Bongo Al? Magic Alex from Istanbul? Blind Jimmy? The Monkey Lady? All those people from the street? They're all gone. Dead," he whispered, "and gone."

Bad Jack left the table and hobbled off down the street. Motta followed him out, and turned north; he took the walk up Telegraph the few short blocks toward Sather Gate, the entrance to the University.

He drifted with the idle traffic of the street, the students all so much younger than he. It had been at Robbie's Chinese Restaurant, an old hangout now erased from the Avenue's memory, that he had written the review of Lisa's first album for *Rag Mama Rag*. Crossing Bancroft, he came to Sather Gate and stood on a spot where he had once taken a club from an Oakland cop.

The tyranny of architecture had seen to it that Sproul Plaza was filled in with benches, no longer a place to gather, foment, communicate. Motta picked a bench and sat down. A retriever with a Frisbee in its mouth nudged his leg. He threw it off in the direction of the Campanile. How many government agents, Motta wondered, had been there among the demonstrators that day, how many forces he had been unable to see at the time? The betrayal had been perfect, complete.

A strong sense of loss welled up, a deep wish that he could roll back the years, rail harmlessly against a building, a university, a billy club.

He wouldn't buy the gun. He would simply return here to Berkeley and live. His son Jamie was here, Diane, and his mother over in Marin. And old friends, who had been right all along: L.A. was the death of the spirit. He could teach. It would be much simpler, a sufficient existence.

A barefoot girl in jeans walked by with a portable radio on her shoulder. Motta heard the vapid, squashed voice of Candy Snow drifting across the plaza. Some feelings rushed up and blurred his eyes. He reached into his pocket and pulled out the letters he had taken from Marty Karp's office: the correspondence from Lisa Wilde's lawyers, the Heller letters—and the odd, random name: Jennings Vaughan. He held them to his face to hide the tears.

He had lied to Bad Jack Horn. He was, had always been, would forever be, a tourist.

Berkeley was a conundrum that answered itself: it had never been the cops, the bureaucrats, the straight world. The beast had flipped over, exposing the belly: it was the dark, secret heart of reality. The enemy he had sought on this very spot long ago—he should have known it then—was his own fear.

Another exit flew past.

Walking back down the other side of Telegraph, the circle he had made to Sather Gate and back seemed to him now a full circle. Or better, a spiral, along whose next arm he crawled hesitantly; whether it led up or down—or neither or both—or none of the above—he could not yet discern. It was a multiple-choice question.

Across the street from the Mediterranean he had to look up at the awning to make sure it was still Moe's. The Moe's he had known, and worked in one summer, had been a seedy, radical bookstore astrew with poetry, posters and anarchist tracts. Now it looked like a Brentano's: tall, two-story glass facade, blond-wood split-tiered stairways inside—spacious, organized, affluent. Only the name betrayed its old homeliness.

Inside there were no familiar faces or spaces. He wandered into the shipping room in back. A girl with glasses and frizzy hair was doing stock inventory. She looked up.

"I used to do that," he said.

"What?"

"What you're doing."

"Shitty job. Want it back?"

He smiled. "I'm looking for someone."

"Who?"

"A guy called The Ferret."

"Ferret?" Her smile told him immediately that she knew him. "Oh. I think he's down in L.A. I haven't seen him for a while. His card's on the board. Look over there."

Next to the back door, among business cards, graffiti, and FOR SALE notices, Motta found it—dirty, greasy, bent:

CONSPIRACIES UNLIMITED
Harpo "Ferret" Beam
Research—Exclusive Information
Theories Included
Reasonable Fees

The telephone number had been scratched out with a ballpoint pen, and another scribbled above it, with a Los Angeles area code. Motta copied it down.

"It's a pay phone in a café in Venice somewhere," the girl said.

"Think he's still there?"

"I don't know," she said, shrugging. "Maybe, maybe not."

Motta stuck the number in his pocket, and walked back out through Moe's to the street. Bad Jack Horn was waiting in front of the Mediterranean. He crossed over to meet him.

"Come on," Bad Jack said, and took off limping southward. Motta followed him around the corner, up Dwight Way. Halfway up the block, Bad Jack went around to the driver's side of an old beat-up Pontiac painted with gray primer, and let Motta in the other door.

They waited in silence while a couple of students passed by on the sidewalk. Motta leaned back against a dirty blue piece of shag rug that covered the gutted seat. It was dank, coffin-like, in the car; it reeked of decay, stasis, a slow settling toward metal dust.

Bad Jack reached into the glove compartment and pulled out a bundle of rags. Inside was a small black revolver and four clips. Motta looked at the blue steel glinting in the sun.

"Ain't it beautiful?" Bad Jack said. "It's a Beretta.

"Go ahead. Feel it." Motta lifted it from the bed of rags. "Careful. It's loaded."

Motta felt the cold surface of the .32 in his hand. Along the side it said: *petro Beretta gardone V.T. Col. 7.65. Made in Italy.*

"You can have these too. Fifteen-shot clips. My price is good, man. New, they cost two hundred and fifty dollars. On the street, a lot more."

"I don't know how to shoot it," Motta said.

"Shoot it? Shit, man. First you load it." He opened the gun handle and showed Motta the clip inside. "Then you flip off the safety, point it, hold tight with both hands, and

squeeze the trigger. Boom. Blow 'em away. Okay? So here.
Put it away."

It was heavier than Motta expected, and bulged a little in
the right pocket of his jacket. "Maybe you oughta get a
holster," said Bad Jack. Motta took two $100 bills out of his
wallet and handed them to Bad Jack, who stuffed them in
his chinos. "Want to celebrate?" he said. "I got some killer
smack."

"No," Motta said.

"Suit yourself." He stuck out his hand, and Motta shook
it. "You're in business, man. I'll see you around the next
corner."

As Motta started to let himself out of the car, Bad Jack
leaned over, looked ominously up at him out of his lone
good eye, and said: "Remember back when you were trying
to deal hash, man? Your problem was you didn't *believe.*
You'd get paranoid. Inside you thought The Man was really
right. So you kept making mistakes. If you're gonna carry a
piece," he said, "you don't got that luxury. You gotta *believe.* Do you, this time?"

"Yeah," Motta said. "I do."

Bad Jack Horn nodded, and pulled the car door closed.

"Hope you get to China," Motta said through the closed
window. He didn't think Bad Jack heard him.

He walked back down to Telegraph, feeling the Beretta's
unfamiliar weight in his pocket. At the corner, the same
long-haired girl accosted him with her petition. She didn't
seem to remember. Motta looked down at it. It said: WOMEN
AGAINST VIOLENCE. She handed him a pencil. Whimsically,
without knowing why, he wrote the name: *Jennings
Vaughan.*

12

Motta sat on a flagstone terrace above Berkeley, listening to the coyote howl of an ambulance drift up from the flats below. Across the blackened bay, San Francisco hung in space like a sparkling jewel, the Golden Gate looping away to a tiny pendant at its end: Sausalito. The smell of eucalyptus and sage blew off the short embankment that sloped at his feet to Panoramic Drive. Beside him, a tall carved wood totem loomed in the night with watchful, sober authority.

A strange afternoon it had been, up in a light plane with a pilot and the woman upon whose patio he now sat, watching Lisa Wilde's ashes flutter down to the sea over Point Lobos, just south of Carmel. Lisa's parents, retired somewhere up on Puget Sound, had not wanted to come, for some obscure reason of conscience; apparently they didn't believe in that form of burial. So, for all the world's acclaim, it had been, in the end, the two of them, Motta and Maggie

Hill, who had witnessed Lisa Wilde's last flight, offshore
from the little cabin where she had written the songs that
had fueled her ascent.

Now Motta watched Maggie Hill coming toward him
across the patio, wearing a Mexican shawl, her silver hair
back in a bun, carrying a roast chicken stuffed with rose-
mary. She set it down on the wrought-iron table next to the
salad, the bottle of wine, a candle flickering in a bowl. Then
she sat and raised her glass.

"To the living," she said, smiling. She tossed the salad and
filled Motta's plate. "They're from the garden, the herbs.
And the lettuce too."

"I can tell the difference."

"It's nice to have a visitor," Maggie Hill said. "I've been
so wrapped up in preparing this show. My late husband's
things."

"He was an anthropologist too?"

"Yes. A very inspiring man." She looked at him across the
flickering candle. "He still is."

"How is it that you met Lisa?" he asked.

"Oh, during the wilder days around here the kids would
come trekking up Panoramic, a bit too far gone on drugs. Or
simply confused. We'd give them food, a place to sleep, a
friendly word. Lisa was one of them."

"So was I," said Motta, "though I never came here. Or if I
did, I don't remember." He smiled. "Which is also a possibility."

"It was a different time, an exciting time. Things were
being born, other things were dying off."

"You must have known Lewis Adam."

"Oh God, yes. He was the most gorgeous young thing
you'd ever seen. Tall, blond, brilliant, riding that damn mo-
torcycle of his. Lisa went appetite over tin cup. They were
so in love, those two. They used to sing. In there."

Motta looked up from his chicken. Maggie Hill was gazing toward the empty living room, a vague frown tinting her face, lost in the clutch of memory.

"Do you know where Lewis is now?" he said.

She turned back to him. "I believe he's in a sanitorium in New Mexico."

"Still struggling with heroin?"

"Oh. So you know." Maggie Hill reached for the chicken. "More?"

Motta nodded.

"Did Lisa stay in touch with him?"

"Lewis? I really don't know. It wasn't necessarily the sort of thing she'd tell me." She gazed at him, curiously. "Are you questioning me?"

Motta felt duplicitous. "I'm sorry."

"I suppose it's all right," she said, refilling his plate. "Anyway, when Lewis and Lisa split up, she came to stay with me. Later, when she had her success, we kept close. She would come up sometimes and stay when things got a bit much. After my husband died, she returned a lot of that support to me."

"You must have met Marty Karp."

She nodded. "Lisa never liked him much. They had an . . . unholy alliance. Recently she was attempting to reclaim some publishing rights he had tied up all these years."

"Yes, I know." Motta looked up from his food. Maggie Hill was gazing at him with a quiet candor.

"Were you lovers?" she asked suddenly.

"Briefly. One spring. Up here. A long time ago." He became aware of the incongruous heft of the gun in his pocket. "I hadn't seen her in all these years. A month ago she agreed to an interview for the company magazine. We met in a restaurant. She told me a little of this struggle she felt she was involved in."

"The art of power, the power of art."

"Yes. That's it."

Maggie Hill darkened and took a deep breath. "The night

before she died she called me. She was very upset. She said
she had found out why."

"Why?" Motta sat forward.

"Why things were the way they were. Why she was getting nowhere with Marty Karp, I suppose."

"Did she tell you what it was?"

"No. She was going to call me back." Maggie Hill's hands
grew agitated; the paper napkin she was holding shredded
in her fingers. She looked away. "She never did."

Motta could feel her distress across the table. They
finished the meal in silence. When Motta had drained the
last of his wine, he looked across at her.

"Do you know why she went to Morocco?"

"To see an old friend, a man she had been close to in
Paris. It was flight, I suppose, to a simpler, happier time. She
had gone through a period of taking various lovers—all quite
exciting, but draining. This last year she'd become more independent, reclusive. Not unhappy, I might add. But in
Morocco, something changed."

A candle flickered in a bowl on the table. Motta sought
Maggie Hill's eyes.

"May I ask you another question?" Motta said.

"Of course."

"Did Lisa ever use heroin? Or morphine?"

"Lisa? What an absurd notion. Certainly not. Why do you
ask?"

"The Coroner's Report says she had some in her blood."

She sat up in her chair, and her eyes blazed suddenly.
"The bastards," she hissed, with a passion that surprised
him. "They'll rewrite history if they have to."

Motta stared at her, astonished. She knows, he thought.

She looked directly back at him. "She didn't fulfill the
conditions of the myth," she said tautly.

Overhead, a helicopter droned lazily down from the
ridge, crossed the moon, and dropped toward the flats.

"This is all so disturbing," Maggie Hill said, pushing her plate away.

They stood and walked down the winding flagstone path, past the dark cactus plants and looming statuary. A blend of scents rose off the garden, threading the air with bougainvillea, jasmine and pine. Above them the stars hung, a profuse choir.

"I saw her killed," Motta said.

"Yes," she replied quietly.

The garden came to an end against a granite hill thick with ice plant and cactus. A breeze rose up off the bay. Maggie Hill tightened her shawl around her shoulders. She looked bereft, alone.

"Maggie," Motta said. "I have something." He reached into his pocket and took out the tiny silver Arabic hand. "I ended up with this. Down in the ravine."

Maggie Hill gazed at it.

"*Allahu Akbar.* God is great," she said, looking up, her green eyes bright. "It's a hand of Fatima. From Marrakesh, surely."

"Keep it," he said.

She held it to her chest. Then she reached out a hand to Motta, and he took it. "I'm happy you came," she said as they walked back to the patio. "I feel you are a friend." Motta again became aware of the Beretta; it made him feel extreme, foolish.

When she returned from the kitchen Motta was standing next to the totem, looking out over the city. He sat down to join her.

"You're going to pursue this," she said.

He nodded.

"Why? Because you loved her?"

"I've always felt that her existence illuminated mine somehow. That our lives paralleled."

"I hope that doesn't have to continue," she said. "If you saw her killed, your life may be in some danger."

When Motta didn't say anything, she said, "What comes next?"

Again, Motta didn't reply.

"I suppose you could use the gun in your pocket," she said quietly. Motta reddened and looked down at his hands. "But then, knowledge itself is a form of power, isn't it?"

He looked up. "What do you mean?"

"You're a writer. You could write an article."

"Who would publish it?"

"Well, *there's* a battle for you." She poured the last of the coffee. "If you take up the sword," she said, "you must ask yourself: At what point will the killing stop? If Lisa's fate leads you to destroy in the name of creation, out of vengeance, or bitterness . . ."

The words hung in the air between them.

"I want an accounting," Motta said evenly.

"For her?"

"Yes," he said. "For her. And for myself."

Maggie Hill turned away and looked sadly out over the city. "I've just lost one dear friend," she said. "Seems I lose too many these days." She turned and looked at Motta. "All I can do, I suppose, is wish you well."

They rose. Then, as they walked through the living room, past the ancient sculpture, Motta saw that Maggie Hill's hands, brushing the sides of her silver hair, were trembling.

At the door she said, "Do you know how vile this whole business is?"

He looked at her.

"My mind has actually been entertaining the possibility that she *was* a junkie."

Tears filled her eyes and began to run down her cheeks.

13

The number on the silver metal door was painted in bright-orange Swiss letters, on a diagonal. Motta pushed the buzzer and waited.

Looking back out across the drab, empty East Oakland industrial street in the late-morning haze, he recalled a conversation with his father, their last before he died. They had been sitting outdoors at Enrico's in North Beach, on Broadway, up the street from his offices on Pacific, having lunch.

"So how is it, Mikey? You making some money?"

"Yeah, Dad."

"Nothing wrong with that."

Motta stirred his coffee and looked out at Broadway. "The topless clubs hang on, don't they?"

"Oh yeah," he said. "Sin. It's recession-proof. Come hell or high water." Sandwich crumbs fell down the front of his fa-

ther's coat; he didn't seem to notice. "I see Diane and Jamie.
He misses you. So does she, if you ask me."

"You're lucky you missed that one, Dad."

"What's that? Divorce?"

"Yeah."

"Shit," he said. "I'm too good a Catholic."

Motta laughed and shook his head. "So how are things?"

"Okay. Slowing down a little. I seem to spend more and
more time with the same clients. My generation, I guess.
More time on estate planning, less in court. Changing of the
guard, eh?"

"You playing?"

"Yeah. They moved it to Tuesday lunches. At the Barn
Door, over on Powell. Businessman's crowd. We got a new
cornet player. A dentist. Great. Knows all the old stuff. I'm
playing a rent-a-clarinet. Sounds like hell. We got buttons.
See? *Swing Lives*. Strictly Chicago-style. Kaminsky, McPart-
land. Got a drummer sounds just like Dave Tough."

"You ever think of retiring?"

"You know, Mikey, I did a divorce case the other day.
He's seventy, she's sixty-eight. Makes you stop and think."
He snorted. "I seem to be running out of causes. How about
you?"

"Same."

"Your mother's Irish spirit keeps me going. She's a beaut,
your mom."

"Let me pay for lunch, Dad."

"Hey! No way! Here!" The crumbs dribbled all over his
lapel as he struggled up to grab the bill.

A week later, he had dropped to his knees on Columbus
Street; by the time the ambulance arrived he was gone . . .

Motta, hearing a buzz, snapped back to the street in Oakland. He pushed the metal breaker bar, stepped inside, and
let it swing shut behind him. He climbed the dark, narrow
wood stairway.

Diane was waiting at the top.

She was wearing white painter's overalls, barefoot, her honey hair long and straight. At the top of the stairs they exchanged one of those joyless, reserved hugs that had come into vogue between them since the split three years ago.

"Come on in," she said softly.

It was a large industrial loft of unpainted wood and high ceilings, with a bank of southern skylights. One corner had been made into a kitchen, another a partitioned bedroom for Diane and her boyfriend Lazarus. A tall white panel painted with clouds and rainbows defined a bedroom for Jamie.

"Jamie at school?" Motta asked.

"Yeah. We have time for tea?"

"Sure."

"What time's the plane?"

"Two."

Motta watched Diane's butt as she walked toward the kitchen. It still amazed him. It was the body he had dreamed of as an adolescent, and had actually found. It had been in his last year of college. She had walked into the newspaper office, wanting to write the Art column. The next day they were in bed—for a week.

"Peppermint? Camomile? Red Zinger? Morning Thunder? Earl Grey?"

"Got any Lipton's?"

"How prosaic," she said. "Is that what Hollywood does to you?"

"Okay. Peppermint."

Motta walked over to the stereo and began to finger her record collection. She always had terrific records.

"Coltrane, Satie, Van Morrison," he said.

"Yeah. Out of all that sixties music, *Astral Weeks* is the only one that's held up."

"Not even Dylan?"

"Nope," she said over her shoulder. "How about you? You're right at the heart of it. The big beat. You must listen a lot."

"At first I did. But it goes dead when you're around it. In the companies nobody listens unless they have to. Except the secretaries."

"How sad."

She brought two cups over to a varnished hatch cover that served as a coffee table, held up by a huge, amorphous bronze sculpture. Clustered around the table were several director's chairs and a handmade couch. A Coleman stove stood to one side. Motta came over and sat down. He immediately recognized an ashtray they had bought once together in Mazatlán. He thought how curious it was that these objects should drift among lives. He felt the ashtray belonged to *them*, him and Diane, forever. They had had so few things to split up at the time: an upright piano, a little furniture, a stereo, forks and spoons—and the ashtray. What right did the interloper have to share it?

Diane sat down opposite him and smiled uncomfortably.

"So how does Berkeley look?" she said.

"Everybody I meet wants to get high."

"*Do* you?"

She gestured toward another ashtray on the Coleman stove with a couple of roaches in it.

"I haven't felt like it," he said, cupping his hands around the tea.

"Don't tell me they don't get high in the record business."

"With avidity. Day and night. A lot of coke, and a lot of pills. Not a very esthetic angle." He sipped the peppermint tea. "So how's Jamie?"

"He misses you. He likes Lazarus, though. They get along." She looked away. "He cut his head the other day running his wagon down a hill."

Motta felt a knot gather in his stomach.

"He's okay," she said, lighting a cigarette. "I didn't say that to make you feel guilty."

"I wasn't," he said testily. "I just would like to see him."

"He won't be home until three. Lazarus picks him up."

Motta gazed at a large painting leaning against the wall, an acrylic of big, bearded Lazarus—Job-like, huge hands and gentle eyes, in his Pendleton shirt—and Diane and Jamie. The new family unit.

"So how's Lazarus?"

"Good. He teaches three times a week at the Art Institute. The rest of the time he's here or at the foundry."

"He still into those big Voulkous things?"

"Yeah."

"How about you? Painting going well?"

"Okay, I guess," she said nervously. "Jamie takes time. I work a couple nights a week. One of these days I'll get a show together."

"You're good."

"I don't know." She stubbed out her cigarette. "Thanks for keeping the money coming."

"Sure."

The air was drawing taut.

"Your mother came over to see Jamie."

"She okay?"

"You didn't see her?" There was a chiding note.

"Not this trip," Motta said. He was becoming agitated. "Listen, I wanted to tell you. I'm leaving the record company."

Diane was expressionless, but he knew it was a blow.

"What it means," he said, "is that I won't be working for a while. I'm going to write you a check that will cover Jamie through the end of the year."

"What are you going to do?"

"Take some time off."

"That sounds pretty cavalier, considering our circumstances." Her voice was brittle. "Will you go back to journalism?"

"I don't know."

"I read that Lisa died. Does this have anything to do with it?"

"What did you read?"

"That her car ran off the road in Hollywood. That there would be an investigation. It was in the *Chronicle.* Mostly about her past. You must have been upset."

Motta didn't answer.

"Jamie will miss the free records," she said.

They fell silent. An Angora cat jumped into his lap and began purring like an airplane.

Motta watched the grief begin to rise in Diane's eyes, like a well filling up. It always came at about this time in the visits. It evoked vaguely erotic emotions in him, and that old desire to help, protect, sympathize. It was what had drawn him to her in the beginning. The doomed heroics of the comforter. Brother Charity. The White Knight. "I miss you," she whispered through damsel tears. "Jamie misses you."

Motta picked up his tea. "I don't know what to say."

"You don't have to say anything," she said softly. "Just let *me* say it."

"Look," said Motta irritably. "I brought this for Jamie." He took a small gift-wrapped box from his pocket. "It's an Eagles watch."

"But his birthday's not until September."

"I know. It was just on my mind. Put it away until then if you want."

"Michael," Diane said, standing up suddenly. "*What the hell is going on?*" She walked over to him, her eyes full of confusion and fear. "You're so—*intense.*"

"Lisa was murdered," he blurted. "I saw it. Whoever killed her may want to kill me." He took one of her cigarettes. "I'm going to try to find out who did it. I came here to get you straight with some money and let you know I won't be able to take Jamie for the summer."

Diane was looking at him with her hand over her mouth in horror. "My God, Michael." She turned, and paced back and forth in front of the Coleman stove. "Were you having a thing with her?"

"No. I was interviewing her. That's all." He was angry at himself; he hadn't meant to tell her anything. It was a reflex, to confide, born of an intimacy they no longer shared.

She stopped in front of the stove and looked at him. "You're not equipped for this, Michael. And what about Jamie? What's he supposed to do for a father?"

"That's the hard part."

"Why do you have to get involved? Why don't you get away, come back up here for a while?"

"I tried it on. It doesn't fit."

Diane lit another cigarette. "Jesus, Michael," she said helplessly. "I can't believe this. It's all so . . . *weird.*"

"I'll keep in touch. I won't have a phone. But I'll call. And Jamie has my love," he said, and added softly: "And so do you."

Diane looked at him, confused and sad. He truly felt sorry for her now. He took out his checkbook and a pen.

"I dreamed of you," she said suddenly, "a couple of nights ago. I dreamed we were fucking. It was great. Like it used to be."

Motta looked up. She was standing over him as he wrote the check. She found his gaze, and he felt the desire, the invitation.

"It's what we did best," he said.

He left the check on the table, and put the pen and the checkbook back in his pocket. Her loins were level with his eyes. A year after they had split up, they had gone to see a fuck movie on Market Street together, then groped in the back of her car. It had been hungry, panicky, brilliant.

"It seems cruel," he said.

"To you?"

"To you," he said. "You've got someone."

"Don't you?"

Motta stood up. "I don't know anymore."

"Lazarus is not . . . He accepts anything. He's a saint," she said. He gazed at her.

"Too much pain, Diane?"

"It's all right," she whispered.

She leaned up and kissed him. Their arms sought, and found, familiar flesh. Motta ran his hand across her back, down over her buttocks, with the certain touch of a sculptor visiting an old creation. Their tongues fed, lashed with salt tears. The richness of familiar breathing, odors, contours and movement drowned them in their most perfect and only understanding. Old codes, rhythms came to life, drummed in their pressed loins. Motta felt a wracking, flushed relief, a submergence in hot, black memory. He was hard with longing, hard with hatred and joy.

Suddenly Diane jumped back, screaming. She dropped into a crouch, her fists before her mouth, her eyes wide with terror.

"*God!*" she shrieked. "*God!*" Sobs coursed through her body like ripples in silk.

This time Motta didn't reach to comfort her.

"It's a friend's," he said. "Don't worry about it."

"No it's not," she hissed, staring at him as if he were a stranger, a maniac, a psychotic intruder. "Where did you get it?"

"From Bad Jack Horn."

Diane turned away.

"I need to wrap it and mail it to L.A.," he said suddenly. "I can't take it on the plane. They check the baggage these days. Will you help me?"

Woodenly, without a word, Diane went to the kitchen. She came back with brown wrapping paper, scissors, tape, a pen, and a wooden shoebox and newspaper.

They sat at the table and wrapped the gun together, putting it into the shoebox, stuffing it with old *Chronicles*, then wrapping it with the paper and tape. Diane cried the whole time. He addressed it to his apartment in Santa Monica.

When they had finished, she said: "Why didn't you buy one in Los Angeles?"

"It takes fifteen days to get a permit at a gun store. And I don't know anyone on the street down there."

"I'll mail it to you," she said softly, "after the airport."

"Send it special delivery. I need it tomorrow."

She stood up, walked emptily to the hand-built closet and took out her coat.

Before they went out, Motta went over behind the rainbow partition and left the Eagles watch on Jamie's bed.

14

It was a soft early-summer evening along a small scrubby stretch of beachfront on the old 101 just south of Oceanside, about thirty miles north of San Diego—an ill-defined sort of community, where ex-military men often settled down after discharge from nearby Camp Pendleton, the marine base, or the naval complex in San Diego; a place where neo-Nazi types and dope-smoking surfers somehow manage to coexist in a kind of languid anarchy among surf shops, an American Opinion bookstore, an organic food market, a couple of garages.

The only sign of life on this evening, other than the ceaseless stream of traffic, was at the south end of the stretch, where a half-dozen American cars were lined up before a one-story stucco building. A pair of carriage lamps with flickering yellow bulbs in the shape of candles hung on either side of double wood doors with fake brass handles bearing coats-of-arms. The sign above the building said, in neon heraldic lettering: *The Charter Arms*. The name was something of a code—it also being the logo of a much-favored line of handguns—giving a clue to the nature of the bar's preferred clientele: Commies, niggers, gooks not welcome.

Inside, in the dim light, it differed from any suburban California cocktail lounge only in the rifle collection locked and bolted behind glass over the bar, and a hefty pile of *Soldier of Fortune* magazines on the counter. A scattering of men sat idly at the bar, drinking, talking a little—but mostly just staring up at the noisy game show on the color television. A lone waitress in a skimpy orange outfit with black net stockings, spiked heels, a lot of boob showing and a pile of teased-up red hair, drifted in and out of her station with a brown plastic tray.

Alone at the back of the room, by the rear exit, two men sat across from each other in a dark-red leatherette booth. The one furthest from the door had a fresh pair of scotch and waters in front of him. He was a big man, in his early fifties, with black, greasy hair curling around his ears, a waxed handlebar mustache, a swarthy, florid face, and purple veins mapping either side of a bulbous nose. A well-worn fatigue jacket of uncertain vintage hung open, exposing a sizable gut. The stub of a dead cigar was clamped between his teeth. His name was Guido Leary.

Guido Leary raised one of his scotch and waters into the air, slopping it onto the table.

"To the Cause," he said, with a certain broad *élan*.

Jennings Vaughan, sitting across from him, gave a stiff nod, but didn't return the toast with his glass of ginger ale.

Guido Leary downed his scotch, then set the glass back down, smacking his lips. He looked over at Jennings Vaughan and shook his head in amusement. "You haven't changed, have you, Vaughan? Always the Puritan. Always the tightass." He emitted a raw, guttural laugh.

Jennings Vaughan sat rigidly erect in his Brooks Brothers suit and his striped tie, gazing without expression at Guido Leary out of his pink, clean-shaven, inert face. A fresh crewcut left his pate shining in the low lounge light.

"You should have stayed out in the field, Vaughan," Guido Leary said. "You got no business stateside."

"I'm on assignment," Vaughan said.

Guido looked at him questioningly.

"Something for a foreign business interest."

Guido Leary looked at Vaughan, bemused. "What about your airplane parts business in New Haven?"

"It's been slow."

"You been dropped out of the lineup for government contracts?"

Vaughan nodded.

"That figures," Guido Leary said. He took his cigar out of his mouth. A strand of saliva followed it to the ashtray. "So you're a corporate stringer now. A hired gun."

"It's temporary," Vaughan said.

"They pay good?"

"Enough," Vaughan replied in a clipped, impassive tone.

Guido Leary looked at Vaughan curiously. "You're one cold fuckin' fish, Vaughan. You know that?" He shook his head and laughed through stained brown teeth.

Vaughan reached forward and picked up his ginger ale. He sipped it carefully, like a debutante, or someone suspecting at any moment to imbibe poison.

"Listen," Guido Leary said suddenly, leaning over the table. "Why don't you come down to Indonesia with me? I'll set you up. I've got my own goddamn little army down there, on an island in the Banda Sea, between Borneo and New Guinea. It's wide open. There's oil. China is opening up. There's Commies to fight. Just like the old days."

"You tried that in Uruguay, Guido. And in the Caymans. It didn't work."

"Hey," he said, throwing up his arms, "those were pilots, Vaughan. Trial runs. This is the *real thing.*"

"Who's paying?"

"Good, clean Texas money. With implicit sanction from Djakarta and Singapore. Everybody's hands off. My only contacts are with local chieftains. It's a perfect setup, I tell you."

"Why are you here?"

Guido Leary looked over his shoulder, then turned back to Vaughan and said, "Buying arms from a combine in San Diego. I'm flying back out tomorrow night." He waved his cigar stub at Vaughan. "I need an adviser, Vaughan. Somebody who knows the ropes."

"No, Guido," Vaughan said. "When this is over I'm going to Washington."

Guido Leary shook his head with sober reproach. "Don't kid yourself, Vaughan. They don't need you down there anymore. They're all busy trying to save their own asses. Helms is running for cover. Angleton's gone. The whole lot. Nobody wants to be seen with you."

"We'll see," said Vaughan tautly.

"You can't go on here, Vaughan," Guido Leary said. "You were never official, you'll get nothing in retirement. You have no protection. You don't exist. If you're smart you'll keep it that way. Don't you see? You've been cut loose, man."

Vaughan pulled back the cuff of his jacket and gazed studiedly at his Timex, as if Guido Leary's appeal had not reached his ears at all.

"You don't see it, do you, Vaughan?" Guido Leary muttered. Vaughan looked back at him with a chill, empty gaze. "You're a legend," Guido Leary went on, "in the secret world. But you've got more enemies than any man alive. Sooner or later your cover's gonna crack. One day, in an underground garage somewhere, or a parking lot—or right out in front of your house. Boom. It could be anyone. From any-

where in the world. I don't have to tell you that." Guido
Leary leaned forward earnestly, and his eyes widened.
"Even someone from the Company."

Vaughan looked back across the table, and for a few brief
moments traces of a strange, shared history occupied both
their minds in the muted corner of the bar. Vaughan and
Leary; Mutt and Jeff; the freelancers; the cold, efficient
urban operative and the flamboyant hedonist bush guerrilla:
Burma, Laos, Greece, Nicaragua, Turkey. Their last common field of operations had been South America. First, São
Paolo, 1967: *Operação Bandeirantes*, the Brazilian "school
of torture"—electric needles, the "Chinese bath," the notori-
ous "dragon's chair"—that had been Vaughan's baby; while
Guido Leary had been in Panama training Special Forces
for Washington to drop into the Bolivian hills to hunt, find—
and kill—Che Guevara.

Then on to Uruguay: Vaughan in Montevideo, training
up the *Escadron de la Mort*, the Death Squad, to torture
and exterminate insurgents; while Guido Leary, up at an old
abandoned airport in Texas, across the Mexican border from
Matamoros, trained Uruguayan police for the FBI's "Bureau
of Technical Assistance," then dropped down with them to
terrorize the Uruguayan countryside.

Suddenly it had all been blown: when the N.L.M., the
Tupamaros, captured the American "adviser" Dan Mitrione
in late 1970, they found the name of Jennings Vaughan in
his wallet. Vaughan and Leary had both been linked to
FBI/CIA presence. From Washington, denials, of course.
Mitrione was accorded a hero's burial.

Then, by cover of night, as had happened so many times
before, Leary was gone, Vaughan was gone; without a trace,
as if they had never existed. Washington, however, had not
been pleased with the *dénouement;* Vaughan and Leary's
stock, along with that of their secret masters, had tumbled
steadily from that point onward.

So it was that the two men now sitting in the Charter

Arms bar, whose lives had traced an arc across the Cold
War sky, were bound by something much more elusive,
more arcane, than liking, or enjoyment, or friendship.

Vaughan looked at Guido Leary. "I'll survive," he said,
with a frightening impassivity.

Guido Leary shrugged, called the waitress over and ordered two more scotch and waters. When she'd left, he
turned back to Vaughan.

And what Guido Leary saw next was something that
quite amazed him.

Jennings Vaughan's frozen demeanor was suddenly broken by an explosion on the right side of his face. The skin
lifted into a sneer, a grin, a grimace; the right eye closed in
a leering, conspiratorial wink. It provided an improbable,
unexpected grotesquerie. Then it stopped, just as suddenly
as it had started; and the face recomposed itself into its
chronic, undisturbed mask. Vaughan remained gazing at
him, as if nothing had happened at all.

Guido Leary's mouth dropped open. "What the hell was
that?" he said.

"A tic. A crossed nerve," Vaughan said grimly.

"You see a doctor?"

"I might need an operation. But they can't guarantee it
will work. Sometimes it causes paralysis."

"You going to do it?"

"No," he said. "It'll go away."

The tic went off again; the effect was unspeakably comi-
cal. "Jesus," whispered Guido Leary, trying not to laugh out
loud.

"It's humiliating," Vaughan said, in a rare admission of
feeling.

"Hell, Vaughan," Guido Leary said. "I've got Philippine
doctors down there who can handle it without surgery. Just
with their hands. Or we fly you up to Tokyo. I've got my
own jet, my own airstrip. What do you say? Christ, man.

You need to relax. You can't stand at attention all your life. How about swimming? You like to swim?"

"No."

"Well, then, I'll set you up in a rattan chair with gin fizzes and all the broads you want. Any color."

The waitress returned with the drinks. As she bent over, mounds of white, freckled cleavage looming into view, Guido Leary, dropping dollar bills on her brown plastic cocktail tray, took it in with unabashed relish. Vaughan averted his eyes.

When she had left, Guido Leary said, "But then, broads isn't your thing. Is it, Vaughan?"

"I don't have time," Vaughan said flatly.

"What *is* your thing, Vaughan? I never quite got that." He looked at Vaughan expectantly, a half-smile on his face, inviting an intimacy.

Jennings Vaughan sat with his hands in his lap, and gazed bleakly at Guido Leary.

"You don't feel a fuckin' thing, do you, Vaughan?"

Suddenly Vaughan's tic went off again. This time it sent Guido Leary into a paroxysm of laughter. His belly shook and his throat clogged up and his eyes reddened and filled with water. He took out a red bandanna and coughed into it. He gazed interestedly at his spittle, then folded the bandanna and stuck it back in his fatigue jacket. When he had finished, he said, still chuckling: "Vaughan, I think that tic is trying to tell you something."

Vaughan stared at him, his gray eyes wide and still and empty, like a pair of silver dimes.

"Listen up, goddammit," Guido Leary said heatedly. "I'm recruiting you. Hell, we had it our way for thirty years. We still can. But not here. Not now. We're out of favor. The pendulum swings. Don't think of it as exile. Think of it as opportunity," Guido Leary said, waving his scotch in the air grandly. "We're samurai, Vaughan. Our masters are dead, scattered to the winds. So we rove the countryside, defending the Good and the True."

"Always the romantic," Vaughan said.

"Well, what the hell else is there to do? Don't you still believe?"

"In what?"

"The Good and the True."

Vaughan looked across the table at Guido Leary for a moment. Then he said: "What sort of money are you talking about?"

Guido Leary shrugged. "It's bootstrap," he said. "I set you up physically. You make your own arrangements, cut your own deals. But it's hotter than a pistol down there. The dawn of a new age."

"I don't work on spec," said Vaughan.

"I'll see if I can sweeten it with a little something. A few grand? Airfare? I can't promise. But I'll try."

Vaughan sat for a while, his hands wrapped around his ginger ale. His eyes flicked around the room. Finally, he leaned forward and spoke under his breath: "This assignment I'm on, Guido. There's a problem. The client is unhappy."

"Did they pull you?"

"No."

"Well, then, what's the sweat? Long as you get paid. Who's the client?"

"Heller."

"Heller? Well, sweet shit. We did a job for them in Colombia. They're alley cats. *They* should talk."

"Nobody has ever questioned my methods before," he said coldly.

"Look, Vaughan," Guido Leary said, "that's what I'm trying to tell you. You can't operate your way here. These aren't peasants, gooks, Commies you're dealing with. These are citizens. This is America, your own fuckin' country. Not some banana republic."

"There is a correct way to do a job, Guido."

Guido Leary sat back and gazed at the man across from
him. It had begun to dawn on him that Vaughan was a man
out of control. "This isn't your turf," he said quietly. "You're
an operative. You've always worked with the implicit sanction of a government. You don't have it anymore. Why don't
you chuck it before you get yourself in deeper?"

"I'm a professional. I don't leave a mess," he said rigidly.

Guido Leary swirled the last of the scotch in his glass. All
his cavalier exuberance had drained away. The man sitting
across from him was gradually coming to resemble some sort
of blunt weapon, or a silent turbine from which no sound
emitted, only a sense of massive, barely restrained force.

"You're crossing the line, Vaughan. You're becoming extreme," he said softly.

Guido Leary was not a man easily alarmed, but he had
seen this before in veteran operatives: the dissolution. In his
business, one did not dwell on consequences. The consideration that the accumulation of actions might leave behind
traces, ghosts, that drifted forward in time, was unac-
ceptable. Now, studying the crumbling, obsessive man at
the table whom he had called here to recruit, Guido Leary
suddenly wasn't sure. Discomfited, he relit his cigar.

"I have to go to a meeting in New York on July tenth,"
Vaughan was saying, "as part of this operation. When this
matter is resolved I may contact you." His voice was a flat,
clipped mechanical drone. All the words were in place, but
the center had dropped out; there was nobody home. The
line between duty and predilection: in the field it was sometimes hard to distinguish. Now, after all these years, Leary
was beginning to see how it was with Vaughan.

"Killing," he whispered. "*That's* your thing, isn't it,
Vaughan? *That's* what makes you happy." His cigar end
glowed in the dark of the bar.

Vaughan looked back at him with an expression beyond
logic, pain, or indifference.

"You are one piece of work, Vaughan," Guido Leary said softly.

He reached into his fatigue jacket and pulled out a matchbook. He scribbled a telephone number on it; then, with reluctance, he handed it across the table. "If you decide to come," he said, "call me from Singapore. I'll have a plane pick you up."

Vaughan took a large black billfold out of his inside coat pocket, placed the matchbook neatly inside it with a fussy exactitude, and replaced the billfold in his pocket.

Guido Leary downed the last of his scotch, threw a ten-dollar bill on the table, and stood up.

"So long, Vaughan," he said, offering his hand. Vaughan shook it stiffly, without getting up. Suddenly his tic exploded again: a snicker, a smile, a hideous, leering wink.

At the door of the Charter Arms Guido Leary stopped and looked back. Vaughan was still sitting there, hand around his ginger ale, looking straight ahead.

Outside, along the beachfront, the waves, thick with summer plankton, glowed a luminous green as they rose, curled, and tumbled to the shore. Guido Leary stood in the parking lot, chewing on his cigar, his hands stuffed in the pockets of his fatigue jacket to keep them from shaking.

Fool Killer

The Fool Killer's comin'
I do believe it's true
The Fool Killer's comin'
I think he's got his eye
on me and you

MOSE ALLISON

Part 3

15

The PSA commuter from San Francisco circled over Los Angeles just after noon. Motta looked down at the thick brown haze that mired the basin. The worst part, he thought, was always the descent. Once inside, the horror was less noticeable. One made accommodations, found ways to pretend it was other than it was.

When Diane had left him off at the San Francisco airport the afternoon before, he had decided to defer his return a day. He wasn't quite ready. He had changed his ticket at the counter, then walked to a nearby airport hotel and checked in.

He had gone to his room, showered, then called room service and ordered lunch. He ate at a table facing east, watching the planes come and go. Afterwards, he had picked up the phone and made several calls.

The first was to the asylum in Albuquerque where Lewis

Adam was supposed to be. He had checked out a week ago, they said; they gave him a number in Santa Fe. He called the number, and the girl who answered told him that Lewis had just left for Los Angeles to seek a new record contract. When Motta told her he was with a record company she got excited. He'd cleaned up his act, she said; he had new tunes; he was on the comeback trail. Then she gave him his number at the Palm Hotel, on Santa Monica Boulevard and La Cienega, a sleazy crash joint on the Hollywood rock-and-roll underbelly. Motta couldn't think of a worse place to stay if someone was trying to get, or stay, clean.

The next call was to the café in Venice where the Ferret was supposed to be. A woman had answered the phone in Spanish. After Motta had reiterated the word "Ferret" several times, she had finally said "Si," and moments later the Ferret was on the phone. He told Motta he was "heavy into some other shit," but yes, they could get together the next afternoon.

Next Motta called Tim Duggan, a senior editor he had been friendly with at *The Rock*. He called him at his home phone in New York. His wife answered and said he was in Hollywood and could be reached at the Chateau Marmont. She was drunk and wanted to know how the hell Motta had been, and if he'd bought his first Mercedes yet, and did he have a starlet on either arm. Motta called the Chateau Marmont and left a message for Duggan, telling him he'd be by the next evening.

Then, filled with wracking, desperate thoughts, he had fallen into a fitful sleep.

Now as the plane rolled to a stop on the landing strip the following noon, all thought had been supplanted by a dull, unremitting dread. Motta grabbed his suitcase from under the seat, and was one of the first off the plane.

He walked rapidly down the terminal corridor and out onto the street. The sun was hot, flat, glaring. The swampy smog assaulted his eyes. He put on the pair of cheap sun-

glasses he had bought in San Francisco, and headed across
the street.

As he entered the parking garage where he had left his
car, and headed up the stone stairwell to the second level,
he could feel already that something was wrong.

Approaching the Citroën, he saw that the left front window had been shattered. Glass was all over the ground next
to it. As he unlocked and opened the door, more glass rained
down over his wrist. He threw the suitcase in back, brushed
yet more glass off the seat with a rag from the floor, and sat
down, shaking.

The next thing he noticed was that the door of the glove
compartment was open. The registration, and the owner's
manual, in French, lay on the floor. Motta briefly entertained the comforting possibility that this was an ordinary
burglary; but the idea evaporated with the realization that
what was missing were his tapes—including the one of his
interview with Lisa Wilde.

Cursing himself for having left the cassette in the car, and
trying to imagine what it would tell someone who played it,
he fit the key in the ignition. The sudden thought that a
bomb had been planted entered his mind; but he convinced
himself that a bomber would never leave such blatant evi-
dence of having broken in. He turned the key: the car
started up. He let the Citroën rise in the air, then backed
out of the parking space, his Michelins crunching on the
glass.

At the pay booth a large, black woman with a blue smock
and blond wig idly held out her hand for the ticket.

"My car was broken into," Motta said gratuitously, handing her the ticket through the broken window.

"Honey," she said. "It happens here every day. We ain't
liable. It says on the back of the ticket. You got insurance?"

"No."

He handed her two twenties. She made change and
handed it back to him.

"Well, y'all have a nice day now, hear?"

Motta drove out on Century Boulevard, then took the circle around and up Sepulveda. A few blocks later he bore left up Lincoln. Bits of glass flew off the window well as he drove. He looked repeatedly in his rearview mirror to see if he were being followed; but he could discern nothing, no one.

At Washington Boulevard he turned left, and drove past the Marina and on into Venice, and the beach. Traffic became a clot of bicyclers, joggers, skateboarders, rollerskaters and random street wanderers—Venice's motley eclecticism parading itself in the bright, innocent summer sun.

He turned right on Main Street, drove north for a few blocks, then took a left between Windward and Rose. Just shy of the beach, he took another left down a one-way alley, and pulled the car over on a dusty shoulder in front of a pink stucco apartment building. He turned off the motor and got out. This time he made sure to leave nothing in the car; he reached in back and grabbed his small suitcase.

He walked up the alley, parallel to the beachfront. Between the buildings he could see sparkling white spume flying off the wavecrests. The heads of skaters and joggers flew past on the boardwalk. The sounds of gulls' chatter rose up into the air, mixed with the waves' crashing. Far out to sea, a thick brown streak lined the horizon.

Motta came to the building he sought, a large old brick retirement hotel. It was very seedy, very déclassé, though no doubt once glamorous, in Venice's palmier days. THE WINDWARD, it said in thick white letters on the side of the building. Motta could see through the glass into the lobby, where a klatch of shriveled, white-haired women in print dresses sat huddled against the implacable boot of time and the riot of youth just beyond the doors.

Adjacent to the lobby was a small café with its own entrance. Motta opened the squeaking screen door of the Windward Café and stepped inside.

A young Mexican woman was behind the counter in an apron, listening to the Spanish radio station. There was dinette furniture, a linoleum floor, bouquets of dusty plastic flowers on the tables, and salty lace curtains blowing in the breeze. The walls bore a montage of Mexican bullfight posters, graffiti, and flyers for various local underground events—films, concerts, demonstrations.

By the back wall sat the Windward Café's only customer, a tall man hunched over a Formica table in a huge old army parka, as if it were the deep of winter. Thick glasses perched on the tip of his nose below a blond bush of hair that shot out every which way like sprung piano wires. Piles of papers, books, magazines were arrayed around him—on the table, the floor, the chairs. There were empty ceramic cups of coffee and an overstuffed ashtray full of Camel butts.

"Hello, Ferret," Motta said.

Harpo "Ferret" Beam looked up, surprised, as if awakened from a deep and timeless dream. He looked first at Motta, then at his suitcase.

"Planning to stay awhile?" he said. He broke into a pale, wide-eyed grin. His face was oddly young behind the glasses, and the hair—ingenuous, almost angelic. As Motta approached him, he proffered a cigarette-stained hand. Motta took it and shook it warmly.

"Here. Sit," Ferret said. Then, realizing that was easier said than done, he took a pile of *Wall Street Journals*, yellowing metropolitan dailies and library books off a chair, and put them on the floor. Motta sat down.

"You want coffee?"

"Sure."

"Marina. *Un café, por favor*," he called to the girl behind the counter. Motta gathered she was the one to whom he had spoken the day before when he had called.

"So," Ferret said, "I haven't seen you since the nuke story. Or was it the tape bootleggers?"

"How've you been, Ferret?"

"Oh, great. I'm into some absolutely amazing shit right now. My own book. I have something going that'll bring down the whole fucking *world*. The Third World War will be triggered by the invasion of *Switzerland*. Think about that."

"Very heavy," said Motta, smiling. "The mind boggles. So you're not working for anybody?"

"On and off. Anderson uses some of my stuff from time to time. Lane, people like that. But I've been getting a little weird for those people. The relationship between cabalistic numerology and world politics is a bit much for them, slops over the edges of their referential grid, shall we say. I'm out of my skull, you know. Just a Ph.D. run amok. If doctorates were dollars, I'd be rich." He shrugged, and grinned sweetly. "Actually, I came down to L.A. to work on a research thing on illegal aliens, Hispanics, for some movie writer. Document the undocumenteds. They put me up at the Bel-Air Hotel with an expense account, the whole bit. They even gave me a title: Counterculture Research Consultant. I went on a research orgy. My information was great—it always is. But my theories caused a bit of a freak." His face opened out into a glowing image of mischievous wonder.

"What did you lay on them?"

"It became obvious to me," he said, "that . . . well, you know how Mexicans are always out *driving?* Not going anywhere, just *driving*. And always *American* cars. Guzzlers. Never Datsuns, right? I discovered that in all probability they were sent here by the Mexican Government with the covert backing of OPEC and Castro to use up *fuel*. And that's just the tip of the iceberg, Michael." He laughed deliciously. "It gets into an old Zapata thing, tied in with conflicts among the German exile community in Mexico City. Ultimately it circles back to the Rockefellers, the Trilateral Commission, smog, and Russian wheat, by a circuitous route which I won't go into right now. Needless to say, the people at the movie company didn't quite get it."

"Surprise," Motta said, laughing.

"Anyway, I'm staying on, working on my book. Interesting place, L.A. The UCLA library is choice. An absolute killer. Also, I have sources down here. But you know, Michael, the Golden Age of Conspiracy was the late sixties, early seventies. The assassinations kept me busy. I was always working. Then Watergate came along, and that was absolute heaven. Now it's slow. But it'll pick up again." He smiled hopefully. "How about you? Still working at *The Rock?*"

"I left a year ago. I've been at a record company."

"Which one?"

"RPM."

Ferret's eyes widened. *"Really?"* he said, with unabashed interest. "Weren't you doing something on them for *The Rock?*"

"Yeah." He didn't elaborate.

"Marty Karp. Now, there's a case," Ferret said soberly. "I've come across a few things on him. Speaking of which, I read where Lisa Wilde was killed."

"Yes."

"The papers said she ran off the road. But I mean that's obviously cosmetic."

"She was killed. I saw it."

Ferret looked at Motta, and his eyes widened. Then he leaned forward, and his voice lowered a couple of pitches. "This is what you've come to me about?"

"That's it, Ferret."

Ferret rubbed his hands, and his blue eyes began to glow. "Wow," he whispered. "I've been *waiting* for someone to turn me loose on the music industry. This is an incredibly juicy area, Michael. It ties in with some other things I've been working on. *Tell* me." He looked like a kid who'd just been handed the toy of his dreams.

Motta looked around the Windward Café. "Is it all right to talk here?"

"Oh, sure. This is my office. Marina doesn't understand any English, except 'Hello' and 'Ferret,' which I taught her so she could answer the phone."

Motta pulled his chair closer and began to speak. He had worked with the mad researcher before, and had no reservations about telling him all.

He started with the taped interview of Lisa, then the details of the afternoon on Mulholland. He told him of his meeting with Marty Karp, and the fight, and how he had later broken into his office and taken the papers on Heller and Lisa's lawyers. He showed him the letters. And finally he told him about arriving at the airport, finding his car broken into, and the missing tape.

When Motta was finished, Ferret drew a deep breath. "You're into some very hot terrain, Michael. Are you armed?"

"I will be, as soon as I pick up my mail."

Ferret nodded. "Good. Now right off the bat I'll tell you a couple of things. I'm into Heller. They're one of the biggest drug cartels in the world. A lot of black market stuff comes from them. Very shadowy, very quiet at the top. Keep a low profile. Operate mostly through other companies. They're all Nazis, of course. So you're looking at that whole thing. They've been moving quietly into everything you can think of during the last fifteen years—munitions, industrial and medical equipment, and more recently, communications and entertainment. Part of a very broad pattern of global corporate control. Did you know they own Multigram?"

"Yes. I know."

"Secondly, you have to realize that it is unlikely that Marty Karp has enough of the right kind of juice to get a Coroner's Report altered in Los Angeles. So you have to face the fact that she *was* loaded. Or, if the Coroner's Report was

altered, you may be looking at outside parties who brought
pressure to bear. Any ideas? Drugs? Mob?"

"No. The guys in the car looked like hired thugs."

"I'll tell you one thing. Marty Karp may not even know
who killed her. Or he may. But I'll bet *he* didn't do it."

Motta looked at him, surprised.

"Here's an axiom: *Where are the profits?* You have to
think *paranoid*, think *control*. Get with it, Michael! Paranoia
is something you have to *cultivate*. It's the black flower of
truth. Another axiom: *In whose interest?* If we're going to
work together, you should start to keep these things in
mind. Lisa Wilde was killed. In whose interest?"

"I just don't know yet."

"Why should Marty kill a meal ticket, albeit a fading
one?"

"She wanted her publishing rights back. Although that's
hardly a killing matter. They've been fighting that battle for
years."

"That's no problem for him at this point, on the face of it.
Where are the profits? What are the numbers in this case?
What are her rights worth?"

"A million. Maybe two."

"Do you know what the business did last year?"

"About four billion."

"And RPM?"

"Around $250 million. But they're in hock up to their
ears."

"If she was killed, it wasn't for the money. Can you imagine how much he's going to get when this merger takes
place? Seven figures for sure. We need to look at some other
stuff, Michael. Also, I wouldn't bother with Lisa's lawyers.
These are perfunctory letters. They don't know anything
more than what's in them."

"Okay, Ferret," Motta conceded.

"Next question: How do you know Lisa wasn't a junkie?"

"How does anyone know anyone isn't?"

"Aha. Now you're beginning to think correctly. Creative paranoia. One can't always tell junkies by their behavior. There are quiet small-town doctors who are junkies all their life, and nobody ever knows. Can you get substantiation that she wasn't a user? Key. Very important."

"I'm going to see Lewis Adam, a guy she used to sing with."

"I remember him. A two-hundred-dollar-a-day man. That should clue you. If he'll talk."

Motta looked at Ferret appreciatively. He was cheered by Ferret's quick grasp of the situation and his enthusiasm.

"I found another piece of paper in the Heller file," Motta said. "I don't know what it means, if anything."

Ferret looked at the paper Motta had handed him, and rolled the name around on his tongue for a while. "Jennings Vaughan . . . Boy, something's vibrating in there. Do you have anything else on him?"

"Nope. Just the name."

"Don't worry," Ferret said brightly. "I'll find him. Let me ask you, Michael, as an exercise. How do you find a man in this society when you have nothing but his name?"

"Telephone books? Police records? Credit card data? Driver's licenses? Census Bureau?"

"Pretty good. I see the old journalist in you. But you have to have *sources.*" He laughed. "That's why I get paid. Which brings me to the next point. How are you sitting?"

"Not too bad. Shall we do it by the hour?"

"Absolutely."

"How about ten dollars?"

"I hope you realize that the fifteen with which I am countering is low. Because there is a considerable danger factor. And because Harpo Beam is the only man on the planet you can come to at a time like this. I am, you must admit, in a class by myself." He grinned proudly.

"Twelve."

"Sold. To the man in the sleeveless sweater. Theory included free of charge. One thing, though, Michael."

"What's that?"

"No checks."

"Cash?"

"No. No cash, either."

"Then, how do I pay you?"

"Gold and silver coins. Half and half. I don't take currency."

"How do you pay for things?"

"In the time-honored manner," he said. He reached down into his parka and extracted a shiny gold Krugerrand. "Courtesy Oppenheimer, DeBeer. Everybody takes this stuff. You should have seen the look on the movie studio exec's face as he brought half a bag of silver to my room at the Bel-Air Hotel."

Motta had to smile. "Okay, Ferret. When do I pay you?"

"When we're done. Now, when's this merger supposed to take place?"

"In two weeks."

"Where?"

"New York. At the Sherry Netherland."

"No sweat. Plenty of time. We'll have it nailed. Let me get into my files on multinationals. Do some library work. Check with some sources." Ferret lit another Camel and looked at Motta. "Let me ask you, Michael. Why are we doing this? For an article, I presume?"

Motta paused. Then he said, simply: "Yes."

"They chased you off last time. What's changed? Why are you willing to face possible loss of life and limb?"

Motta sat quietly for another minute before he said: "There's a tiger in my path."

Ferret nodded wisely.

"Well, any conspiracy scholar is hip to the fact that the tiger is always there. It's just sometimes you see him, sometimes you don't. When you do, and those big green eyes are staring right at you in the night, and he's licking his chops, at least you're galvanized to the situation. Maybe you make a good move, maybe you don't. But one thing is for sure: if you stand still, you get ate."

"You got it, Ferret," Motta said.

"Life becomes very vivid, eh?"

"It does."

"So I suppose you could say paranoia is a great blessing. It comes from the gods. It's a state of constant creation. It attunes you properly to an ominous environment. And that, in a way, is a bit of freedom. Because truth begins where reality leaves off. Axiom."

"Do you charge for the sermons?" Motta laughed, and drank the rest of his coffee.

"No. It's part of my calling. Shards of a certain cumulative wisdom. A divine madness, if you will." He giggled with delight. "You know, Michael, your problem fits in tangentially with my old rock murders alphabet theory."

"What's that?"

"Well, of course Janis was killed. So was Jimi Hendrix. And Jim Morrison. And Jim Croce. You can put Jean Seberg in there too, if you like. What do they all have in common?"

Motta waited.

"The letter J. Simultaneously they went after the K's, of course. Kennedy, King. Now they're down to the L's. Lisa Wilde."

"Who's *they*, Ferret?"

"Aha. That's *the* big question. That's why I'm in this line of work." His face shone with a saintly fervor. "Boy," he said. "Jennings Vaughan. That name is rattling around in my brain like a pinball . . ." He looked at Motta, suddenly serious. "I'll get him. I never fail."

"Will you call me?"

"No. You call me. In a couple of days." He gestured toward the phone booth by the café door. "Did you know that all phones are tapped? Do you know who runs the phone company, and what the relationship is to the government, and the intelligence agencies? Axiom: *Any means of communication is an instrument of control.* Apply that to your situation. And I'll get to work. I'll have some preliminary stuff for you by the time you call."

As they stood and walked toward the door of the Windward Café together, Motta looked over at the strange, gentle madman who now appeared to him in the unlikely guise of a savior.

"*Señor?*"

Motta turned toward the counter. The Mexican woman was smiling expectantly.

"Sorry," Motta said. He walked over to the counter and paid her for both their coffees.

At the door, Ferret looked at Motta with concern. "Caution, my friend," he said. Then, as Motta opened the screen door, Ferret said, "Michael?"

Motta turned back around.

"Many are chosen," Ferret said. "But few are called." He broke out into a wide, enigmatic grin.

Outside, in the streaming sun, a kid on a skateboard suddenly rammed him, sending him careening back up against the brick building. The kid stopped and looked sheepishly up, awaiting his chiding. But Motta just waved him away.

He turned and walked toward his car, feeling oddly buoyed by the blithe, zany presence of the paranoid in the Windward Café.

16

Motta turned the Citroën into the lot next to his apartment building and pulled it up to the boardwalk. An afternoon breeze had come up, whipping the acrid smell of kelp in off the sea. He got out of the car, went through the formality of locking the door with the missing window, and walked up the boardwalk toward the building.

The building, an old pink monstrosity with fluted deco columns along the front, had been built in the Twenties as a luxury hotel. Then, during the war, it was commandeered for Coast Guard troop housing. Later, under different names, it had drifted into senescence, to become finally a whore's and artist's hotel, a classic waterfront dive. Motta, once visiting a rock star who took legendary weeklong drunks down here, had fallen in love with its tawdry elegance and decided if he ever came to Los Angeles he would stay there. By the time he arrived it had been somewhat sanitized into apartment units, but ghosts remained: the Isadora Duncan theater on the second floor, the frescoed ceilings, the massive lobby, the seedy bar along the front.

Motta walked through the tall doors into the lobby. Deciding against the unreliable elevator, he started up the stairs. In the darkness of the enclosed stairwell he found himself looking back over his shoulder, peering around each new corner. He was, as Ferret would say, cultivating paranoia.

At the fourth floor, he took the hallway to his apartment. Then, turning the key in the lock, he felt the door suddenly draw open, pulling him forward into the room.

The windows were wide open, the curtains blowing in the breeze that ran in off the sea in the white light's glare, sucking the door inward. Motta's breath clogged in his throat.

At his feet were two dead goldfish.

A spider fern, ripped from its planter, lay strewn across the carpet. The dining-room table lay on its side, its objects scattered on the floor. Food stained the walls. The stink of rotting orange juice flooded his nostrils. Bits of broken china crunched under his feet as he walked dazedly into the room. It had been thoroughly trashed.

Posters had been ripped off the walls and slashed. A standing lamp lay across the couch, its neck broken. His records had been dumped out of their covers into a pile. The refrigerator had been gutted; spilled food smeared the kitchenette linoleum.

Motta walked absently through the flat, nausea welling inside him.

"Amanda?" he called out. But there was no reply.

He wandered emptily through the ruins of the bedroom. The bed had been upended. Clothes, ripped from the closet, lay in a heap on the floor. In the bathroom, shaving cream had been sprayed all over the blue tiles. The cloying smell of a broken cologne bottle dizzied him; quickly he closed the door.

"Mr. Motta?"

It was an old man's voice calling.

Motta walked back out to the main room to find Mr. Shuman, the landlord, standing in the doorway, gaunt and quivering, his mouth hanging open, staring at the wreckage.

"Quite a commotion up here last night," he croaked sourly. "You and the missus have a quarrel?" The comment infuriated Motta. Old Shuman was an unabashed racist who always leered at Amanda, spoke condescendingly of her to the other tenants.

"I was away. Someone broke in."

"They take anything?"

"I don't know yet."

The geezer shook his head. "Neighborhood's just getting worse and worse. Had a man killed upstairs last week."

"I'll get it cleaned up," Motta said.

"Where's the missus?"

"She's away." Motta reached for the door, inviting him to leave.

"Get that cleaned up now," he said, "if you want your deposit back." Then he held up a package in his waxen, mottled hand. "This came for you. A few minutes ago. You owe me two dollars."

Motta saw, with aching relief, that it was the box containing his gun. He took two dollars from his wallet, handed them to Mr. Shuman, took the package, and closed the door. He could hear the scuff of the old fart's slippers as he padded off down the hall.

He turned back to the room, and took idle stabs at righting the chairs, the table, Amanda's emptied aquarium. Then, where the dining table had been dumped over, he saw a note on the floor, smeared with plum jam.

M.—

Got back from Nashville. It was good. I wiggled my rusty dusty with *class*. Some redneck cracker abused

me in the first class of the plane coming back. I couldn't
believe it. What a shitty society this is sometimes. I have
to get some space. Clear my head out. I'm worried
about you. Me. Us. I'm at Bessie's. Call if you want.
Don't if you don't. Time to take a deep breath. Kunda-
lini. Love you, honky. Sad tonight. Feed the fish.

Love,
'Manda

Motta looked at the dead goldfish on the carpet. She had
left then, before the break-in. He went back into the bedroom. Her clothes were gone from the closet. Peering into
the bathroom, he saw that her makeup kit was gone too.
When it rains, he thought dully, it pours.

He walked back through the other room and straight out
the door.

At the south end of the corridor he opened the fire exit
and stepped outside onto the roof of the wing that extended
out from the fourth floor. The dazzling beachfront spread
away below, sunning summer crowds teeming like insects.
In the parking lot he saw his Citroën. Someone had put a
beer can on the hood.

And then, several cars beyond his own, his eyes suddenly
came to rest on another car.

It shone in the late afternoon light, its tinted windows
rolled up. Motta would recognize it anywhere, to the end of
his days: the black Mercedes—the car from Mulholland. His
heart pounding, he slipped behind a tin roof turret and
watched.

For a minute there was nothing. Then the door opened,
and the smaller of the two men he remembered got out,
walked forward, and leaned against the hood of the car. He
was dressed in a white Panama suit and hat to match. He lit
a cigarette and began to smoke it idly, gazing out to sea.

Motta slipped back inside the building and walked
quickly down the hall.

Inside the apartment, he didn't need to synthesize any paranoia; it was right here with him: the men who had killed Lisa, broken into his car, gutted his apartment, were staking him out. He went to his closet, took out an extra shirt and jeans and stuffed them in the suitcase he had brought from San Francisco. Then he crawled around the floor by his upturned desk until he found a small picture of Jamie in a cracked frame; he stuck it in the suitcase.

Then, there on the floor, he realized they had taken something else: his address book. He thought of his son Jamie, and a panic seized him. They would have his number, his address. A terrible vision bore in upon him and made him gasp out loud.

He scrambled to his feet, unwrapped the Beretta from the package, loaded in a clip and stuck it in his belt at the small of his back. The other clips he put in his suitcase. Then he threw on his jacket, grabbed the suitcase and left the apartment for the last time.

This time he turned north, and walked up the corridor to the other fire exit. There was no roof on this side, only a fire escape. He opened the emergency exit, stepped out, and began a quick descent down the side of the building. The bottommost stair still left him a fifteen-foot drop to the ground. "Jump, sucker!" some kid yelled from below. Several people in swimsuits were looking up at him: a burglar, they must think, a guy skipping out on his rent. Motta prayed they wouldn't try to stop him.

He jumped to the ground, landing on his feet. Then, with fierce authority, he pushed through the onlookers. Nobody stopped him.

He ducked into the boardwalk crowd and began walking rapidly north, toward the pier. Looking back at one point, he could just see the figure of the small man in the Panama suit, leaning against the hood of his Mercedes, still smoking. He turned and plunged on through the surreal panoply of beach life—chess players, gymnasts, bums, musclemen—until finally, a long ten minutes later, he arrived at the pier.

He walked quickly up the ramp among the children and balloons and bicycles and dogs, past the merry-go-round and the hot-dog stand. Arriving at Hank's Fish and Chips, he slipped inside and sat down at the only empty seat at the counter, sweating from the heat and the tension and the tweed jacket that hid the Beretta. He ordered a beer, then said to the waitress: "Is Hank here?"

"He's in back. You want to see him?"

"Yes."

Moments later Hank came out—a balding, bearded, portly gnome in sandals. He had a copy of *Billboard* in one hand, and an old Gibson acoustic guitar in the other.

"Working on a new tune," he said softly, sheepishly, in a long drawl. "Haven't seen you in a while, Mike. How you been?"

"Okay. You?"

"Not bad," he said, standing behind Motta's stool. "Say. You ever hear anything back on that tape I gave you?"

Motta, like anyone who works at a record company, from the mailroom on up, found himself prey to constant pitches by indomitable hordes of tape-bearing aspirants. They come from everywhere, with a song, an act, a band; everyone wants into the business. Hank, like so many, had come out to Hollywood with his dream and a batch of mournful, illiterate country ballads about lost love. For years he had written, with little luck. But the word "failure" had no meaning for him. Supported by his eccentric café, an artist's hangout in winter and a tourist trap during the sunny months, he wrote on with dogged, unquenchable hope. Motta, unlike some, found this something to admire.

"Hank," he said guiltily. "I haven't heard anything." He had never passed the tape on to Len Woolf, as Hank had asked. He knew it was hopeless. Instead, he had left it in his car. Now he realized, with some irony, it had been stolen.

He wondered briefly what arcane revelations the thugs in the Mercedes would manage to extract from Hank's cracked, baying rendition of "She's Leavin', I'm Grievin'," "I Cried All Weekend," and "Heart, Don't Fail Me Now."

"I got some new ones that are better, anyway," he said bravely. Motta felt like a dog.

"Hank. Is there someplace where we could talk for a minute?"

"Come on in here."

Motta followed him into a dim, narrow passageway stacked with china, linen supplies, and canned goods. "I need a little help myself," Motta said. "A place to stay for a few nights."

"Sure, Mike." Hank looked down at his suitcase. "Lady problems?"

Motta nodded. That, at least, was a partial truth. Hank nodded in sad commiseration. Yes, he knew all about lady problems.

"Well sure, man. You can stay at my place over the merry-go-round. No problem. I ain't even there. I'm staying with my lady up in Topanga."

"I'll pay you."

"Oh. No way. It's yours. Long as you want." Hank smiled out of his warm, brown, wounded eyes.

"I need a car too, Hank."

Hank looked at him with surprise. "She take your car?"

"It's just for tonight."

"Use my old Chevy. It runs. I ride my Harley in summer." Hank fished out the keys to both the car and the apartment.

"I appreciate it," Motta said, trying to let Hank know that he meant it.

"The Chevy's out back in the lot. There's beer in the fridge."

Motta walked back down the pier, ducked behind the hot-dog stand, and climbed the rickety wooden stairs that ran up back of the merry-go-round, the deafening sound of

German march music from the calliope punctuating each
step. He opened the door at the top, and walked down a
short hallway with inside windows that looked down on the
merry-go-round, where children bobbed with mindless rapture in the flickering shadows.

Hank's apartment was a long narrow room, like a railroad
flat, divided off into a kitchen at one end. The south side
was all windows, facing down the coast—a spectacular view.
Old unstrung guitars, stacks of demo tapes, music trades
and copyright forms were piled along the walls. A faded
madras spread covered the bed by the window. The riotous
calliope strains of "Bicycle Built for Two" pulsed through
the walls.

He set his suitcase down at the foot of the bed, then took
his Beretta out of his belt and put it under the pillow.

As he walked around the flat, an almost sweet breeze
blew in on him through an open window. Outside, a blood-
ied sun fattened over the burning brown sealine to the
west. He went to the kitchen and opened the fridge. There
were a couple of sixpacks of Coors, some stale American
cheese, and rotting vegetables. What the hell, Motta
thought, I'll live on beer and hot dogs for a while. Then he
saw an unopened bottle of Pernod on top of the fridge. He
took a twenty out of his wallet and stuck it under an ashtray
by the sink. He opened the Pernod, poured a little of the
clear liquid into a glass, and watched it turn a milky yellow
as he added water from the tap. Pernod and hot dogs: that
was a little more tolerable.

Sipping the drink, he walked to the bed and sat down. He
took out the note from Amanda, read it over, and let the
hurt enter him again. He was not surprised; it was what he
had wanted, in a way, without having said it. But it didn't
lessen the pain any. He looked out at the sea and considered
calling her. But he knew he really didn't have anything to
say to her right now.

Then he suddenly picked up the telephone and called

Oakland. Thank God, he thought, when Diane answered. Over her uncomprehending protests, he reiterated the same command several times over: Get Jamie out of there for a week. If you can't take him away, send him to your parents, or my mother. He may be in danger. I'm sorry, but that's the way it is. When Motta was satisfied that she'd gotten his message and would acquiesce, he hung up, limp with relief.

Hank had left the latest copies of the music trades on the bed. Motta reached over and opened *Record World.*

On Page Three was a brief story on Lisa's death, simply stating that her car had gone off the road up on Mulholland, and that the police were investigating. There were appropriate accolades from various industry figures, including Marty, who was quoted as saying, "This is a blow to all of us who were close to her. She was a great talent who surmounted tremendous personal difficulties."

Fucker, Motta thought. He's already planting the seeds of her defamation.

The article also dredged up the old "Muse of our time" quote from *Newsweek.* And Motta saw that they had used one of his own lines from a *Rock* review: "An artist of passionate perceptions, whose melodies and lyrics rend the veil of appearances . . ." He didn't read on; he knew the rest by heart. The article concluded with a mention of RPM's plans to rush out a *Greatest Hits* package as "a tribute to a fine artist."

On the same page, in a box, Motta read a brief, unconfirmed report that RPM was to be sold to an unnamed entertainment conglomerate; "RPM Prexy Marty Karp could not be reached for comment."

Opening to the Charts, the Top 100, Motta saw that Candy Snow's single, "So Hot, So High," was listed at Number 8, with a bullet. Her album was Number 25, also bulleted. Motta, stunned, let the magazine drop to the floor.

It's controlled, Michael.
What's controlled?

Culture. Art. What we get to see and hear and feel and think.

He wondered why he hadn't realized it earlier: some sort of massive hype was in—all the way.

He gazed into the glass of milky Pernod. He was alone now, cut off from everyone except Hank and the Ferret. There was only the force he could not see, the force he felt himself slowly swinging in opposition to, the way a star constellation swings into perfect mirror with its twin nebula.

He tipped the glass and let the tepid liquor drip down his gullet. Then he lay back on the bed, took his Beretta out from behind the pillow, lay it across his belly, and waited, neither anxious nor calm, for nightfall.

17

Eddie Malone pulled his leased red Mercedes into the driveway of Marty Karp's hillside home at the top of Benedict Canyon and parked it in front of the garage. He walked heavily up the gravel path to the door of the sprawling one-story modern house, hesitated, then rang the bell. Waiting, he looked anxiously out at the stain of smog that hung over the city like a shroud. Perspiration bathed his fat, florid face. He took a wad of gum out of his mouth and tossed it into the ivy.

The door opened. Hedda Karp, Marty's wife, stood in shorts and gold wedgies and a blouse, a white clipped poodle next to her, with a sour, expectant expression. Her legs were overtanned, mottled, papery, like a pair of salami casings, her face glossy with lipstick and suntan lotion, her hair a coiffed silver-blue. Gold jewelry gathered up the arm that held a cigarette in a rhinestoned holder.

"Hello, Eddie," she said nasally, indifferently, without really looking at him. "He's in the pool." She stepped aside to let him enter.

Eddie crossed the threshold, and Hedda disappeared off down a hallway. He crossed the white carpet of the tall, beamed living room with indoor Hawaiian plants, a brick fireplace, and expensive kitsch furniture. Two teenage boys, one fat, one skinny, were huddled in a corner, absorbed in a video game.

"Hiya, Mark," Eddie called out to the skinnier one.

"Hi," he replied, not looking up from his video game.

Eddie opened a sliding glass door at the back of the living room and stepped outside onto the flagstone veranda. A barbecue, hanging plants, and wrought-iron patio furniture defined the sheltered area beyond which, bordered by oleander, hibiscus and a row of tall pines, lay a slanting hillside lawn that dropped off into the San Fernando Valley, where the smog lay even and thick all the way to the dim, distant San Gabriel Mountains. A rubber raft floated in the center of a kidney-shaped swimming pool, buoying the wiry, tan body of Marty Karp, wearing blue trunks, talking into a cordless phone, surrounded by papers. Eddie heard him bark into the yellowed, clotted air: "Philly! Why the hell is it always Philly? Can your guy deliver or can't he? Tell him I want to see some numbers by tomorrow night or I'm gonna pull him!" There was a silence, as Marty scratched his chest. And then: "Fuck him! We got stuff breaking. I don't have the time. Tell him to shit or get off the pot!"

He slammed the phone down and looked up at Eddie, standing uncomfortably on the edge of the veranda. He broke into a smile.

"Eddie! Eddie! You're back! How was Vegas?"

"Can we talk, Marty?" Eddie called out glumly, hovering in the shadow of the green corrugated plastic overhang.

"Sure." Marty rowed himself over to the side of the pool with his hands, like a paraplegic in a chair, and clambered up out of the raft. He padded, dripping, across the flagstone, holding his trades and his cordless telephone. He looked fit but for a small roll of fat that obscured the upper line of his trunks.

"Eddie," he said excitedly. "Did you see the trades? Candy's a monster. The single's Eight with a bullet, the album's Twenty-five. She's doing the talk shows this week. We're putting her out on tour. Absolute dynamite. We got three million units shipped already. And Lisa's album is breaking. We did it, Eddie!" He reached up and gave Eddie's porky, slumped shoulder a squeeze, then sat down in a plastic deck chair by the wrought-iron table and gestured for Eddie to do the same. "Kippel called," he went on exultantly. "Today's June thirtieth. We made our numbers. We're in. A week from Friday we cut the deal in New York with Heller. Hedda!" he yelled. "Can we get some iced tea?" When nobody answered, he laughed and made an exaggerated gesture of masturbating himself. "Broad's either on the phone or getting her hair done or spending *my* money on Rodeo Drive." He looked at Eddie, his eyes shining with triumph. "We're going to be rich, Eddie. I mean fuckin' *rich*. So *tell* me, for Chrissake. How was Vegas? Those guys should get some kind of award. I mean they did some kind of number. They delivered."

"Well, Marty," Eddie said, starting in slowly, nervously, stumbling over the words. "Lucchessi wouldn't talk to me. But his number-two guy would. Martoni. He talked plenty. He told me a lot of things, Marty." Eddie's words were careful, gently testing, ominous. He knew Marty wasn't going to like what was coming next.

Marty was looking away out over the garden, his manic exultation already cooling in the presence of the perspiring, hangdog lieutenant across from him. "So tell me already," he said edgily. "What did they say?"

Eddie sat, shoulders hunched, disconsolate. "How come

you didn't tell me, Marty?" he said, his voice swollen with distress.

"Tell you what?"

"How you paid Vegas for the Candy Snow?"

"What's the difference how I paid for it?" Marty said sharply.

Eddie looked at Marty, full of hurt and betrayal.

"Oh, come on, Eddie," Marty said impatiently. "So what's new? We've done this before. It's all I had, Eddie. Besides," he said, spreading his hands out, palms up, grinning. "Does it matter anymore?"

Eddie shook his head doggedly. "That wasn't right, Marty," he said.

"Look Eddie," Marty said, full of exasperation. "It was a simple deal. I put it up on a six-month guarantee at a million and a half. We buy it back with the Heller money. Plus Vegas gets a piece of what they make for us on the Candy Snow. It couldn't be sweeter. Vegas gets paid. We make our numbers. Heller gets their company. See, Eddie? Simple economics. Everybody is happy."

"Everybody is not happy, Marty," Eddie said slowly. He sat with his hands in his lap, head down, reluctant to go on.

"Come on, Eddie," Marty snapped. "Let's have it. What? What?"

Eddie spoke without raising his head. "Martoni said you gave them dirty paper."

Marty's eyes narrowed. "What the hell is that supposed to mean?"

"Your collateral was no good."

"Bullshit. What are you talking about?"

"They said you didn't have clear title. You had no right to put it up as a guarantee."

"That isn't true, Eddie," he said hotly. "What do they know about my stuff, anyway?"

Eddie squirmed and looked away across the garden. "Somebody saw papers. In your office," he said.

"*What?*" Marty sat up. "*Who* saw papers?"

Eddie Malone looked across the patio table at Marty, wounded and afraid. "How come you done that, Marty?" he moaned.

"Eddie, shut up," Marty spat. "What *I* want to know is *who the hell was in my office?*"

A black maid in a white uniform came out onto the veranda with two iced teas, then silently withdrew. Eddie Malone, sweating uncomfortably, resumed his melancholy report.

"There's somebody from outside on this, Marty."

"Outside? What do you mean 'outside'?" Marty's eyes glittered, brown and hard, like almonds.

"Some guy came to the casino. Older guy. Not Italian. A real cold fish, Martoni said. From back East."

"Go on," Marty hissed.

"Ten minutes after he left, Lucchessi told Martoni about the dirty paper."

"Guy with a crewcut, and a tic in his face?" Marty said under his breath, leaning forward.

Eddie's mouth dropped open. "Yeah," he whispered. "That's him. How'd you know, Marty?"

"Jesus!" Marty slapped his forehead with the palm of his hand.

"What, Marty? What?" Eddie began to wring his hands.

"That's the guy from Heller."

"What guy?"

"Vaughan's his name. Jennings Vaughan. He called me the week before Lisa died. Came over to the lot. Looked around."

"What'd he say?"

"Nothing. Just how much they looked forward to the acquisition, that kind of stroke. Said he'd see me in New York for the negotiations. Ivy League dresser. Cold as ice. And that goddamn twitch."

"He's the guy what saw your papers, Marty," Eddie

Malone said breathlessly. "When Lucchessi found out, they wanted to pull. But it was too late to stop buying the hit. Now they're pissed off at you, Marty. Very pissed off. They don't trust you so good." Eddie's voice swelled in an anguished blubber. "They're dangerous bastards, Marty. Like I told you. We never shoulda got mixed up with them."

Marty swore, and swore again. He fell silent, and sunk down inside himself somewhere. Eddie waited, and watched him. All Marty's *élan* had drained away. He was taut, drawn in, with his hunted, asp's look, his eyes hot and jumpy. Eddie could almost hear Marty's mind working, like some sorting machine, chewing up data, sifting it. Marty was afraid too; Eddie could tell. It didn't happen often; but when it did, you could read it easy. But there was something new that came from Marty of late, an effluvium, a vibration, that Eddie couldn't quite dig yet. *Megalomania* was the word Eddie Malone would have wanted, had words been one of his tools of thought, which they weren't.

"So they know everything," Marty said at last, softly.

He shook his head in a manner that Eddie couldn't quite interpret. Eddie was afraid he was going to blow. But then Marty just looked out across the oleanders with a kind of childlike amazement.

"You know something, Eddie?" he said.

"What's that?"

"Everybody is a motherfucker to somebody else."

"How's that, Marty?"

"See, I'm the big fish around here. But I'm just bush league to these guys. *They're* the real motherfuckers." A faint smile rose and blew across his face like one of the hot Santa Ana winds that sweeps the canyons of L.A. every fall. He reached back, grabbed a blue monogrammed terrycloth robe off the chair, and wrapped it around him. "I always thought the real big guys, like Heller, were legit. But they're not, Eddie. They're just like us. We know how *we* got this far. They're no different from us, Eddie. Just heavier."

"I don't get it, Marty," Eddie said unhappily, his wet, sandy brows knotting. Marty was outstripping him again.

"Don't you see why they told you all this? So you'd come and tell me. They want me to know they have my ass in a sling. *They're* the real motherfuckers." Marty seemed to be experiencing some great, dawning revelation. "If I squirm, they hang me out to dry just like *that*." He snapped his fingers. "So that's how the big boys play," he whispered with a kind of awe.

"We got big trouble, don't we, Marty?" Eddie Malone said.

"Not if we play along. Accept exactly what has happened. Then everybody makes out. Heller gets their company. Lucchessi gets his profits. We get our sale. But we have no room to move in now. Understand? We have to go it their way."

"All this stuff ain't right, Marty," Eddie lamented. "We shouldn't have gone to them."

"I know, Eddie. But we can't change anything now. We have to run with it."

"And Lisa, Marty. What about her?"

"She's dead, Eddie."

"Yeah. She's dead," he wailed. "Why? And this whole thing of her being a junkie. It ain't true, Marty. Is it?"

Marty leaned forward, intense and hard, and looked right into Eddie Malone's eyes.

"The queen must die," he said.

Eddie looked back at him blankly.

"You don't understand what I'm saying, do you?"

Eddie shook his head.

Marty gazed at him with a cruel scorn.

"She was a junkie," he said emphatically.

Eddie was helplessly confused. He didn't know what to believe anymore. "What about her reputation, Marty?"

"How about we get Motta to write a book about her life sometime? How's that?"

"That number you ran on Motta. In your office. Did we have to do that?" Eddie Malone's dogged, inarticulate sense of wounded honor lashed futilely at the dark waters closing in around him.

"Hey relax, Eddie," Marty said gently. "What are you saying? He's no kid. He'll be all right. He'll come back after he cools off, and it'll be business as usual."

"I'm uncomfortable, Marty. Very uncomfortable," Eddie said, fidgeting in his patio chair. Sweat from his flanks dripped through the white plastic slats onto the ground beneath him.

"Eddie, please. It'll be over in ten days when we take the meet in New York. Now button up. We didn't know this was going to happen. This guy from Heller scares me, whoever he is. But it's not something we can change. What's most important is we don't panic."

"Hey, Marty?"

"What?"

"You don't think Motta's gonna stick to that story of his, do you? About Lisa getting murdered?"

"Not if he ever wants to work in this business again." Marty darkened. "Look. He's a writer. Understand? No clout, no juice. As long as he can sound off a little, he's happy. Trust me. I know his kind. I bought him off before. People don't change."

Eddie Malone sipped noisily, inconsolably, on his iced tea, which was no longer iced but warm. Something thick caught on his lips. He spat, and a dead fly wheeled on the surface of his drink. Eddie winced distastefully and put the glass down.

"Look, Eddie," Marty said, the hard, cold cokehead flame rising again in his eyes. "What's most important is that we made our numbers. Candy's album is a monster. Lisa's album's going to be hot. Dig it, Eddie. We made our numbers. Stop worrying about Lisa. Christ, Eddie, you look like a piece of cheesecake. Take your shirt off. Get some sun. Personally, I think her commercial potential was finished. You want to take a dip? I got some trunks. She was asking for trouble, Eddie. That's what she got. How about some lunch? You want a chicken salad sandwich?"

"The word on the street, Marty, is nobody's ever seen a hype go in like the Candy Snow. There's talk."

"Good. Gives them something to look up to. See how the big boys play. Let them dig it, Eddie. Let them respect it."

Eddie Malone glanced over at his boss, whose swelling visions of power sang out across the veranda, the lawn, the pool, like jagged, dancing electric beams.

"Don't," Marty was saying, "look a gift horse in the mouth."

"Huh?"

Marty laughed his little viper laugh, as Eddie looked desolately back at him.

"Hey, Marty?"

"What is it now, Eddie?"

"You said I'd see some money out of this. How much you talking?"

"Oh, Eddie," he said, standing up and throwing off his monogrammed robe. "Don't ask me about it now. I haven't figured anything out. But there'll be plenty. Don't worry about it. I always took care of you, didn't I?" He walked over and patted Eddie Malone's broad, beefy back.

Then Marty turned, sprinted across the lawn, jackknifed, and dove into the chlorinated turquoise waters of his pool.

In that instant, everything froze in the sad, gray, moist hound's eyes of Eddie Malone: a David Hockney painting: the tail of water from the splash, the plastic deck chairs, the steaming, veined tiles, the carpet of green lawn, the silhouette of the San Fernando Valley: frozen, as Eddie's thumbs played with each other in his sweaty lap, and a dissonant mix of warring feelings, full of all the things he was coming to know, gripped him. Some precarious balance between need and honor hung by a thin thread; mute stirrings in the breast of the lumbering Irishman who didn't use words to think, but whose soul possessed no less a moral threshold because of it.

A terrible possibility was entering his mind.

Time began to move again: the splash; a spray of water falling through the air; the thump as Marty's body hit the pool; and the slightest of breezes coming up over the Benedict Canyon ridge, rippling the tips of the pines, and turning Eddie's perspiration to a clammy chill.

Somewhere in the depths of the pool's blue-green waters, Eddie Malone's meal ticket had just disappeared.

18

Darkness, it seemed, would never come.

Finally, somewhere near nine, with traces of daylight still ribboning the sky, Motta saw out over the ocean a paltry display of emergent stars, signaling the descent of night. He got up from the bed, jammed his Beretta in the back of his belt, and slipped out of the apartment. In the entranceway, he saw through the arched interior windows the frozen silhouettes of the dancing horses below, free at last from their tyrannical march master, the calliope.

Outside, the pier was a dark, tossing sea of debris, its sunlit joys a gone memory, the arcades and cotton candy stands boarded and silent, their vendors somewhere far away in fitful sleep. In the parking lot out back he found Hank's old Chevy, covered in dust. Someone had inscribed on the hood in tight, careful Gothic lettering, the ubiquitous Chicano graffiti: *K13*—it meant "Born to lose; dope; being out on the streets." Someone else had scrawled in the dust the more prosaic gringo message, "Wash Me." Motta got inside and turned the key; as Hank had promised, it started up. With the lights still off, he turned the car around and cruised slowly out of the parking lot and up the ramp to the pier's entrance. At the cross street he turned on his lights. A pale-yellow outlaw moon, fresh and full, hung over the city ahead.

Taking a zigzag path through the small neighborhood streets of Santa Monica, he studied his rearview mirror the way a pilot would eye a bomber sight. He could discern no tail. By the time he hit the lavish, wooded lanes of Brentwood he was certain he wasn't being followed. He reached behind his back and patted his .32. When, where, he wondered, would the black Mercedes find him next? He sped up, and hit Sunset Boulevard around Holmby, west of Beverly Hills.

To break the tension, he flipped on the old AM car radio. Sliding across the dial with a turn of his fingers, he heard the day's display of music—all the neat playlist categories whose magic demographic numbers the music trades delineated each week: the rise, and fall, of product. He settled on a rock station, rolled down the window, and sped up Sunset, letting the motion take him.

Music had once been a window to Motta, through which he saw greater realities, found sense and solace. He used to scrimp to buy records, stand in line for hours at concerts, crowd backstage to meet the stars. Somewhere along the way, the window had become a wall. He seldom bothered to open the cartons of new records he received free every month from the companies, and rarely listened to those he did. He couldn't remember the last time he'd sung in the shower, hummed while walking, let a love song define his emotions, abandoned his body to the beat. If one's life was a melody, his was inaudible; certainly, it wasn't something you could dance to. His world had become soundless, a bathysphere. Perhaps that's what Amanda was always trying to tell him, with her talk of Jamaica.

Jazz, country, soul, news, weather, sports. Rotating the dial nervously again, he approached the west end of the Sunset Strip, feeling the dangers of the night, and its thousand neon eyes. One could tell a society's values by its tallest structures, someone had once said. The towering church at the center of a Spanish village, the statues of Easter Island, the Kremlin. America was medical buildings and banks. Death and money. The doctor with the priestly wand of the stethoscope; the banker with his mysterious cultish green paper. As Motta passed the tall glass-and-steel office buildings on his right that guarded the entrance to the Strip, he acknowledged the ascension of a new god: the Media. The consolidation of music, art, film, words—all the things that people did with their minds and senses—into a massive global interlocking enterprise, run with all the efficiency of a bank, was virtually complete. The circle, as Monk Purcell had said, was closing. The borders of the mind itself had been stormed, crossed, and conquered. The last crossover: The Age of the Prerecorded Mind.

Remember you're theirs. Be what they want you to be. Do that, and you will always be loved.

CANDY SNOW. A REFRESHING DEBUT. ON RPM RECORDS AND TAPES.

It loomed in the night, a massive, fifty-foot-high neon board specially prepared for the Strip, blotting out the moon. She glowed invitingly, blinking on and off, pert and naughty. So hot, so high. So sex, so dope; painted into beauty in her spandex outfit by the consummate hand of the German refugees at Foster and Kleiser, the billboard company, where Motta had seen them work from tiny gridded reductions to make their dot-perfect, monstrous paneled images. *Impingement.* Brief sanctification. To own the night.

You succeed into impotence. It's Faustian. You can become a very famous hollow shell.

Motta rode the stream of traffic to the far end of the Strip. The Chateau Marmont Hotel rose up on his left, a huge old dirty sandstone structure with a movie history, where those with an aversion to plastic—conspicuous at the Continental Hyatt House down the street—still bedded, sometimes for a night that turned into years. Motta took a left, wound around behind the Chateau, and parked in a red zone on a small, narrow one-way street.

The entrance was at the side, a courtyard with a small lawn marked by rusted window casings, and peeling muraled ceilings on the arched walkway to the lobby. Inside, faded Persian rugs, pitted chandeliers and a motley wall display of dusty oils defined an aura of wearied literacy. A girl, dressed punk, in black, with ruined sagging eyes and dyed pink hair, sat smoking behind the desk. She gave him Tim Duggan's room number with an unstudied Quaalude languor.

Motta started up the narrow polished-wood stairway; he still wasn't ready for elevators. At the fourth floor he traversed a silent musty corridor to the front of the building. He came to a door at the end of the hall. It was slightly ajar. He knocked.

"Enter!" called Tim Duggan's familiar, perennially cheery voice.

Duggan was sitting on a faded-purple velvet couch in the center of the small suite, watching a silent TV, his stockinged feet up on the table, balancing a glass of red wine on his chest. There were a dozen different California wine bottles on the table—several empty, one freshly opened. A Nagra tape recorder, cassettes, and a pack of Senior Service cigarettes completed the table display. On the floor, a British edition of Pound's *Cantos* lay open. Through a leaded-glass bay window at the end of the room, the electric night city quivered like a gelatin.

"Michael," Duggan said. "How the hell are you?" Tim

Duggan struggled to his feet, in a show of residual good breeding, and reached for Motta's hand.

Duggan was Motta's age, perhaps a year older, tall and thin, with sandy hair and a kind of East Coast preppie feel that ten years of debauch had not managed to erase. His face was pale, aquiline, animated by a patrician flippancy, or carelessness which Motta imagined him to have been born with. He had on pale linen slacks, and a blue silk shirt with a tie loose at the collar. He was dangerously bright, and wrote like a demon.

"Join me in a quiet lush?" Duggan had already drained two different pinot chardonnays, and was well on into a Taylor burgundy.

"Why all the grape, Tim?" Motta asked, sitting down in the matching velvet chair opposite.

Duggan switched off the TV and lit a cigarette. "I spent yesterday up in Napa, checking out your local vineyards with a bunch of old immigrant millionaires, getting swacked out of my gourd on samples. Pretending I know a good nose from a bad stink. Me. Wine articles. Can you imagine?"

"Why not?" Motta said, smiling.

"I thought of you yesterday. I wasn't that far from Altamont."

"Oh, I'd say you were."

"Right you are. Good metaphor for the changing times. Altamont was hardly wine for us, was it, old buddy? So how are you? You look a little peaked. Flat on your feet. An absence of bounce. Under the gun? The weather? Deadlines? I presume they have them out here, too?"

"Something like that." Motta leaned back in the faded, overstuffed chair, feeling the gun settle into a soft pressure against his back. "So what's up these days, Tim, besides wine stories?"

"Oh, silly stuff. Features, rock gossip. Things on cities. New dopes that have been discovered. Profiles, interviews. I take a lot of terrific trips. Like this one." He grimaced.

"Your esteemed former publisher and editor mostly sits around Elaine's, hobnobbing with the *Interview* crowd. We're just an advertising organ for products. Who cares? I've made my peace with it." He made a cynical *moue*, and when Motta didn't pick it up, continued. "I don't even know what I'm looking for anymore when I go out on a story. Most of the guys went to work for the record biz, like you, or drifted off, their brains fried, or tried their hands at a novel, or the movies. A few are still around, like me, but nobody gives a shit. Rampant, terminal cynicism. The best minds, and all that tripe . . ."

"Sounds deadly."

"It is. How's tinsel town?"

"Tinselly. As advertised."

"And RPM?"

"I'm on leave for a month."

"Leave? How do you work that?"

"It's a long story." He reached for one of Duggan's cigarettes.

"And how's Mr. Big?"

"Marty? A mad little Napoleon."

"I read about Lisa, of course." Motta nodded, waiting to see what Duggan knew, or didn't. "The *Times* said she ran off the road."

"Yes," Motta said, volunteering nothing more.

"Sad for you, I suppose, being an old *aficionado*. And exswain, as I recall."

"I thought she had some good work left to do."

"Did you see her much out here?"

"No. Hypecraft is deceptively rigorous. It consumes a lot of time. Writing copy, producing radio and TV spots, booklets, brochures."

"We're going to do something on her. A glorified obit, basically. It's already in the works. You'll be quoted liberally, by the way. My orders."

"That's all?"

"I'm afraid so. She hasn't been exactly what you'd call *sizzling* lately." Duggan reached for his burgundy. "By the way, speaking of sizzle, I heard a hot one today."

"What's that, Tim?"

"I heard she was on junk. Lisa."

"Who told you that?"

"Arlene. Your new publicist at RPM. The one with the sublime chuggers. She sort of leaked it, over drinks at Musso's. Said it was on the Coroner's Report."

"Don't bite, Tim."

"Oh, really?" His eyebrows went up.

"The reason I came to see you," Motta said, leaning forward, "is to sound you about a piece for *The Rock*."

"What on?"

"Lisa."

Duggan looked at him, mildly alarmed. "Still holding the old torch?"

"No. I just think there are some things to be said. About her death."

Tim Duggan squirmed uneasily on the velvet, and did some quick damage to his glass of burgundy. "How about you? Vino?" Motta accepted a glass from Duggan's thin, tremulous hand. "We're going with a two-column reprise of her high points, and a stock shot. Probably that last album cover. That great Monk Purcell photo in the restaurant. That'll be it, I'm afraid."

"So you're not open to a story?"

"No," he said simply, "I'm sorry, but no."

You're not a reporter anymore. You work for the company.

"Why?"

"Frankly, Michael . . . Oh, shit. How do I say this? I think there's a lingering negative vibe, a feeling you left the ranks for Hollywood. That sort of thing. And there's been a shift in public consciousness. You know that. Lisa is not *courant*." Duggan looked at him with an apologetic frown.

"Besides, we just aren't doing the sort of thing I gather you have in mind anymore. No corruption in the music industry. No dirty linen. We treat it all in the form of news briefs, same as any metropolitan daily, or magazine. We tried it once, remember? Shaking the pole. We got burned. All the labels pulled their ads. We had to eat crow, come begging to Hollywood. We realized where our bread is buttered. We're willing to do stuff on nuclear, the environment, old Vietnam things. But we won't mess with the business. Christ, you should know. You got shot down on your Marty Karp piece. Sorry, old buddy. *Cosas de la vida*. You know I'd like to say yes."

Motta swirled the wine around in the stemmed glass. Outside, a police siren revved up somewhere. He heard a couple of fenders crunch. "You used to be such a firebrand, Tim."

"Do I detect moral qualms?" Duggan said archly. He looked at Motta with weak ill-humor. "From you, of all people. The one who left *El Rock* to work for the guy you were investigating. Really, Michael. Sentiment is unbefitting the *métier* toward which you once aspired." He kicked an empty wine bottle to the floor with his stockinged foot. "But I'll tell you what. Out of respect for an old *confrère*, I'll scotch the junk rumor. Even though we'll get scooped by somebody else."

Motta let the good dry burgundy slide down his throat. It was warming. Little else in the room was. "Thanks a lot," he said softly.

"Anyway," Duggan said. "On to brighter things. Know where I can get laid?"

Motta looked up, surprised. "I thought you remarried."

"I did. So? That's another peace I've made with myself. Pardon the pun."

"There's ass right outside your window. All you can eat. Boys and girls."

"Diseased flesh, you mean," he said, with a fey wave of his hand.

"Try the Century City Hotel bar."

"Just thought I'd ask," he said dispiritedly. "Where do *you* park your little red wagon these days?"

"I was living with someone until recently. An actress. A black girl. Jamaican."

"How exotic and hip. What happened?"

"Too much TV."

He looked quizzically at Motta. "You'll have to explain that one."

"You know how when you have the TV on in the bedroom with your lover and you're lying there and your hands fall apart? Too much media action. Deadening. Love doesn't weather it well."

"Is that some sort of neo-McLuhanism?"

"Just idle thoughts, Tim." He was missing her, badly. "When are you going back?"

"Tomorrow. I'm finished. I did the wine thing, and another interview this afternoon. Talk about nowhere city. Candy Snow. Cottage cheese for brains. Sitting up at Grossman's new mansion in Bel-Air, stoned out of her mind on Valium in her silks in a corner, awaiting her imminent enshrinement as the new culture deity. Pathetic. Grossman did all the talking."

Motta turned cold inside. "You're kidding," he said, trying to keep his voice steady.

"That's what I mean, Mike. Things have shifted. You getting the picture? She's garbage. But it's orders from above. Part of the hype. It says here she's hot. The charts. We don't get to decide that. If it's happening, we cover it."

Motta put his wine back down on the table. He had lost the bouquet somewhere.

Tim Duggan was blushing, chagrined. "Hey. What's going on here?" he said petulantly. "You're embarrassing me. *You're* the guy who came out to glitterland to do hypecraft. *I'm* supposed to be the purist here." Motta listened as Duggan, his tongue loosening, rose and walked unsteadily toward the window. He stood in front of the city lights in his socks.

"So where were we at? Space age dilettantes with a fake revolution." He gestured toward the book on the floor. "Like old Pound says. *Usura.* Economics runs art, has since the fifteenth century. It's all just candy. Every so often you look down and see what you're eating. And it's poisoned shit." He sloshed wine on the carpet. "I mean I still get high, but I don't. It just cauterizes me. No visions anymore. I'm just walking the line of my own sanity. Shit. Aren't we all?"

"What would make you cross that line?"

"The loss of my expense account. No more Bloody Marys at the Sherry bar. I mean it's not even a question of corruption or compromise. It's one of survival. Civilized behavior is a very fragile thing. Reality's a Swiss cheese. But you can't stand there gaping at the holes. You have to get on with it. Another drink?" He had gotten himself back to the table and was brandishing the remains of the Taylor burgundy.

"No," Motta said.

"My theory," Tim Duggan went on, lighting another cigarette, "is that this country had two great revolutions. The thirties and the sixties. Both aborted. Hemingway blew his brains out. I have a feeling we'll be just sitting around our rooms in the year 2000 listening to Dylan preach to us on the tube, Mick Jagger show us his operation scars. It started with *A Hard Day's Night,* and ended at Altamont. Commercially, it ran from Clive Davis' trip to the Monterey Pop Festival to the ascension of John Denver, or something like that. But I'm not going to stew my brains about it. I'm riding a cushy carpet woven from that revolution, or whatever it was. I helped create it in my little way, and I'm going to ride it until it stops. Or maybe it never will. That's okay with me, too."

"So it's wine articles and Candy Snow."

"Pert and perky. Hot and high." He grinned, his teeth red from the burgundy, and slumped back onto the velvet couch. Motta was beginning to see he was wasting his time.

"Hey, Michael," Duggan said, slurring. "Is RPM being bought by Heller, the emperors of dope?"

"Looks like it."

"Well, I've got one for you," Duggan said mischievously. "So's our rag."

Motta looked at him, not even trying to disguise his shock.

"That's the skinny in the corridors. Soon to be signed, sealed and delivered. *The Rock. A Publication of the Heller Group.*"

Motta felt another layer of illusion melt away. He knew he had to leave quickly.

"How about the *National Enquirer?*" Duggan was saying. "No, I'm serious. They pay well. Send them your piece." He laughed drunkenly. Motta stood up and reached down for Duggan's pale prep-school hand.

"What are you going to do?" Duggan asked, looking up at him with watery, fearful eyes.

Motta turned toward the door. "The next thing," he said, "to quote one of your old lines."

Tim Duggan gazed stupidly after him. "I envy you," he blurted.

Motta turned and looked back.

"You're struggling again," Duggan said. "Fucker."

Motta left the door ajar, as he had found it when he arrived.

Hank's Chevy had a ticket on the windshield. Red zone. Fifteen dollars, it said. Motta stuck it in the glove compartment, started the car, and drove the circle street behind the Chateau around to the Strip. This time he headed west, retracing his earlier drive in the opposite direction. The night, and the street, were swelling with human traffic. In front of the Continental Hyatt House, a phalanx of limos announced the arrival of a supergroup to play for Forum. Maddened, shrieking groupies clustered around the cordoned entrance.

At La Cienega he turned left and dropped down the steep hill, heading for the Palm Motel. The jeweled landscape stretching away before him looked oceanic, a heaving algae on the surface of some great water. He could see the lights of planes, like dragonflies, settling in over the airport. Nursing Hank's spongy brakes, he let himself slowly down the grade.

He was immensely disturbed by the encounter at the Chateau. He saw in the reflection of Tim Duggan how far, and how fast, he had traveled. Was he madder now? Saner? The chilling reality of Heller's acquisition plans; the betrayal of culture; the hype: it was in, all the way. Some massive power shift was occurring, while Motta slid downhill in a beat-up Chevy.

He was desperate to hear from the Ferret. Time was drawing short. The RPM/Heller merger meeting was ten days away. His only comfort, and it was a meager one, was that he knew he had begun to break his own media bondage. But to do that, he realized, was to become an outlaw. The media was the law. One conformed to the culture profile, or one was on the outside, sealed off. Cultural dissent, he reflected, was as terrifyingly absolute as political dissent.

Were they any different, actually?

It's a war.

Traffic slowed in the right lane at the foot of the grade. There was a jam-up. He heard a siren. Smoke was curling up from buildings he couldn't see, to the right. A fire truck crossed by below. He idled the Chevy and waited.

If it *was* political, this cultural dissent, then what was one's stand? Restoration of the Maori way, with the artist as shaman? Dismantling of the media machine? Pull the plug? Burn the tapes? Were there to be Mad Bombers of the Media? Axiom: *Any means of communication is an instrument of control.* Watching the control being assembled, piece by piece, where did one jump in and counter it? The media, unlike politics, was an empire that conquered by *inclusion.* It had no overt wars. It didn't isolate and attack the dissident entity, the antisocial, the hermetic, the beat, the hip, the punk. It *embraced* it.

The artist exchanges his kind of power for this other kind, which destroys him . . . Truth and beauty . . . You begin to feel like a sacrificial lamb . . .

At the foot of the hill at last, he took a right turn on Santa Monica, then came abruptly upon the source of the fire: the Palm Motel. Fire trucks, ambulances, police—the entire panoply of official overkill that met the slightest deviation in public decorum in Los Angeles—every stolen car a Vietnam, every drunken black man a terrorist—milled and performed with swollen authority.

He followed the slowed traffic until he was past the fire trucks, then pulled the Chevy into another red zone, in front of a gay bondage shop. He could see the smoke piling up into the sky, crossing the full moon, which hung straight over the city now. He stepped across several thick hoses and quietly inserted himself into the crowd of Palm habitués— punks, porno queens, hustlers, rockers—gathered on the semicircular lawn in excited disarray.

Several rooms along the top floor of the two-story stucco structure, black and gutted, smoldered as firemen completed their dousing. Charred furniture littered the driveway, the acrid smell drifting through the clotted air. Moving closer, Motta saw a solitary figure sitting on the ground in the driveway, a pair of police officers behind him. He was barechested, wearing only jeans and boots. Handcuffs pinned his arms behind his back. His right hand was freshly bandaged. He was tall, thin, pale, with long blond hair. One of the lenses of his rimless glasses was broken, and he trembled softly. He was staring down between his legs. Motta moved a little closer and bent down.

"Lewis Adam?" he said.

After a moment the man turned and looked up at Motta. Out of a pale, waxen face that bore distant memories of light and intelligence, empty blue eyes gazed up at him, the pupils like two tiny pencil points. Motta saw the fresh track marks on the arm.

"Nodded out," one of the cops was saying to a fire official. "With a cigarette in his hand."

A fireman came toward them from the wreckage holding a burned Gibson guitar in one hand, and in the other, charred makings: spoon, syringe, dropper, and a Western tie-up belt studded with inlaid pieces of New Mexico turquoise.

"Lewis?" Motta was right next to him, crouching down. "Lewis. I have to talk to you."

Lewis Adam turned away and gazed emptily up at the smoldering building.

"Lewis. Was Lisa a junkie?"

Lewis Adam, if he heard the question, didn't register it by expression.

"*Was she?*"

Lewis Adam looked up at the cop standing above him. Then he turned to Motta.

"Who isn't?" he whispered languidly.

"*Bullshit, man,*" Motta said, grabbing his arm. "I need to know. It's important, if you loved her."

Lewis Adam turned away and looked down at the ground. It was a long silence. He seemed to be staring at his foot.

"She was clean," he said softly.

"Not once?"

Lewis Adam looked up at Motta. "Never. Ever."

By the time Motta got back to the street the fire trucks were beginning their withdrawal. So, he knew, was Lewis Adam. Looking back, he saw him being shoved into the back of a black-and-white. And who would post bail this time? Who was left?

Motta found another ticket on the window of his car. That made two in a half hour. He climbed in, stuck the ticket in with the other, and started up the Chevy, his mind racing with the engine.

So much for Lewis Adam's comeback, he thought as he pulled away from the curb. Running for his next destination, Motta thought about the junkie's last words—words which Motta took as an act of goodness—as the siren rose up behind him into the night, and billows of black smoke poured across the moon.

19

Luigi's was an Italian restaurant just south of the Strip, a hangout that catered to the older generation of mid-level music business types, largely ignored by the hipper denizens of The Roxy, the Troubador bar, or Roy's. Luigi's, favored by the likes of Joe Ruffino, RPM's toupeed VP of Marketing, was also something of a Musician's Union haunt, frequented by older players whose only gigs these days were the free funerals every Local 47 member got if his dues were paid up when he died.

Motta pulled Hank's Chevy into the lot next door. He made his way among the Strip's nightcrawlers, slipped inside the door, and stood for a moment in the darkness until he could discern a fat woman greeter in a flower print dress, holding menus.

"Geno?" he asked.

"In back. Follow the drumsticks."

Motta did as he was told, moving past the booths and half-full tables with checkered cloths and the oversweet smell of tomato sauces, until he picked up the tap-tapping of drumsticks.

Motta found him at a back table, in a black Naugahyde booth—a small man, partially bald, with a black shirt and a string tie, a beer in front of him.

"Geno?"

He looked up at Motta, popping gum, his mouth open, idly drumming paradiddles, flams and ratamacues on the tablecloth.

"Do I know you?" he said.

"Motta," Motta said, punching home the ethnic flavor. "I talked to you once. I was doing a story on tape piracy."

"Oh, yeah."

Motta opened his palm and let a $100 bill appear. He slipped it across the table toward Geno.

"I need some information" were his words accompanying the gesture.

Geno put down his drumsticks, picked the bill up, held it to the flickering candlelight, pulled at it, snapped it. Satisfied, he slid over in the booth and gestured for Motta to sit down. Then he picked up the sticks and began again. They were a worn, striated pair of Ludwig 7b's, a stick Motta somehow recalled from his brief fling at drumming with a terrible Bay Area band called Brain Soup; tired of hauling around the equipment, he had finally switched to flute, at which he had even less aptitude.

"Any relation to Jake LaMotta?" Geno said.

"I get asked that. But no."

"He was some fighter."

"That's what I hear."

A jukebox emanated Billy Joel somewhere in another room. Geno started up a soft rhythm to it on the tablecloth.

"Who you with, Motta?"

"RPM."

"Marty know you're here?" His eyes hardened.

"No."

"Good," he said emphatically, and eased. "So what can I do for you?"

"Tell me about Candy Snow."

He chuckled softly and rolled his eyes. "You mean the Snow Job?"

"Snow Job?"

"That's what they're calling it on the street. Biggest hype what went down since anybody can remember. Somebody's greasing a hit for that broad like you wouldn't believe. That ain't even news."

"How extensive?"

"Well, they bought all three trades. They bought the racks, and the retail outlets. You been into the stores on the Strip lately? They each got three hundred units stacked right up at the front, beneath the mobiles and a twelve-foot poster of the broad on the wall. And that's all they play in the stores, day and night. That goddamn 'So Hot, So High.' They even got it on the box in *here*. And there's the radio too. They bought that."

"How do they buy radio, Geno?"

"Well, in the old days, they just bought it with the green. Everybody's hand was out. Then after the payola scandals it switched over to broads, trips to Vegas, cars, things like that. And dope. Lots of dope."

"How do they do it *now*?"

"Well, the guy from the label goes into the station, visits the PD, the Program Director. And he says—Hey, Joey. Remember that time I let you debut such and such a single on your station? Remember the time we got you the contest prize, sent you and your old lady to Hawaii for two weeks? Remember that nice clean coke we scored for you last Christmas? Now this is one I really need. I need it bad, more than anything I ever brought you before. And by the way, we got another contest coming up. A trip to Europe.

And I got a friend here, he's in town for a few days, he's got some fine weed. I'll have him give you a call. And hey, use my limo while I'm here, okay?—What's the guy gonna say? Like maybe these two went to P.S. 100 together, you know? Or his kid needs a job, he wants to break into the business. Go check out the last names in your company directory sometime. Then match them with the last names of people out there in distribution, radio, promotion. Check it out. You see? So that's basically the way it is. A lot of favors pile up over the years, things you can call in when you need to. Sometimes you even use a little threat, some strong arm on somebody. A little nudge. That's my line of work, when drumming gigs is slow, like recently. I'm in what they call Collections. Me and Bunny, my partner. We get hired by independent guys, never the big labels directly, to drive around in the lim, stop some guy on Rodeo Drive, just remind him he owes somebody some money. You hip? That's usually enough. Bunny, he's about seven foot, see. We been known to crack a kneecap now and then. But I mean all this is peanuts next to the Snow Job."

"How do they do the stores, Geno?"

"Same idea, basically. They got what they call a full-returns policy, the companies. The stores can return anything they stock for full credit. So it's no skin off their ass if they stock millions. They can always send it back, you dig? Trade it in for other product. No risk. So they're like a display window for the companies. That way the stores get all the product they need, and the labels get exposure. Everybody wins. That's the idea. It's got some problems, though, which is why you see the industry suffering. You can only keep the hype in so long. Some of this product is so bad you couldn't move it with an atom bomb. And records are getting too expensive. Kid used to come in, buy six or eight. Now maybe he buys one, two. Last year the companies took back millions in returns that they can't do nothing with. But on something like the Snow Job, they can still pull out the stops. They say, 'Hey, we need this one. We'll give you special terms.' That kind of thing. And you're looking at a network of favors again. And if there's other people involved, guys outside the business, know what I'm saying? You're looking at a lot of clout, a lot of favors."

"The Mob, Geno? Is that what you mean?"

Geno tapped out a little pattern with his sticks, shook his head, and smiled to himself. "See that there? That's a triple ratamacue. There's hardly any of your young rock drummers can do that. It takes chops. Schooling. The kids coming up today don't get their basics. All they know is a backbeat, and a couple of fills they pick up off somebody else's record. Buddy Rich. Now there was a drummer. Ever heard about the battle he had with Krupa? It was Carnegie Hall. Krupa came out on the stage with a big set. Gongs, cymbals, two bass drums, the works. Buddy Rich, he comes out with just *one bass drum*. And a chair. That's all. And he cuts him. Cuts him to shreds. You dig?" Motta laughed, and waited while Geno demonstrated a few more beats. "Listen," he said finally. "I'll tell you this much. There's a lot of juice behind the Snow Job. More juice than Marty Karp's got. Or any record company's got. A lot more."

"So the Mob *is* in on this."

He shook his head at Motta, and smiled with tolerant disdain. "You wasn't around when Jimmy Petrillo run the Musician's Unions. But I went to his funeral, back in fifty-nine. You shoulda seen it. Thousands of guys weeping, carrying on. Some rough trade was there. It looked like a Cosa Nostra funeral. You hear me? Don't kid yourself. Those guys is still around. They still run the business."

Motta nodded, and waited to see if Geno would give him any more. Geno snapped his gum and did another lick. "That's a flamadiddle. *Da*-da-da-da. See, you do them fast, you get a nice, cool thing going. Rudiments. That's what they're called. You hip to the Rudiments? Your young drummer today, he don't got that down."

"Geno. Do you know anything about Lisa Wilde?"

"Lisa Wilde? Run her car off the road up on Mulholland. Died. That's what I know."

"You heard anything about that?"

"Hey, man," he said, looking aggrieved, put upon. "Like I don't know everything. Things happen. Maybe she run off the road, maybe somebody helped her. Who knows? Life is mysterious. Could be somebody wanted her gone. I don't know. I didn't know the broad. Was she on dope?"

"No."

"Funny sex?"

"I don't think so."

"Hey. Maybe she was too good, you know? That can happen too. But I wouldn't mess with that if I was you. Unless you got eyes to end up down a ravine yourself."

"Okay," Motta said.

"Okay is right. But I tell you the Candy Snow is some item. I mean you hear guys talking, and they got *awe*. It's put some life back in the street. Most of the guys thought those days was over. But they ain't. That don't change. That kind of thing, it's always there."

"Geno, thanks." Motta reached over and shook his hand.

He nodded, and drummed out another lick. "You ever dig the New Orleans drummers? They do a modified march thing, like a street beat, but with a *lope* in it. They call it *second line* drumming. It's some kind of stuff. Check this out." He played a riff, chewing his gum, his little head bobbing, and Motta nodded appreciatively. "Where you parked?"

"In the lot."

"Go out back, by the door here. Tell the attendant you was here to see me. Don't tip him. He's my stupid nephew from Buffalo. Wants to be a rock star. Can't play his ass. Two chords is what he knows. Thinks he's the next Jimi Hendrix."

"Thanks, Geno." Motta got up, slipped out behind the

booth and, with the tapping of the sticks following him, took the fire exit door into the alley.

He saw a wall opposite him, with graffiti on it. He heard the door close behind him. There was a shuffling of feet. The next thing was a tremendous, booming pain in the small of his back.

Then something hit him across the chest, in the sternum, knocking his breath away. A fist loomed, and crushed into his mouth. He could feel his nose cracking, and at the same time his feet went out from under him.

As soon as he hit the ground a boot was kicking his head. Another heel dropped in his groin, bringing a scream of agony. Nausea swept him, blood rolled in his mouth. He struggled to keep his eyes open, tried to move his arms, cover up. But a silhouetted figure was straddling him, pounding his face over and over with what he dimly knew was the butt of a pistol. A boot kept ramming the side of his face, splitting his ear, causing an unutterable agony of pain.

The final perception was of the loss of resistance, a yielding to the darkness, the brim of the Panama hat of the man straddling; and the foreshortened, winking neon face of Candy Snow, bigger than the sky, blinking on and off, far above him on the Strip, her lips seeming to flash the words over and over: "So Hot, So High."

20

A strange pair they were, sitting in deck chairs on the narrow, cracked cement porch that fronted the old crumbling adobe hotel set in the granite hillside above Avalon Bay. Below them, small craft glided and bobbed on the shimmering waters in the midday sun, the strand thick with summer tourists.

The old gray man sat in his pajamas and a maroon robe, a plaid blanket wrapped around him as if surrounded by the deepest London fog, a mottled hand held up to his face, sucking hungrily on a Camel.

Next to him, huddled in his old army parka, papers scrambled in his lap, a dulled pencil in his fist, wild blond hair sticking out of a brand-new cowboy hat that shaded his angelic, pallid scholar's face from the sun, was the Ferret.

The two of them watched the ferry turn slowly around in the harbor.

"You could have come over on the seaplane for a couple bucks more," the old man wheezed. "They only take fifteen minutes. 'Course they crash a lot." He worked on his Camel a little more. "Saw one go straight down the other day. Sweet as you please. Nothing wrong with the planes. It's the pilots that're no good."

He turned and looked suspiciously at his visitor.

"How'd you find me?" he asked.

"I came across an old book of yours," Ferret said. "On Asia. *Cochin China After the War.*"

"You must be some kind of ferret, all right. Book's been out of print for thirty years." The old man, Malcolm Dickens, stubbed the Camel out in a small metal ashtray in his lap with a map of Catalina at its center.

"Somebody at AP in Los Angeles seemed to think you were out here," Ferret said.

Dickens looked out across the water. "Yeah. This is my little Elba. Haven't been to the mainland in five years. Winters are lovely. Summers, too many tourists. Used to be a grand place, this island. See that ballroom down there? That's where the Hollywood crowd would come in their yachts. Dancing, booze, women . . ."

"That was a very good book you wrote," Ferret said. "You knew Asia well."

Dickens grunted. "AP gave me three months off to write it. In nineteen forty-seven. I thought it would pay my way out. Never did, though. Worked the rest of my life for them. I was what they call an 'informed source.' Used to quote myself in my own stories."

Ferret, eyes burnished with fatigue, peered over at the old man from beneath the brim of his cowboy hat, and waited. The smell of sage drifted off the browned summer hillside behind the old, sagging, bougainvillea-twined hotel.

Dickens looked stealthily over his shoulder, then back at Ferret. "Think you could spare me another fag?" he said guiltily.

Ferret fished around in his parka until he came up with one, and lit it for the old man.

"Look at these things," Dickens said, staring with grim pleasure at the Camel's burning tip. "A man should be able to design his own end. Mine happens to be nicotine. But the nurses don't let me smoke. Another erosion of freedom, in my view. Emphysema. I've got an oxygen machine in my room. Only use it at night." He coughed beneath his blanket. "So what do you want from me, Mister Ferret?"

Ferret leaned forward earnestly. "I've been trying to get some information on a man. But all my sources are dry. He simply doesn't exist. The only thing I have is an old war record that puts him in Southeast Asia in early nineteen forty-five. But then it ends suddenly. Expunged. He seems to have disappeared after that. Went completely invisible. You knew Asia as well as anyone. I thought I'd try you. You're my last resort."

"What was his name?"

Ferret said the words "Jennings Vaughan," and Malcolm Dickens became very still and silent and shrunk down beneath his blanket. His cheeks hollowed out like bellows. He sat for a while and smoked. Finally, he turned and looked balefully toward Ferret.

"Why?"

"Someone I know wants to find him."

"Friend or foe?"

Ferret didn't give him an answer; but it was a professional silence. His eyes held bright with hope, and appeal, and an invitation to the old man to speak.

Dark emotions played around Dickens' face in the harsh sun. Ferret took his Camels and matches out of his parka and placed them on the peeling, rusted little metal table that sat between them. Dickens looked darkly out of the corner of his eye. Ferret, gripping his pencil, waited hopefully.

The old man settled back in his chair and closed his eyes

and let the smoke curl up into his face. And Ferret, flushed
with anticipation, watched memory slowly reach its gray,
curling fingers inside to take hold of Malcolm Dickens.

"First time I ever set eyes on Jennings Vaughan," he
began, "was in a tent not far from the Burma Road, in nineteen forty-five. A sweltering February night. I was with AP,
running with a British intelligence unit headed by a guy
named Arthur Cross. God knows what ever happened to
him . . ." He lit a fresh Camel with the butt of the old one,
and squinted out at the sea. "We had come over the mountains from India, chasing the Japanese survivors of Imphal
across the Chidwin River. MacArthur had landed at Lin-
gayen Gulf on January ninth, and launched an offensive toward Mandalay. The taking of Burma was only a matter of
weeks . . ."

Ferret, nodding encouragement to Dickens as he spoke,
began to scribble eager notes.

"Our group had broken off on our own, heading up into
the Shan States to make contact with some of the old
sawbwas, the feudal lords who ruled all of northern Burma.
The idea was to help organize insurgency forces against Ba
Maw, the nationalist who was heading the struggle to oust
the British from Burma.

"Just outside of Kentung we ran into some Americans.
They were supposed to be there running guns through these
same reactionary sawbwas, across the hills into Yunnan and
Chungking, to fortify Chiang's troops in South China. We
ran for three days with the Americans as they advanced
north toward Lashio . . ."

Dickens paused, gasping for air. He took from the pocket
of his robe a small spray, and hungrily inhaled a squirt. A
moment later, he continued.

"That first night we sat in a tent behind mosquito netting,
drinking Guinness stout magically procured by a smiling
young U.S. Army captain, fresh out of Williams College.
Jennings Vaughan . . ." He darkened, and coughed into a

Kleenex. "He had established himself as something of an entrepreneur. You know the type. If somebody needed nylon stockings, or a swing record from home, Vaughan was the man to see. He seemed to have people flying goods in from Bangkok, Hong Kong, even San Francisco.

"The following afternoon Vaughan invited me to accompany him on a run up ahead of lines. He had a sawbwa contact he was to meet. This young black fellow, a private named Green, whom everyone agreed was the best saxophone player in the U.S. Army, was assigned to drive us.

"We slipped up a rutted road behind lines in a khaki jeep piled high with shiny new U.S. machine guns and ammo. It seemed like a safe penetration. All of Burma knew the American troops were advancing, and the further north we got, the less resistance there was left.

"The village turned out to be a small bunch of huts beside a clogged, muddy river. As we pulled into the clearing the Shan ran to meet us, smiling and waving. Their leader was a fat sawbwa smoking a Churchill cigar, an American machine gun slung over his neck. He spoke to us through an interpreter as we stood in the clearing.

"And then as the village boys began hauling reed satchels across the dirt toward the jeep, I suddenly realized what Vaughan was up to . . ."

"Opium," Ferret said, nodding.

The old man looked over at Ferret sharply, a little surprised. "Yes," he said. "The Shan States manufacture fifty percent of the world's supply. As I watched the Shan boys load bag after bag into the back of Vaughan's jeep in exchange for the guns, I knew those guns would never reach China . . ."

Dickens paused to put out his cigarette, and shifted under the blanket.

"We were standing in the clearing," he went on. "Vaughan, with all the illicit glee of a schoolboy, was busy orchestrating his trade. Suddenly I heard, *Tenno Heike Ban-*

AP. One day I was up in the Rockefeller Center building, trying to get some scoop from Bill Donovan and some of my old OSS pals who were busy forming the Central Intelligence Agency. On the way down I found myself in the elevator with none other than Jennings Vaughan. He was dressed those days very much Ivy League, East Coast Establishment, crewcut and all. He was, as I understood it, not working directly with CIA, but on some sort of call, or retainer, on things having to do with Southeast Asia. The talk those days was of organizing the Meo tribesmen through the opium-rich Golden Triangle, setting them up as a 'bulwark against Communism.' Of course I knew what that meant . . ."

Dickens paused, and smiled bitterly. Overhead, the sun had passed over the ridge, throwing the two figures on the porch into shadow. Dickens pulled his blanket tightly up around him.

"Then, as I stepped out of the building onto Fifth Avenue, I saw something which shook me to my bones. Private Green, that gifted young saxophonist who had saved Vaughan's life that day in Burma, was sitting in Vaughan's green Packard, in civilian clothes, his eyes glazed with heroin. And at that moment, I knew that Vaughan and the others had found a new opium market to replace China: Harlem, and the streets of New York City . . ."

Ferret, in quiet ecstasy, scribbled furiously.

"See, the poppy was refined," Dickens went on, "into pure number four heroin in processing plants throughout Southeast Asia. Then they brought it into the city, with the Mafia as its errand boys. Luciano would be set loose from prison later that year by Governor Dewey. Of course, he went on to organize the Corsicans in Sicily and Marseilles to process and ship heroin from Turkish opium.

"Anyway, there on Fifth Avenue, as inklings of all this dawned on me, I saw this pale, pinched woman, trailing two kids in shorts and camel's hair coats, climb into Vaughan's

zai! Sniper fire tore into our midst. I hit the dirt. Two Burmese fell with us, wounded. And Private Green, the black
jeep driver, took a hit in the leg. As Green fell he purposely
took Vaughan down, and lay across him to protect him.
Then Green, using his handgun, fired into the tree. The Japanese soldier dropped like a rock, thudded on the dirt, and
bounced a couple of times.

"I saw Vaughan get to his feet and look down at the jeep
driver who had just saved his life. Green was struggling up,
holding his thigh where the bullet had ripped it, blood seep-
ing through his fingers. All Vaughan said was, 'Shoot him,'
pointing to the emaciated, near-dead Japanese twitching on
the ground. But Private Green couldn't raise his gun.
Vaughan snatched a carbine, jammed a clip in it, and went
over to the Japanese. Holding the gun several feet from his
face, he fired the entire clip into him."

Malcolm Dickens looked up at Ferret, ghostly pale.

"May I?" he said, his tremulous hand already fishing for
another Camel.

"Well," he said, lighting up again, "later I heard that
Vaughan had arranged for a Purple Heart and a discharge
for Green. But I knew it was less out of gratitude than a
desire to seal Green's lips . . ."

An afternoon breeze had come up off Avalon Bay, carrying salt spray across the porch to settle on their lips. Dickens
went on with his tale, as Ferret, rapt, listened.

"As we left the Americans and trekked up along the Sal-
ween River, watching the Shan chieftains arm themselves
for the battle against Ba Maw, I saw that the days of the
British *raj* in the Far East were doomed. Southeast Asia
would soon be run by the Americans. And the Americans
would fall heir to the opium trade. But coastal China,
opium's vast perennial market, would be closed off by Mao's
takeover. The Americans would need a new market. But
where? . . . I couldn't figure it out.

"In early nineteen forty-six I was back in New York with

Packard. It struck me as strange that such a man would
have a family, a domestic existence, that he would produce
life of his own. Must have struck her, too. Because some
time later, around nineteen fifty-one, I heard she killed herself with a shot in the temple—after dispatching her two
children the same way."

There was a dark and bitter pause. Ferret stopped writing, and looked up to meet the pale gaze of Malcolm
Dickens.

"Is there more?" Ferret asked gently.

Dickens looked out at the shadows lengthening over the
bay, and nodded.

"Keeping tabs on him became a kind of melancholy
hobby with me. I've got a file on Vaughan in my room back
there." Ferret sat up, scarcely able to contain his excitement
as Dickens nodded over his shoulder. "I'll tell you this,"
Dickens said, his eyes narrowing. "He's the only man in my
life I would kill on sight. And I'll bet I'd have to fight my
way through a crowd for the privilege of being the first."

A sudden cool wind rose up off the bay to brush the granite hillside. Malcolm Dickens quivered quietly in his blanket, and looked off to sea.

"If you want to catch the afternoon ferry," he said, "you
should get going."

"Would you be willing to show me that file?" Ferret ventured.

The old man turned and looked at him for a long time
through the dimming air. Finally, he nodded his assent.

Ferret helped Dickens struggle up out of the deck chair.
He guided him into the old hotel and down a long linoleum
corridor to a gray, musty room where plastic curtains,
crusted with salt, whipped in the breeze.

21

"Mike?"

There was the slightest awareness of the presence of light: nothing more. Light, interrupted; then a gradual sense of pattern, resolving into a dim perception of movement. Then the parallel sound, with as little significance as the shadow: *"Mike?"* A third element: the blind sensation of total pain. The shadow, the sound, the pain: a single event. *"It's me. Hank."* Shadow, sound, pain. *"Somebody called. Found you in an alley."* There was the flickering concept of a source for the sounds, a speaker, a world outside where the light and the shadows lay. *"Picked you up. Three in the morning. Day before yesterday."* The question was inseparable from the pain, the light. Consciousness differentiates; unconsciousness merges. The pain was a filter, a steady state. For an instant, the shadow tinged green, took on a person's shape: then it was mere light again; the inter-

ruption of light; silence. *"You been out the whole time. Can
you hear me?"* But the sounds were disconnecting, dissolv-
ing, details drowning. And then even the light and the
sound went out. There was only pain, and unconsciousness.

The next light was different: a brighter light, with less
shadow, the sounds more complex, vivid. The green he saw
this time was paler, and he recognized—what little he could
discern through tiny slits—a wall, bathed in sunlight, the
wall of Hank's apartment. And the sounds were of the sea,
beach revelers, the implacable militance of the calliope. A
weekend, he thought. It's so noisy.

He must have moved then, for pain shot down his right
side. This brought with it a mental inventory, a gradual iso-
lation of the body's specific myriad pains. He tried working
his right arm; it was like attempting to lift a car. Bells rang
storm warnings in his head. His stomach, and his groin, felt
like kicked-in walls. Each limb he tried in turn; each fought
him.

A gull cawed. The calliope marched. A dry fern came into
focus, hanging from the ceiling in a red pot bound in ma-
cramé. The sea thundered distantly. He smelled fresh coffee.

He contemplated the idea of raising his body for a long
time before attempting it: levitation might have been easier.
Sitting upright somehow at last, he saw he was wearing the
same clothes, and they were bloodstained. Slowly, he
wheeled his legs off the bed and let them drop to the floor.

Through swollen eyes he made out across the room, sitting in an old crumbling wicker rocker before a round oak
table, in a cloud of smoke, hunched over papers piled high in
his lap, draped in his old army parka, thick glasses down on
his nose, the spectral figure of the Ferret.

"What day is it?" Motta made a viscous sound through
thickened lips.

Ferret looked up, startled, out of red-rimmed, haggard
eyes of his own, and broke into a smile.

"You're awake," he said cheerily, "leading me to conclude that you're alive."

Ferret removed his papers from his lap and put them on the table. Then he stood and ambled over to the bed. "Coffee's made. I brought Danish. Man, you should see yourself." Ferret, towering above him, gazed sympathetically down at what Motta gathered were the ruins of his face. "Are you . . . of a piece?" he said.

"What day is it?" Motta repeated, burbling.

"July Fourth. Independence Day. The bikini locusts are swarming." He gestured out the window. "Coffee?"

As Ferret walked off toward the kitchen at the back of the flat, Motta attempted the feat of standing upright; he found it less difficult than he had expected. His groin throbbed in time to his head, and his right ear felt like somebody was twisting it and wouldn't let go. The blow to the small of his back had left an imprint of pain which he now realized was from his own gun. "My Beretta," he whispered anxiously, turning back to the bed. It was lying there. Precious good it had done him, he thought.

He limped off to the bathroom, using the aid of the walls as he went. The dusty mirror gave him back a hideous visage: both eyes were still puffed, though the purple had already gone to yellow. A blue welt adorned the bridge of his nose. His right ear looked like a small eggplant. Blood caked his upper lip, through several days' growth of beard; he bathed it gingerly, feeling the sting. Gradually he concluded, vanity aside, that the total damage consisted of a broken nose, possibly a couple of cracked ribs, and various bruises, sprains, lacerations; if there was worse, it hadn't hit him yet.

He worked his way back to the apartment's main room, where Ferret had brought an orange ceramic pot of coffee and a pink cardboard box full of Danish pastry to the oak table. Outside, beyond the arched windows, the sun beat

down on a vast, shimmering infestation of holiday sun-
bathers, stretching all the way to the end of sight.

Ferret had propped pillows in the wicker chair in front of
the table, faced it toward the windows, and now stood solic-
itously by, inviting Motta to sit.

Motta, settling into the chair, gazed at the steaming coffee
cup, gripped it, sipped it, and felt life returning. Even the
sticky cheese Danish tasted good. He let his eyes drift out
along the silvery, sun-whipped surf, thick with swimmers.
Ferret had taken a chair next to him; Motta could feel his
anxious, coltish impatience, his waiting, his concern.

"How did I get here?"

"Somebody found you in an alley behind Luigi's two
nights ago. They got Hank's name from the car registration
and called him. He went and picked you up."

"How did *you* get here?"

"There were two numbers in your wallet. Amanda's and
mine. Hank called Amanda, but she wasn't home. He left a
message and the number here on her service. Then he called
me at the Windward. He didn't know what the hell was
going on. Still doesn't. He was afraid to take you to a hospital." He looked anxiously at Motta. "Know who it was?"

"The same guys. One I couldn't see. But I recognized the
little one sitting on my stomach pistol-whipping me." Motta,
wincing with the pain's replay, cradled the coffee cup in his
lap, let the steam rise into his swollen face.

"How did they find you?"

"I went to Luigi's to see a guy named Geno, a collections
man, to buy some information on Candy Snow." Motta
gazed up at the gaunt, wired visage of the Ferret. "You
don't look much better than I do."

"Oh, I'm okay. A week's worth of library pallor. And I
was up all night," he said, smiling shyly, sucking a Camel,
"on this." He nodded toward the unruly pile of papers on
the table, scarcely able to conceal his excitement.

"You got stuff?"

"Michael," he said intently, "I've got the keys to the high-way. Tell me when you're ready."

Motta wasn't ready, couldn't imagine being ready. All he felt was the desire to forget, hide, slip back into darkness, find sleep again and enter it. He swallowed more coffee, and pushed weakly against the body's ceaseless, punishing signals of pain.

Ferret was over the table, fussing with messy stacks of ruled notebook paper, a mad, smudged schoolboy in science class. There were razor-tipped pens, pencils, pads of blank paper. He was setting up with a ceremoniousness befitting a State Department briefing, this maniacal blond Rasputin in the army parka in the 90-degree heat, hair shooting out like mattress coils. Motta could feel Ferret's zappy glow of anticipation; the merry-go-round playing; the wicker rocker squeaking; the doleful swing of the dry fern in the clay pot; the hysteria of the holiday crowds outside; the strong coffee and oversweet Danish; the seedy apartment room.

"Okay. Anytime," Motta murmured through swollen lips.

He found himself staring into the eager, angelic face, the wild red eyes, magnified through the thick spectacles, earnestly seeking his own. Aching with lassitude and pain, Motta settled back in the chair to listen.

"First," Ferret said with mock formality, "a moment of silence for a vast network of confidential sources who shall go unnamed but not unappreciated." He put his hand over his heart. "And to you, my friend, for having delivered me my consummate piece, my opus, my Divine Comedy." He grinned fiendishly.

It was Ferret's saving grace that he was never far from self-mockery; and Motta found himself once again oddly cheered, endeared by him, as he had been that day at the Windward Café.

"End prelude," said Ferret. "On to the great debrief. Now let me say that we're going to draw a long bow. So grant me the apparent *non sequitur*. There's method. Revelation is never far behind. We're going to mix theory and fact, because we'll need both to unravel the vile machinations of our cast of characters." Inspired eyes gleamed, mystic hands hovered over his papers like a Ouija board as Harpo "Ferret" Beam prepared his grand exposition.

"You comfortable?" he asked.

Motta closed his eyes. "Yes, Ferret," he whispered, comfort an unimaginably distant state.

"Okay. Here we go. Now. Let's open with a tidbit. A shard. There's a Japanese word. *Giri*. Do you know it?"

Motta shook his head, twitching as a bolt of pain shot down his back.

"*Giri*. It means obligation, or owing. It has to do with honor. If somebody does you a favor, helps you out, you *must* return that favor, at whatever cost. Not to do so is dishonor worse than death. Okay? Cut to New York City, nineteen forty-two. Japanese being rounded up and shipped to so-called 'internment camps' all along the West Coast. A pharmacist in New York City, one Tadao Suzuki . . ." Here he brought one of his fingered sheets close to his face. "What is known as a *kibei*, a Japanese born here but educated in Japan. A very efficient and good pharmacist. And a U.S. citizen. One of his customers, a man named Giuseppe Martoni, kept Tadao Suzuki and his family out of the camps by getting them papers saying they were Chinese, and letting them stay at his house in New Jersey. A large favor, for which Suzuki and his family owed very big giri. All right? Now follow me, Michael. We're going to make a diagram. A *visual aid*, as we used to call them in high school."

Motta opened one eye and watched Ferret take a blank sheet of paper, turn it longways, and write, over to the right, south of center, in a tiny, illegible hand, the name of "T. Suzuki." Opposite, on the far left of the page, he inscribed, in equally tiny letters with his gray razor-tipped pen, the name of "Giuseppe Martoni."

"Onward," he said, looking up brightly. "Now. Another

deductive riff: Bogotá, Colombia, nineteen seventy-one. The laboratory of a Colombian professor of chemistry is blown up, killing himself and his assistants. He had just sent a report to his government demonstrating how penicillin imported from the United States and Germany could be made locally for one-twentieth the price. It set off a wave of price-fixing scandals against international pharmaceutical firms all over the world. The worst offender? The Heller Group, with an annual nine hundred and twenty-seven percent profit, all of it taken out of the country."

Motta watched Ferret laboriously enter Heller's name in a box, in large letters, in the center of his page, near the top. Outside, the sun had already begun its long summer arc of descent. A wave of nausea passed over him; he fought the urge to sleep.

"Time," Ferret said, waving a fresh Camel, "for an axiom: *It is in the Western governments' interests economically and politically to support international drug production and consumption.* All the major drug-producing countries are Allies. It is the way we keep our friends in business. It gives them an export, us an import. Licit and illicit drugs, the line gets thin, bleeds over into international drug cartels. You can't discuss economics and politics without acknowledging this key fact. A *thematic* element, Michael. We will draw on it later."

A breath of salt spray blew through the window, and Motta inhaled it hungrily as Ferret continued his strange litany of paranoid *arcana*, slurping coffee, spilling it on his pages.

"Ever heard of Ernst Kaltenbrunner? No. Okay. Nazi. S.S. head. After Heydrich was killed by Czech partisans. Extermination squads in Eastern Europe. Nineteen forty-four. Did you know he was Director of Interpol after the war? A genocidal killer, running an independent international crime-prevention body. You hip to that?"

Ferret stopped suddenly, sensing unrest, and looked hesitantly over at Motta. "You with me?"

I have gone, Motta thought, to the madman for the cure.
This is the height of folly. The idea that the ravings of the
sweet fool in the parka, eagerly scrambling his dirty ruled
papers, could counter the palpable messages in his flesh, the
compelling argument of physical pain, was absurd. He felt
humiliated, whipped, unutterably depressed, wanting only
to sleep and forget. A shattering complacency possessed
him. He and the Ferret; simply a couple of refugees from
the real world, speculative freaks from the college towns,
ghosts of the Café Mediterranean.

"What are you saying, Ferret?" he mumbled. "How does
it relate?"

"Hey," he said, touching Motta's arm gently. "Hang in.
We're getting there." Ferret gazed at his rudimentary diagram, with Heller in the center, somebody named Suzuki on
one side, someone else named Martoni on the other. "I can
see," he said, chastened, "that I'm losing you on the hors
d'oeuvres. Let's go for some meat."

Ferret then launched into an elaborate, astonishingly detailed history of Heller, from its early days in antibiotics
after the war to its present positions and holdings, and
its global operations in entertainment and communications
through Multigram, complete with names, dates, figures. It
was a brilliant précis, all tinged with an aura of evil complicity, and it stirred Motta out of his torpor. Then Ferret
began to spin it out further into an excitable rap on the history of Heller's financing, which, he suggested ominously,
led right to the doorstep of the American banks, finding it of
tremendous significance that Klaus Heller, Junior, the president of the company, was a member of the Trilateral Commission. This led, by a path which eluded Motta, to a quick
improvisation on the Masons, a mystical group called the
Thule, the ancient Egyptian Order of the Snake, and the Il-
luminati. Somehow Ferret even managed to work in the

name of Aleister Crowley. Then he brought it all back
around to a triumphant inferential scenario of conspiratorial
control of global communications by multinational corporations. It was a bizarre, spectacular *tour de force.*

"So you see?" Ferret said, frothing, chugging coffee. "For
a company that grosses four hundred and twenty billion
legit every *year,* even the thirty billion their Multigram entertainment empire brings them is rather small. So why all
this fuss about a foundering little record label?" He raised
his pen in the air significantly. "They want the *line.*"

"Capture the radio station and you've won the revolution," Motta said.

"Right. Extend that principle to a more sophisticated look
at media. Or, to use my axiom: *Any means of communication is an instrument of control.* Heller wants the
line. Financially, it's an insignificant acquisition, very minor.
They don't care if it's in the red or the black. They can
pump it up with capital, or tie it in, cross it over with their
other media companies, or let it lie fallow. But it's leverage,
an entrée into the music business in America, a chess piece.
Keep an eye on the *inner* line, Michael. Think *cultural control.* Dissemination of ideas. You with me? This is *key.*"

"Heller is buying *The Rock,*" Motta offered.

Ferret grinned triumphantly. "There. Wouldn't you
know?"

And Motta, stirring in his chair, found himself being led
further into Ferret's cabalistic vision of complicity.

"Now, *who* exactly is Klaus Heller, Senior? A Nazi, who
ran with Kaltenbrunner in Eastern Europe. I have his S.S.
number right here. He is also a former *morphine addict.* A
junkie drug company owner. Check *that* out. Where is he
now? In a Zen monastery in Japan! He's been there for
fifteen years. The son runs the business, this same son who is
on the Trilateral Commission, who is also a member of Kaltenbrunner's Interpol. An *adopted* son. Okay? I just want
you to get a feel for the scope of this thing, who the players

are in the game. Our *dossier*. You can't get answers in conspiracy thinking without a good dossier. So we've got our Heller up here . . ." He wrote in below the Heller box: *Heller Sr.*, and *Heller Jr*. "And over here we've got little Suzuki, and over on the other side, Martoni . . ."

He seemed momentarily lost, confused. Spittle had formed on the corners of his dried lips. He ran his trembling, inkstained hand through his bushy hair, fingered his paper piles indecisively. "Wait. Wait . . ." The sun was fattening in the afternoon sky, and the revelers' shouts seemed to grow louder with the lowering day. Motta felt the insistent pulse of the calliope beyond the walls as the throbbing of his own head.

Then suddenly Ferret lit up again. "Got it. Closer to home now. *RPM*."

Motta gazed through the widening slits of his eyes as Ferret drew a box below Heller, in the lower center of the page, and entered the letters: *RPM*.

"Here we have a company that grossed two hundred and fifty million last year, with a forty percent returns rate. *Forty percent*, Michael."

"And no hits on the horizon," Motta interjected, struggling up in his chair. "When I was doing my article on RPM for *The Rock*, I discovered that the lot is mortgaged up to the hilt. With three different banks. They've been in the red since the day they opened their doors. Awash in a sea of credit. A classic house of cards."

"A company *in extremis*."

"Edge city."

"So they must sell or die," Ferret said excitedly. Hastily, he wrote in Marty Karp's name on his diagram, above RPM, and drew a short line connecting them. "Now. Tell me if I've got it right. Marty came out to California in the sixties, picked up Lisa. Founded RPM with loans off her publishing royalties. Brought some of his cronies out, like Eddie Malone, and Jay Kippel." He wrote in Eddie's name under the

RPM box, and next to it, Kippel's. "And Marty pyramided RPM all the way up, using profits to pay off old loans and take out new ones?" Ferret said.

"Yeah."

"He never, ever got ahead?"

"Never. I'm sure of it."

Ferret's face opened in a beatific smile as carefully he wrote in Lisa Wilde's name in a large box to the right of RPM, in its own space. "On to the queen bee," he said. "Do you know what sort of deal Lisa had with RPM?"

"A standard artist's contract," Motta said, warming to Ferret's line of attack. Struggling against the urge to sleep, he began to speak, and found that by doing so his head slowly cleared. "I saw it once up in Legal. Nothing special. Normal royalties, production budgets. She was also a partner in RPM Corporation, one of those closely held California corporations. The principals were Marty, Kippel and Lisa. It's all on record with the state. I checked it out when I was doing my article. She probably never went to a board meeting, if they even had them. She may not even have known the corporation existed until this year."

"When she changed lawyers."

"Right. Kippel was her lawyer until this year, when she went to the guys whose letters I took from Marty's office."

"A big threat to Marty, this assertion of independence."

"Sure."

Ferret stood up, went to the window and paused, arms waving, looking like some wild, psychedelic albino *sadhu*, the yellow afro coils of his hair backlit by the falling sun.

"Now Lisa's publishing rights," he said, "form the bulk of her estate. They lie *outside* RPM."

"Yes," Motta said. "They're a labyrinth. Various companies in various names down through the years. Wildflower, Karp & Wilde, LW Songs, going back to the early days. All very vague, scrambled."

"And Marty, *with no legal authority,* has always adminis-
tered them."

Motta nodded. "An informal arrangement. It's quite
common."

"Now these are the same publishing rights Marty used to
leverage the founding of RPM, right? The point being that
he's used them before."

Motta sat up. "Yeah," he whispered. "Now you're getting
someplace."

Ferret strode back and forth before the window, consulting a crumpled sheet of paper, grinning mischievously.

"And Kippel," he said. "What do you know about him?"

"Quiet. Crafty. Came out of the Seventh Avenue garment
trade, I think."

"Good. Now watch closely, Michael."

Ferret rushed back to the table, grabbed a pen, and stood
excitedly over his diagram. "We're going to connect up
some of our lines. Remember Giuseppe Martoni over here?
This is *Joe* Martoni. His son." He drew in, below the father's
name, the son's. "And way over here. Remember Suzuki?
His son Tom, who went to Columbia University and became
a good toxologist, *now works in the Coroner's Office in Los
Angeles.*"

He looked over at Motta impishly, then drew a long looping line across the page between the two names.

"Martoni Junior?" he went on. "Let's see what happened
to him. Well, he followed in his father's footsteps, became a
small-time Mob guy, went to work for a man named
Lucchessi, who was on the board of the Garment Workers'
Union. Jay Kippel worked, as you said, on Seventh Avenue.
He was introduced to Marty Karp twenty years ago by none
other than *this same Lucchessi.* Later, when Marty hit it big
in Hollywood, Kippel was on the next plane out! Now watch
this, Michael."

Motta stared, astonished, as Ferret next drew, in a large
box above RPM and below Heller, in the center of the page,

the word: VEGAS. Then he wrote beneath it the names of
Lucchessi and Martoni. "We are closing in on our cabal," he
said, with a diabolical leer. "*This* is where Lucchessi and
Martoni are today. Lucchessi is part-owner of a couple of
casinos, a very rich and influential man in Mafia circles.
Martoni is his second in command."

He brandished his pen in the air victoriously. Then he
brought it down to the page and entered a line from Kippel
to Lucchessi, and another from Marty Karp to Lucchessi. He
looked up at Motta, his eyes ablaze. He knew he had him.

"How the hell did you find all this out?" Motta whispered.

"Conspiracy, Michael, is an *industry*. I am not alone in
my trade. I have colleagues. More of them every day." Ferret smiled modestly.

Motta sat back in his chair, amazed.

"Now," Ferret said. "Let's call upon the work of one of
my esteemed colleagues. Mafia Marvin."

"*Mafia Marvin?*"

"Mafia Marvin has a network of switchboard operators in
the Vegas telephone exchange who monitor calls in and out
of the casinos for him. Information which shall go unremarked by you." He raised his eyebrows significantly. "On
the morning after Lisa Wilde was killed, Martoni called
Suzuki from Vegas. The Coroner's Report was released the
following day, with the heroin/morphine story. *Giri*. Obligation. Remember? Martoni and Suzuki, who grew up in the
same house together during the war."

"What did they say?" Motta asked, dumbstruck.

"I can't get the content of the calls—Marvin keeps them
to himself—but I can tell you that they happened. *That* is
how your Coroner's Report got fixed. *If it got fixed*. Let's not
jump to any conclusions."

"It got fixed," Motta said. "I found Lewis Adam. He
confirmed it. She wasn't a junkie."

Ferret nodded slowly. "But can we believe him?"

Motta thought back to the dazed, ruined figure in front of the burning Palm Motel, and the empty eyes that looked right through his own. "Yeah. I think we can."

"Okay. If so, that eliminates an entire category of possibilities. Now, there is some other Vegas phone business I should bring to your attention. Six weeks ago Kippel called Lucchessi. An otherwise unremarkable event, except that Marvin says he has no record of them having spoken in a year and a half. Now, the Mob's been involved in the business since speakeasy days. Kippel's call is not in itself news. But it's the *timing* of the calls that draws our attention. A flurry of calls followed, then a night trip to Vegas by Kippel and Marty Karp five weeks ago. I can even tell you the airlines. Courtesy, once again, Mafia Marvin."

"They went there to buy the Snow Job," Motta said, struggling up again in the rocker.

"The Snow Job?" It was Ferret's turn at incredulity.

Motta recounted the revelations of Geno, the little tablecloth drummer at Luigi's. He told Ferret the anatomy of buying a hit, and how it was being done on a massive, unprecedented scale for Candy Snow.

"Good," Ferret said when Motta was done. "This confirms our thesis that RPM has been in a scramble for money. Which leads us to the next question: Why? They're about to make a huge sale, get all the money they could ever need from Heller, enough to pay off every debt under the sun. Why buy a hit?"

"Because they think they need the record sales to secure the Heller deal. Beef up their books. Disguise all the returns."

"I agree. Now, *we* know that Heller doesn't give a good shit if RPM is rich or poor. They just want the string to the balloon. But obviously *Marty* doesn't know that. Otherwise he wouldn't be fooling around throwing water on the flame, courting the one thing that Heller fears most: *scandal*. This

is *immensely significant*. I think it's time to draw in a few
more lines on our great design here."

Outside, the sun was sinking toward the horizon as Motta,
fighting the pain and exhaustion and weariness, watched
Ferret draw a thick, strong line from Lisa Wilde to RPM,
and a similar one from RPM to Vegas.

"Onward," he heard Ferret say. "Let's call up one of our
axioms. *Where are the profits?* For RPM it's in selling to
Heller. For Heller, it's in buying RPM, for reasons which
we've discussed. But where are *Vegas'* profits? We haven't
found them yet. RPM is worse than broke. Vegas doesn't
work on spec. No amount of favors would account for something of the magnitude of the Snow Job. What did Marty
use to buy the hit?"

"His own money?"

"He's got it. A girlfriend at TRW ran it down for me, to
the penny. But is it his style to put up his own money?"

"No. He lets his corporations take the risks."

"But he can't put up RPM's money. Not with Heller's
lawyers and accountants looking in on the figures. So what
does he have," he said, grinning with conspiratorial glee,
"that is neither the company's nor his?"

"Lisa Wilde's publishing rights," Motta whispered,
amazed at the obvious truth of it.

"Yes! *The same ones Marty used before to start RPM!*"
Ferret exulted. "A couple of million dollars' worth, more or
less, at this point, right? They lie outside the company. He
puts them up as a guarantee, even though he has no legal
right to them, never did. Right in the middle of this, Lisa's
new lawyers want to see the books. Marty is threatened. He
writes 'Pricks!' in the margin of their letters."

"You think the lawyers knew what was going on?"

"No. Or they would have made a noise by now. They
were just trying to do what they were hired to do—get her
publishing away from Marty. But the big question, Michael,

is . . ." And here Ferret paused and raised his pen in the air. "Did *Lisa* know?"

Motta sat back in his chair and recalled the trembling hand proffered him out the window of the silver Jag that afternoon at the foot of the canyon, and her pale, burning eyes.

"*I need to talk. It's important . . .*"

"She knew, Ferret," Motta said emphatically.

They both fell silent, and let the sea roll between them for a few minutes.

Finally, Motta said: "Somehow she found out. But how?"

"There's only one person who could tell you that," Ferret answered. "The person who had her killed."

"Marty?" Motta said.

Ferret stood over the table, rolling his pen between his fingers. "See, I have a problem with that. It's so *extreme*. He would have to admit he'd lost control of her. Like killing a part of himself. Would Diaghilev murder Nijinsky? Destroy her, yes. Because he hates her, always has. Unconsciously, he *must*. The *inner* line dictates that. But murder her? You met with him. Does he look like someone who has admitted he has lost control?"

"On the contrary. He thinks he's in total control."

"He's still operating off that myth?"

"Yes."

"Who else would have known about it at the company?"

"Kippel. Possibly Eddie Malone."

"Would either of them have broken ranks and told her?"

"Hard to conceive. Certainly not Kippel. Eddie liked her. But Marty has him in his pocket."

"Next possibility. Vegas found out that Lisa knew. They killed her to keep her from speaking out. Maybe they also found out that Marty had put up rights he didn't even own as collateral, and they wanted to punish him by knocking off his meal ticket."

"But she *wasn't* anymore," Motta said. "Her last album was a stiff. Her sales were way down."

"That makes it even more interesting," Ferret said. "So her death would mean a *Greatest Hits* album, and undoubtedly a surge in the sale of her old albums. Right?"

Motta nodded.

"That would guarantee Marty could pay Vegas with the profits from the record, whether the Heller deal came through or not. And it would cause a surge in Lisa's publishing profits, which Vegas is holding. So that sweetens their take too."

"That's a plausible guess," Motta said.

Ferret turned and rushed back to the window. "The only trouble I have with that, Michael, is the *motivation*. Vegas is deeply into entertainment on a daily basis. They're old friends of Kippel's. They can't go around dumping innocent people in ditches. Even if they're upset with Marty, or think she might know something, they have to live with it tomorrow. These things get around. They don't operate that way as a rule. I have a hard time imagining Lucchessi originating that order. Again, it's so *extreme*."

"But there's nobody else to consider," Motta said. "We've run through all the players in the game."

Ferret came back to the table and stood, pen raised, retracing in the air the space from Heller to RPM and back again. Then he went into a kind of reverie, a fragmented rumination, his pen waving back and forth like a dowser's wand above the surface of his diagram.

"Dope . . . Heller, dope . . . Vegas, dope . . . Candy Snow, dope . . . Symbolically, Lisa the antimatter in the drama . . . A *cultural dissident* . . . Not amenable to *control* . . . *Big stakes* . . . There wasn't *time* . . . She *had to go* . . . Darwinian considerations demanded it . . . natural selection . . . *Her very existence was discordant to the greater process* . . ."

Ferret's face suddenly began to spread into a saintly, beatific glow. He turned and rushed back to the window.

"Time," he said, "for the joker in the deck."

He turned back to the room, his eyes wild with apocalyptic revelation. *"Time for the joker, Michael. Michael?"*

But Motta was fast asleep in his chair.

22

A series of sudden explosions brought Motta struggling up out of sleep, thrashing in the wicker, seized with panic. He fumbled in the dark for his Beretta, but it was somewhere far across the room. On his knees, still half-asleep, he scanned the darkness, trying to discern the source of the attack. Finally his eyes came to rest on a silhouette at the window.

It was Ferret, gazing idly out into the night, smoking, watching the sky.

Motta got to his feet and walked to the window.

"Beautiful," Ferret said. "Chinese really came up with something, didn't they?"

The launching area must have been next to Hank's apartment, just out of sight. Crowds were milling in the pier parking lot; and all along the beachfront, lit by sparklers, fires and flashlights, Motta could see huddled figures in the sand. A sudden hiss rose from below, then the "whoosh" of the ascent: a moment later, far above, a multicolored hydra erupted, brightened, wheeled, and fell in a fiery fountain arc, giving off a delayed battery of pops; then it dimmed, and slowly dissolved into the night.

"They must do this every Fourth," Ferret said wondrously. "It's been going for an hour."

"What time is it?" Motta asked, still feeling foolishly shaken by the manner of his rude awakening.

"Around ten. I think we're about to see the finale." He peered through the dim at Motta. "You fell asleep at the end of Act Two," he said chidingly.

"I'm sorry."

In the silence that followed, Motta became aware of his body and the pains it still bore. Touching his face gingerly, he found that the soreness had subsided, and with it some of the swelling. "You look a lot better," Ferret confirmed. "Almost human," he added, chuckling.

Outside, it had grown quiet. "Here it comes," Ferret whispered excitedly. A group of hisses, one after the other, burst from below. Ferret was looking up into the sky with all the ingenuous delight of a child.

A frenzy of whirligigs, showers and spins blossomed in the sky, hung, and fell in a machine-gun splatter of noise. As the last spark was swallowed by the night, a chorus of whistles, cheers and applause broke out along the beachfront. Then the shadowy sea of onlookers began to shift, disperse, drift away.

Ferret gazed at Motta in the dimness. "Shall we?" he said.

He turned on a lamp beside the table, then went to the kitchen to make coffee. Motta saw the erratic bunches of papers strewn across the table, documents whose peculiar import was known only to the Ferret. On top was the diagram, and Motta saw that Ferret had filled in something new: a box, to the left of center, in its own space, placed triangularly relative to Heller and RPM. It contained no name, only a question mark, drawn in with a pen, then retraced, over and over.

"What's this?" Motta asked as Ferret returned with a fresh pot of Hank's coffee.

"The Invisible Man," Ferret said devilishly, pouring out two cups.

Motta recalled the afternoon's exposition as if through a haze. In memory, it seemed insubstantial, speculative, a mad *récitatif,* leaving only a sense of things awry, dire forces poised at the edge of vision.

Ferret gazed measuredly over at Motta by the lamp's dim glow. "You ready?"

"Let's go."

Ferret pushed his glasses up on the bridge of his nose, then undertook the ritual fingering of the papers, his long hands fluttering like birds' wings. His forefinger ran up to the top of his diagram to Heller, then traced a line down to RPM. "Let's look at Heller for a moment, considering them as more than a passive party, simply waiting in the wings for the acquisition to take place."

Motta stirred and reached for his coffee, bracing himself for Ferret's next onslaught.

"International corporations, Michael, operate much like governments. They have their own intelligence operations, and they also work closely with existing governments and their intelligence arms. There's a rather thin line between the two, actually. The CIA, for example, has an office that does nothing but deal with corporations overseas. Now," Ferret continued, "we made the point that Heller doesn't care much about RPM's financial situation. But they do care about their *legitimacy.* Ironic, considering Heller's own past. But all the more reason to make sure they don't take a tainted company into the fold. They have to thoroughly check out anyone they're going to buy. And," he said, his eyebrows raised significantly, *"they have the resources to do that."*

"You mean you think Heller knew what was going on?"

"Marty is naive enough to think they wouldn't. But I'm not."

The dreamer, Motta thought, calling the pragmatist naive: Was his whole world turning upside down?

"Heller," Ferret went on, "has a security office in every country where they have a major interest except the U.S., which they handle out of London, operating under the name of Brighton Pharmaceuticals, an inactive drug firm, run by an old ex-British Intelligence man named Arthur Cross."

Motta, watching Ferret shuffle his papers, marveled again at the unexpected breadth of his resources.

"Now dig," Ferret went on, "that Heller *must* purchase an existing American company if they want in. The political and social climate is not right for a German firm to start up their own label here. Economically risky, and ethnically inappropriate. They *need* RPM, the last large independent record label left. So imagine that Heller found out that Marty had gone to Vegas and bought the Candy Snow with bad collateral, and that Lisa was snooping, and decided it was worth their while to bypass, remove the threat themselves somehow, before Marty stepped on his own dick, so to speak."

"How would they have found out?"

"Same way we did."

"I think that's a very long shot, Ferret."

"Are we to assume," Ferret said, "that *our* investigative resources are better than *theirs?* Flattering, I admit, but . . ."

"Okay," Motta conceded.

"Let's check it out a little further, Michael. It is unlikely they would want to go to Vegas themselves, even if they have contacts there, which of course they do. After all, they're in the same business. Drugs. But that would risk more scandal. And Mafia Marvin has no record of direct contact. However, neither are they willing to stand by and watch the acquisition fall apart. So let's imagine that they didn't undertake this directly, but *through an intermediary.*"

Motta saw the dancing brightness in Ferret's eyes, the conspiratorial mania mounting again, as outside the night had fallen silent, only the sound of the sea lapping against the shore.

"Allow me to introduce," Ferret said, waving his finger excitedly over the box with the question mark in it, "The Invisible Man. The joker in the deck."

He reached a soiled fist into the pocket of his Army parka, extracted a yellowed, dog-eared newspaper clipping, and laid it down in front of Motta, smoothing its edges ceremoniously.

Motta, leaning forward, saw a faded image of a small office, antiseptically furnished, with desk, typewriter, couch. On the wall were two pictures: one of a jet plane, with the letters *USAF* on the side. The other photo was of a young man in a World War II American Army uniform, in a jungle. Also on the wall was a plaque, a diploma of some kind possibly, its lettering too small to read. Sitting at the desk was an older woman, with a fifties hairdo. And in the foreground, leaning against the desk, was a man of about forty, in a dark Brooks Brothers suit, with a crewcut, exhibiting a very bland smile.

"You are looking," said Ferret happily, "at what well may be the only photo extant of Jennings Vaughan."

"So that's him," Motta whispered. "The man in the Heller file. Where did this come from? Who is he? Some aerospace engineer? What's the plane . . ."

"Jennings Vaughan," began Ferret, "is now fifty-five years old. He was born in Meriden, Connecticut, of solid New England stock. He went to Williams College with some other figures who later helped design the postwar world. During World War II, he ended up in Southeast Asia . . ."

Ferret, consulting his fistfuls of notes from the files of old

Malcolm Dickens, launched into a reconstruction of Jennings Vaughan's career. The names went by like a National Geographic travelogue: Burma and Laos in the forties; Vietnam in the sixties; Brazil and Uruguay in the seventies. Ferret sketched in Vaughan's apparent connection to the entire panoply of seamy international activities that has since become a matter of public record: coups, assassinations, torture, drugs, shady business dealings. "And nowhere," said Ferret fervidly, "is there an official trace of this man. I've had my Freedom of Information Act guys comb everything. My foreign guys. My CIA guys. In official terms, *he simply doesn't exist*. It would take an actual invasion of Langley to pry out his name. If it weren't for this guy Dickens, I never would have found him."

Motta kept staring at the photo, struggling to match Ferret's chilling monologue with the smiling, empty visage in the office in New Haven. It just wasn't working. Emphatically, he decided that Ferret's paranoia had finally overtaken him.

"A note in passing," Ferret was saying. "Vaughan's wife killed herself and their two sons in nineteen fifty-one. A shooting. Very grisly." He picked up another piece of paper from the table and brought it close to his face. "Remember that lab in Colombia that was blown up, Michael? It was done by a crazy right-wing American mercenary named Guido Leary, *hired by Heller*. Know who owned the plane that spirited Leary off in the middle of the night to Mexico City? Jennings Vaughan. Are you getting the picture? *An operative with no official existence*."

Motta, listening to Ferret's litany of evil, continued his search of the photograph for some trace of the sadism, the corruption that Ferret alleged hid beneath the bland, pleasant face.

"So we come to the Watergate period," Ferret said. "Vaughan was out, along with scores of others. Back to the airplane parts business. But the only government contracts he'd ever gotten were through the good offices of his friends high up in the CIA. So where does that leave our man? Broke. And *persona non grata* in Washington. Where did he go for work? His experience is too colorful, too international for local police work. So he hires out as staff, or as a stringer, to these global corporations, who have virtually replaced the governments anyway, right?"

Motta looked up to see Ferret's face flushed with revelation, arms outstretched, pleading for credibility.

"So I am inviting you to consider, Michael, the possibility that Heller suspected things were not kosher with RPM. They needed to find somebody with Mob contacts to quietly go in, find out what was going on, and attempt to remove any danger. *They hired Jennings Vaughan.*"

"Where's the proof?" Motta said.

"All right. Proof. First, you found Vaughan's name in Marty Karp's file on Heller. Secondly, the day after Lisa Wilde's death *he sent a telegram to Arthur Cross at Brighton Pharmaceuticals in London. From a casino in Las Vegas.*"

Motta sat back in his chair, stunned.

"What did it say?" he whispered.

Ferret shrugged. "I haven't the slightest idea. Does it matter?"

"I suppose not," Motta said.

"Now, Vaughan must have either called Marty Karp, or come out to see him, which is more likely. That's when Marty scribbled his name on the notepad and stuck it in the Heller file. Vaughan probably introduced himself as a representative of Heller, quite likely as a member of the negotiating team, for reasons which will become clear shortly. He took a look at the situation, then made his decision."

"To kill Lisa."

"Basically, yes. But I think the way it happened was *he had Lucchessi put the contract out on her*. Maybe he paid him with Heller money, or traded off old favors going back to heroin days in New York, and kept the Heller money himself. Who knows? Who cares?"

"But why didn't Vaughan just let Heller know what was going on? Heller could have called Marty and said, 'Cool it. You've got your deal. We don't care about the money. Just stay away from Vegas. Don't make scandal.'"

"Things were too far along. Don't you see? The hit was being bought. If Lisa already knew about it, calling it off with Vegas wouldn't necessarily keep her from speaking out. And Vaughan's solution, by his very nature, would be to eliminate her."

"It's so fantastic, Ferret. So extreme."

"Exactly," Ferret said feverishly. "*This* is our extreme man. An efficient man. A killer. A man who thinks expeditiously. In his world, one simply removes obstacles. He has the same problem all ex-intelligence men have working Stateside. He's a mad dog, trained to kill foreign enemies, turned loose on his own citizenry. A gun pointed at its owner. It's not the first time we've seen this in recent years, is it?" He looked up at Motta significantly.

"From his angle," Ferret went on, "it looked like Lisa might expose Marty Karp. His job was to protect the deal. His solution was to have her killed. But Lucchessi's guys goofed it, and left a witness: *You.* Now, at Vaughan's behest, they're trying to clean up their mess by driving you off. If they can't, they'll kill you."

Motta looked up to meet Ferret's concerned eyes.

"*Jennings Vaughan,*" Ferret said slowly, "*had Lisa Wilde killed. Now he wants to kill you.*"

Motta stared dully down at his hands, unable to speak.

"Now one more thing, Michael. I took a long shot, and checked with a travel agent contact. Yesterday afternoon Vaughan bought a one-way ticket to Singapore. From Kennedy Airport. On July eleventh. *The day after the acquisitions meeting at the Sherry Netherland.*"

"That means he'll be at the meeting," Motta said.

"Most definitely."

Motta gazed at the man in the photo a final time. It would have been so much easier were it the image of the little man in the Panama hat who had beaten him. Or even Marty Karp. Their rationales were so much more transparent: greed, fear—simple criminality. But that made them victims too, and hard to hate. This man, however, was beyond criminality; in his impassivity, he was the consummate physical expression of the art of power—a cold weapon, carefully forged in extreme heat. He, unlike the others, acted out of *belief*. Therefore, thought Motta, he was culpable. If Ferret's speculations were correct, Jennings Vaughan was somebody one could truly hate.

"You think he had Heller's blessing, Ferret?"

"Moot point," Ferret said. "But my guess is no. I think he went beyond orders. His own logic, his *hubris*, his extremism, led him to kill her. But what was Heller going to do? He had to be allowed to cover his tracks."

"What about Marty? Did he know?"

"My surmise is that Marty was as surprised as anyone. It made him very nervous. He figured it was Vegas that hit her, Vegas that fixed the Coroner's Report. Instinctively he decided to take their story and run with it. So he made up the heroin routine. What else could *he* do? He was hemmed in. In his mind, putting up a stink would nix the sale, if not worse. He probably felt a mixture of remorse and relief. After all, he'd been killing Lisa slowly for years. Now it was over." Ferret shook his head sadly. "See, I think you're looking at a big stone rolling down a hill, with Lisa in the way."

"So killing her had the effect of committing all the players to their courses of action, locking the whole drama in place."

"Yes. The terrible thing is that maybe Vaughan was *technically* correct in killing her."

"Except for the witness."

"Right. *You* are the only loose end. *You* are the difference between it working out or not."

Motta turned away toward the window, letting the meaning of Ferret's words sink in. It was like being told that the tossing dream from which one expected to awaken momentarily was in fact reality itself—endless and inescapable.

Ferret had bent over his diagram and was etching in the name of Jennings Vaughan in the box, over the question mark. He drew in three lines leading away from Vaughan: one to Heller, another to Vegas, and a third to RPM.

"There you have it," he said, putting his pen down. "That completes the puzzle."

"A fantastic piece of work, Ferret," Motta said.

And mad Ferret grinned, basking in Motta's honest admiration.

"Actually," he said, "I must confess I felt my own paranoia abate when I found Jennings Vaughan. He is the *gray area* in life that drives people like me a little daft."

"I wish we could get some sort of corroboration. A smoking gun. Something hard."

"I know," Ferret admitted. "Conceptually it's airtight. But it wouldn't hold up in court."

Motta stood up and walked to the window. A night breeze had come up and drifted into the room, harsh and salty. He watched the faint silvery line of the shore. The thought that he now stood between Heller and the acquisition, as Lisa had done before him, brought with it both terror and resolution. *You begin to feel like a sacrificial lamb.* He had moved into the breach, the empty space she had left behind. *If he chose.* He was the dissident entity now, the piece that didn't fit, the cultural outlaw. Recalling the afternoon in the ravine on Mulholland, Lisa's crumpled body in the Jaguar seat, he thought how incomprehensible it had seemed at the time. Now, if he and Ferret were correct, they had followed the string all the way back to its source. It was a knowledge that left him with an aching emptiness. A sudden desperate desire to see Amanda rose up in him like a storm.

He gazed out into the night, listening to a repetitive banging from somewhere behind him, mixing with the crashing of the sea. It sounded like someone hammering, or doing construction.

"What's that?" he heard Ferret say.

Motta turned around.

"The door?"

The banging stopped.

They listened in the silence together. Then the knocks resumed.

"Better let me check," Ferret said. "It's probably just Hank."

Ferret walked to the end of the room, and down the narrow hallway leading to the front door. Motta ran to the bed, took out his Beretta from under the pillow, flipped off the safety, and waited.

A moment later Ferret came back, accompanied by the fat, sweating, miserable apparition of Eddie Malone.

"Mike," he said, wringing his hands. "Mike. Jeez. We gotta talk."

23

Motta stood at the window of Hank's apartment long after midnight, waiting for the emergence of Eddie Malone into the parking lot below.

Eddie had stayed a couple of hours. He had been unwilling to talk in the presence of the Ferret, so Motta, trading ecstatic whispered congratulations and thanks in the hallway, had settled with Ferret in cash instead of the gold and silver coins he had originally requested, and promised to call him in the morning at the Windward Café.

Then Eddie Malone, sitting on the edge of the bed, sweating in anguish, had spilled his guts. He told Motta of his visit to Vegas, and of Lucchessi, and Martoni, and how Marty was buying the hit. He told him, too, of the stranger from outside, the one with the crewcut and the tic in his face, the man from Heller. And bit by bit, in his own fashion, Eddie had confirmed Ferret's scenario.

Motta had listened with admiration to the pathetic, tortured figure trying to explain why he had secretly decided, only a few hours earlier, to break with the man he had served loyally all his life. It was because of Lisa, he said. He knew now that Motta had been right; somebody had had her killed. So he had called Amanda and persuaded her to tell him where Motta was staying.

"Who was it, Eddie? Who killed her?"

But Eddie had just shaken his head back and forth. "I dunno, Mike. I just dunno."

"What are you going to do?" he had asked Eddie Malone as his terrible recital had drawn to a close.

"Who knows?" Eddie had said, staring at the floor. "Maybe go back East. Look around the street. I got nowhere to go."

Now Motta watched Eddie appear from out of the shadows of the building below, and drag his broken, lumbering frame across the empty parking lot toward his car.

"This stuff's no good, Mike," he had said just before he left. "Get out of here. Take Amanda. Don't get mixed up anymore with those guys. Let them have it."

Eddie was halfway across the lot when Motta saw the outline of a car directly below. It moved out of the shadow of the building into view: the black Mercedes. Only its parking lights were on.

Motta froze as he watched it move slowly forward, trailing Eddie Malone. Eddie, nearing his car, didn't seem to notice. He was busy fishing the keys out of his pocket.

The car made a wide arc, then wheeled around until it faced Eddie. The lights went on suddenly, pinning him in the beams.

Furiously, Eddie worked the key in the lock.

Motta saw the black car's window lower.

Eddie turned toward the window where Motta stood, and his mouth opened in a mute, helpless cry.

"Eddie!" Motta yelled out.

Then there were two quick pops, like muted echoes of the fireworks earlier in the evening. Eddie's body convulsed: once forward, once back. Then he slumped down the side of his car, his right arm upraised.

The Mercedes accelerated and came straight for the merry-go-round building.

Motta knew he was trapped. The only exit was the front. He took his Beretta out of his belt and threw on his coat. Traversing the hallway leading to the front door, he could hear the Mercedes idling outside just below and one of its doors open. Then he heard the footsteps at the bottom of the stairs.

Opposite the front door in the hallway were the series of small arched double windows that looked down on the merry-go-round. Motta ran to one and twisted the rusty handle. He managed to force it open and pushed the windows inward. The faint shadows of the carousel horses loomed in the dark below. The footsteps began their ascent. As Motta climbed through the small windows, he could see his own shadow from the hall light casting a giant reflection on the far wall of the merry-go-round. The footsteps reached the top of the stairs just as he dropped the fifteen feet to the stone floor below.

He scrambled up and ran across the room. The front of the merry-go-round was a pair of tall, ancient sliding wood doors that opened onto the pier. He fumbled frantically at the point where they met, feeling for the latch that would free them. Above, he heard the knocking on the door. He felt in the darkness, filling his fingers with splinters from the rough wood; but he couldn't find the latch.

The door above shook. Then a pair of kicks sent it crashing in. The sound shuddered through the building.

Motta scrambled back into the room, jumped onto the carousel, and crouched behind a gilded horse. Squeezing his gun in both hands, he pointed it toward the open window and waited. The figure came into view, gun drawn, back lit

by the hall light: Motta saw the familiar silhouette of the
Panama hat. The man paused at the open window and
peered in. Motta's finger tightened on the trigger.

Then the little man turned and passed on into the apartment.

Motta ran back to the door and resumed his search for the
latch. This time he found it and flipped it off. The tall wood
door groaned on its runner as he slid it open. He heard the
rush of footsteps back into the hallway above. There was a
shout: "Hey!" And then a shot rang out.

But Motta was already outside, running up the pier toward the shore, hugging the side of the building. Behind
him, he heard the Mercedes door slam, and the car start up.
When Motta reached the end of the building, realizing the
car would race up the pier and overtake him, he jumped off
into the sand below. It was a short fall. He got up and
ducked beneath the pier. Then he ran up the sand toward
the road, zigzagging among the tall, creaking struts of the
pier. Overhead, he heard the Mercedes, unable to ascertain
his direction, slowing.

He stumbled up an ice-plant bank at the sand's edge, and
paused just at the point where the pier abutted the road. He
stuck his head up and peered carefully back: the Mercedes
had stopped midway up the empty pier, and the little man
had gotten out; he was leaning over the edge, looking down,
his gun drawn.

Motta stuck his Beretta in his pocket, dashed onto the
road—into full view—and ran straight ahead for the cross
street. Just as he hit it, he heard the roar of the Mercedes.

He turned right and raced along the sidewalk, next to a
motel. At its blinking neon entrance he saw an empty taxi
turning slowly around in the driveway. Motta flagged him
and jumped in.

Hunched in the back of the taxi, he watched the Mercedes pass slowly by.

The taxi pulled out onto the street, turned left, and drove off in the opposite direction.

Motta fell back, exhausted, onto the seat.

The cabbie didn't want to take him there; he said he wasn't comfortable in the black neighborhoods at night. It wasn't the ghetto, Motta said to no avail, just a nice middle-class black neighborhood south of Hollywood. Finally he agreed to pay the cabbie extra.

They pulled off the freeway at La Brea and drove south into Baldwin Hills. Motta had him turn left at the main intersection, drive a few short blocks into a residential area, and drop him off in front of an eight-unit apartment. Relieved, the cabbie sped off.

Motta walked through the central courtyard, past the lanai chairs and the tropical plants. Mounting the stairs on the left side, he went to the second apartment at the back, rang the buzzer, and waited.

Across the way, an old black woman in a nightgown had pulled her curtain back and was peering disapprovingly at him.

The door opened, and Amanda was standing there in her blue terrycloth robe, her hair in curlers, her mouth open.

"Sweet Jesus," she whispered.

He rushed in, and they held each other. She reached behind him and pushed the door closed. Motta felt the flow of her tears against his cheek.

Then she stepped back to look at him, and shook her head.

"I swear," she said, wiping her eyes with the sleeve of her robe. "Every time I see you you're all beat up."

"Where's Bessie?"

"Out of town. Ran off with some soul singer. You know how she is."

Amanda turned and went to the kitchen to make tea. Motta followed, and stood over the stove with her.

"I've been so worried," she said.

"I'm sorry," Motta said. "Nashville was good?"

"Got another movie out of it. I play a *boutique* owner this time. Suppose I'm moving up in the world." She shrugged. "What about you? Where've you been, anyway? Who'd you fight with this time?"

Motta told her a little, but not much. He told her about the thugs who had beaten him; but he didn't say anything about Eddie Malone.

"What now?" she asked, when he had finished.

"Spend the night with you," he said. "Then I'm going to New York."

She frowned, and took the cups of tea to the table in the living room.

"Well," she said, sitting down. "Know what I'm going to do? I'm going to take that check that's coming in a couple of days from the Nashville movie, and go down to Jamaica for a week." She looked at him, her eyes pleading. "Sure wish you'd come."

Motta looked up at the flocked ceiling. These middle-class apartments, he thought, they build them all the same. But he was comforted by the quiet room, and the tea, and her. Even his hands had stopped shaking. "I want to," he said. "Very much."

"That night at the Grill, Michael. You were puttin' me on, weren't you?"

"I didn't want anything to happen to you."

She looked down, stirring her tea. "You have more jive in you than I gave you credit for," she said.

"The men who tore up the apartment," Motta said. "They dumped out your goldfish."

"Oh, well," she said softly.

When they had finished their tea, they went into the bedroom. Motta lay down next to her.

"Monk Purcell quit RPM," she said. "Know what's he's going to do? Go to New Mexico and paint. His wife called, says he's all excited. Like a little boy. Says he looks ten years younger. He's even getting off the pills and the whiskey."

Motta smiled for the first time in a while.

"What about you, boy?" she said, looking at him with concern.

"I'm already out. There's just one more thing I have to do."

"You did battle," she said. Her eyes were filling with distress. "Can't you just back off now? Let fools play?" When Motta didn't answer, she grew agitated and turned away. "It's that Lisa Wilde again, isn't it?"

"No," he said. "It was. But not anymore. Now it's just me." He looked at her. "And you," he whispered.

Amanda reached over to the table next to the bed, dimmed the lamp, and switched on the radio. Some nice black music pulsed softly out into the room; it was like a balm. For the first time in a long time Motta found he was actually hearing it—and it sounded real good.

He took his gun out of his jacket pocket and lay it on the bed table. Amanda watched him and shook her head. Then he reached over and took her in his arms, kissed her, let his hands move under her robe and find the soft parts of her body. She began to undress him.

"I'll be waiting for you in Kingston," she said before their bodies went under and drowned out the light and the music and the words and the pain, "so don't you be breaking my heart."

They whispered beneath high, massive Iberian chandeliers in the old, ornate Union Station in downtown Los Angeles the next morning, she unable to understand why he was taking the train instead of a plane. "To rest," he answered, thinking how they would be watching the airport, how he had no place to hide, really, for the four days until the acquisition meeting at the Sherry.

She waited distractedly outside the telephone booth while

he called Ferret at the Windward Café and told him of the sad dénouement of the evening before—Eddie Malone's affirmation of all they had suspected, then his murder, and Motta's escape.

"You're going," Ferret said.

"Yes."

Then Ferret said, "Don't assume anything."

"What do you mean?"

"Vaughan will come looking for you. You have to figure he'll find you."

He kissed Amanda, long and sweet, next to the silver siding of the Southwest Limited.

"Jamaica" was the last thing she said.

He told her he'd book a plane, but he didn't know how to tell her he didn't expect to be on it.

Phonograph
Blues

My needle has got rusty
It will not play at all

ROBERT JOHNSON,
"Phonograph Blues"

Part 4

24

Motta lay, fevered and aching, on a berth in the narrow Pullman compartment, watching the train blow steam through orange trees and palms and pink stucco buildings in the tiny San Bernardino Station just east of Los Angeles at twilight. And it seemed as if all the weariness and the madness of the last few days were coming down around him at once.

As the train began its slow, lurching eastward haul across the flat, browned California summer scrub and up through the mountain pass, night fell like a gavel. In the window he could see the reflection of the tiny metallic cabin suspended against a racing shadow of darkness.

He struggled up, took a fresh notebook out of a black vinyl shoulder bag Amanda had given him, and sat down at the small fold-out table by the window.

He began to write the story of what had happened.

And as he wrote he found that, in the telling, a great sense of relief came, and a burden lifted off him.

He started with the day of the killing, and the ride up Mulholland. He described the car, the men in it, how they had pushed Lisa's car into the ravine. He wrote of Marty Karp's attempt to dissuade him from telling the truth, and his defamation of Lisa: the junkie story. He laid out the financial situation at RPM, its shaky history, its present straits. And he wrote of little Jay Kippel—his strange past, his Mob connections.

Later in the evening he stood up, stiff and sore, and stepped out into the corridor. He pushed past a portly, pink-faced man in a dark business suit just outside his compartment, and went to the dining car—only to find it closed. He paid a porter to slip him a sandwich and a soft drink from the kitchen, took it back to the cabin, and ate in the dark—a dry roast beef sandwich on white bread, and a Coke—as the train began its surging run across the Mojave beneath a sea of iridescent stars.

He woke up around midnight, covered in cold sweat. Outside, the train was slowing; he saw the NEEDLES sign: they were leaving California. An ancient, solitary stationmaster in shirtsleeves waved them through.

"When a culture is murdered," he scribbled in the notebook, *"what bleeds?"*

In the morning, he didn't remember having written it.

He was in the dining car early, eating eggs alone among jabbering tourists in the high, cheery town of Flagstaff, pale-white mountain sun glinting off the train's striated Plexiglas windows. The same fat man he had seen outside his compartment the night before took a seat at the next table, ordered cereal, read a folded *Wall Street Journal.*

Motta hurried through his breakfast and lurched back down the narrow swaying corridor, his hand burning from coffee in an Amtrak paper cup.

As the train dropped down onto the dry Arizona flats,

Motta wrote on feverishly. He found that when he tried to recall Ferret's wild, baroque exposition of two nights before, it dissolved, evaporated; in memory, it had the quality of a dream. What Motta was left with were not the ravings, the paranoia, but the facts: and these he wrote down with all the precision he could muster. He wanted a tight *dossier*—irrefutable, damning, beyond contention. He knew it would have to be that; nothing less would do.

In the Albuquerque station he looked up to see Indians selling expensive jewelry on the platform. He thought of Lewis Adam, the gaunt junkie musician in turquoise jewelry at the Palm Motel. And that old Indian in a blanket on the platform: could he be the same one he had seen as a child, coming West with the family (his father, restless, eyes burning and distant and hopeful, stalking the corridors), seeking open space, liberal thought, an unbroken horizon line? It had been the old Super Chief. *The Atchison, Topeka and the Santa Fe.* As in the song. *Route 66.* As in the song.

Now, the Western experiment lay in ruins, the song over, the promise unfulfilled.

And as the train headed out across the flat, scorched summer wastes of eastern New Mexico, Motta, setting down his tale, had foretastes of his own doom: something to do with a reversal of the evolutionary process, back eastward, back into the belly of the beast, back into destruction, pain, conflict, death. War had found him at last, a war whose existence he had never been willing to admit.

Telephone poles blurred past like grave markers: In the distance the red mesas were still, stony, silent; at his feet the ground raced by with a blinding, maniacal clatter, a soundtrack to the words he was hurling up against forces to whom he, like Lisa before him, was but an insect, something to be squashed, eliminated.

He had a name for his piece now: *The Killing of Lisa Wilde.*

In the afternoon, in the passage between cars, he listened

to a French couple speak lyrically of the romance and wonder of the American landscape, the Indian prairie racing
past. Motta wished he could feel it with them, as once, ages
ago, he had.

In the domed lounge car, where men played gin rummy
and drank beer and families rocked mindlessly eastward, he
saw the same large, solitary man standing at the bar. He was
wearing a Hawaiian shirt, smoking a cigar.

Motta, certain now the man was a tail, rushed back to his
compartment and locked the door.

Was he going mad?

He sat at the table and rechecked the clip in his Beretta,
enacting the ritual that had become like breathing to him.

Petro Beretta gardone V.T. Col. 7.65. Made in Italy. He
could say the words in his sleep. He reached forward and
turned the pistol on the table, faced it forward, eastward, in
the direction he was going, and closed his hand around the
cold black grip. This weapon, Bad Jack Horn's "piece," had
become an extension of his body—familiar, comfortable, easy
—it's eventual use as certain, it would seem, as the hand that
gripped it. He had come within inches of killing already, at
the merry-go-round; he knew now he could do it. Was that
the gun's destiny? Was it the same as his?

He released his hold, the sweat from his hand bright on
the grip from the dancing prairie sun outside.

"You could write about it, couldn't you?" Maggie Hill had
said that night so long ago on the patio in the Berkeley hills.

Maybe he could.

As he wrote on, detailing everything he knew about the
Heller Group—the strange, addicted passage of Klaus Heller, Senior, and the cold machinations of his adopted son—he
chose to avoid Ferret's leaping, half-remembered speculations on Nazis, Interpol, the Rockefellers and beyond. But
he did tell of Heller's willingness to hire a killer to ensure
their acquisition of RPM Records. And Motta thought he
could see now a clear vertical line, as Monk Purcell had

once suggested, running from a stoned kid at a concert all the way up to the supplier, who in three days' time would own *both* the drug and the music—a deadly vision of music as soporific, a numbing instrument of social control.

Night fell as the train left Colorado and entered Kansas at a crawl, inching across the dark wheatfields. Near sleep, he saw the Dodge City sign, and thought again about the fat man with the pink face in the corridors, the restaurant, the lounge.

Vaughan will come looking for you. He will find you.

He awoke on the morning of the second day in the Kansas City station, his head full of root strains of American music: Charlie Parker, Count Basie, Joe Turner—all out of Kansas City—and further downriver, the delta blues of Robert Johnson, Leadbelly, King Oliver.

He took out the newspaper clipping of Jennings Vaughan that Ferret had given him, and smoothed it on the table. Staring at the image of the crewcut, smiling man in the antiseptic office, he thought: *Jennings Vaughan is a virus, lodged in a tubercular host, the purveyor of a dead, colorless, silent, ordered world that threatens to become our own. His greatest crime may be that he neither sings nor dances . . .*

Suddenly, gazing down at the image of spiritless, puritanical functionalism in front of him, Motta was overwhelmed by the presence of Lisa Wilde. She swept in upon him: Lisa Wilde, *la grive*, the canary, in flight. And Motta knew now that he had truly loved her. There could be others; but none would he ever love in that way. What he loved in her was what he was coming to imagine he could love in himself: a dream, an essence, a reason to live and act. And he knew that what he was about to do he would do, quite simply, out of love. And he knew that he would never again allow the allaying or the repression of that love.

He saw, at the same instant, gazing at Jennings Vaughan's image, that he was the antimatter, that which must be cast

out, the messenger of destruction, the virus. He was his
enemy, as he had been Lisa's. They stood in essential opposition, as fundamental as the play of dark and light.

The train was crossing Illinois, the fields thickening into
towns: Chillicothe, Streator, Joliet. Motta stayed in his room
as the train made its slow entry into the Chicago yards on a
hot, dirty day. Relieved, he watched the fat, pink-faced man
in his dark suit step onto the platform with his suitcase in
one hand, attaché case in the other, and start to walk off
into Chicago.

But no: there he was, glancing back at the train. Motta's
hand tightened around the Beretta: the man was looking
directly at him.

Vaughan will come looking for you.

Just before the train left, the man got back on.

Had he gone to phone New York with their arrival time?
You have to figure he will find you.

Vaughan: would he be waiting?

Motta rushed to the tiny cabin commode and plunged his
face into a metal basin of icy water, fighting to break the
surging, mad stream of thought.

On the third morning, as the Broadway Limited chugged
eastward out of the valley of Pittsburgh, Motta closed his
notebook, satisfied that he had written it all. He began to
put it away in the shoulder bag; but then he took it out
again, sat back down at the table, and wrote something
more.

*Peter Goldmark's invention of the long-playing record
launched a revolution. It allowed a multiplicity of ideas to
flourish, enabled selective private listening, turned music
into a special carrier of culture, a message-bringer. On July
10th, this era threatens to come to a close: the last major
independent record label will be sold to a German multinational drug corporation. This establishment of centralized
control has been accomplished by design—and by murder.*

Like a colonized people, we are being turned in upon ourselves. We are fed, and feed upon, images of conflict, emptiness, violence, whose source we cannot see. A world is being constructed in which all the cages can be left open, because all memory of freedom will have been lost.

It would be nice to think that out of the shards of our experience, out of the wars and disillusions and crimes, we could commit ourselves to struggle to renew our own sense of promise, reconnect ourselves with the larger work of the past, restore our own feelings of magnitude and joy, flow back toward that which is alive, profound, rich. Could we see ourselves again, before it is too late, as an ardent, spiritual people, involved with the universe and its expressions in our own lives?

As afternoon light latticed the dry summer Pennsylvania birch woods whipping past, he wrote, *Sing the sun up, for if we don't, it may never arrive.*

Then he was staring at the gun, and the image of Vaughan, and thinking of Lisa. And all the conflicts and contradictions entered and possessed him, became his own flesh, crystallized into a dark resolve.

25

It was less a question of vanity than *correctness* that gripped Jennings Vaughan with a cold, frustrated fury as he gazed into the morning's mirror.

It hung now, like a flag on a windless day, the entire right side of his face. For two days he had awaited its reanimation. At this point he would have welcomed even the return of the tic, or any sign that the wooden, waxen, yellowing half-mask—the red of the lower part of the right eye slowly, balefully exposing itself—had not petrified forever. He reached his hand up and massaged it—to no avail. He tried smiling; but only the left side moved, presenting in reflection a hideous gargoyle snarl.

Nothing could bring Jennings Vaughan more anguish than the idea that he might actually *look* like what he *was*. It was an existential affront: that his final enemy—after he had outlived so many—should emerge from *within*; his cover dissolve like melting wax; his soul assert itself, find perfect expression in the slumped, hardening diagonal mask in the bathroom mirror.

Grimly, before the glass, he adjusted his Ivy League tie—the striped, dangling cloth of legitimacy which, along with the suit, the socks, the shoes, all of it purchased only a few blocks away—he had grown into as into his body, years ago, the way a monk takes the robes.

A knock at the door caused him to turn away from the mirror; he crossed the dim Gotham Hotel room—rigid, erect, ruined—and admitted a waiter with breakfast and a New York *Times* on a tray. Vaughan signed the bill, averting his face; the waiter left.

He chewed doggedly on soft-boiled eggs and toast, using the good side of the face, the way an animal chews: as if to choke back the perfidious interloper into the bubbling depths from which it had sprung.

When he had finished he stood and walked to the window. Parting the curtain slightly, he peered bleakly down at the bustling, bright Fifth Avenue summer hordes of morning nine stories below, like some horrible Quasimodo in his bell tower.

Letting the curtain drop, he turned back to the half-darkened room and began to move through a series of precise, measured actions.

He placed a chair in front of the desk, to the left of the mirror above it, so he would not have to look at himself. Then he took a brown attaché case from beside the bed, and put it on the table. He turned the digits of the combination lock and opened it: inside were a number of papers. He began to go through them methodically, starting with the topmost one.

It was a telegram, nine days old, dated June 30:

FRANKFURT MOST UPSET WITH YOUR SOLUTION STOP BAL-
ANCE OF YOUR FEE WITHHELD UNTIL SUCCESSFUL CONCLU-

SION OF MEETING JULY 10TH SHERRY NETHERLAND HOTEL
NEW YORK STOP YOUR PRESENCE MANDATORY STOP IN
MEANTIME PLEASE ENSURE AGAINST ANY UNTOWARD RE-
PERCUSSIONS FROM YOUR ILL ADVISED ACT STOP

ARTHUR CROSS ESQ
BRIGHTON PHARMACEUTICALS
LONDON

Vaughan, glowering, put the telegram on the table. Next
he took out a manila envelope postmarked "San Francisco"
two days earlier, with no return address. He slit it open with
his fingernail, turned it over, and slid out an 8 x 10 color
photograph. Tiny bits of glass rained onto the table; the
photo had been ripped rudely from a frame.

Vaughan gazed at a somewhat younger Michael Motta, in
a borrowed blue suit, standing in a garden, his arm around
Diane—she in white lace thrift-shop antique dress, a tiara of
daisies on her head. They held glasses of champagne, looking innocent and silly and smashed, emanating a tentative,
woozy happiness. In the background an older man, gaunt
and grinning, in a minister's collar beneath a Nehru jacket,
held a joint: a hippie wedding, in somebody's long-forgotten
Berkeley backyard. Vaughan turned the picture over. The
inscription:

Diane and Michael Motta
Wedding
June 1st 1971

Turning the picture face up again, Vaughan studied it for
a moment, then placed it on the table. He reached back into
a compartment built into the attaché case and took out a
small handgun: a Walther PPK/S :380 semiautomatic of
dark-blue steel, with a semi-matte finish. He placed it on the
table next to the picture.

Then Vaughan walked over by the bed and removed from a tan suitcase a pair of black sportsman's gloves, perforated on the back. He slipped them on, wriggling his fingers forward until they were comfortable. Back at the desk, he picked up the Walther and wrapped his right hand around the cross-hatched Bakelite grip with deft, professional fingers. He cocked it once, by pulling the whole top back, and pointed it toward the window—holding it first up to his sagging right eye, and then, not satisfied, to his left. He pulled the trigger: it was unloaded. Then he took from the same compartment in the attaché case a seven-shot clip and loaded it into the butt handle of the Walther.

He loosed the button of his coat; a holster was strapped across his shirt. He put the gun in the holster, adjusted it so that it rested just below his left rib cage, then rebuttoned his coat. He took off the black gloves and put one in each pocket of his suit.

Then he sat back down at the desk.

The next item he took from his attaché case was an Amtrak national train timetable. He turned to a section marked "Eastern Schedules," and to a page listing the two trains from Chicago:

The Lake Shore Limited
Chicago-Toledo-Cleveland-Albany-Boston-New York

the first said. And the second:

The Broadway Limited
Chicago-Fort Wayne-Pittsburgh-Philadelphia-Washington-New York

Vaughan removed a blue Parker ball-point pen from the inside pocket of his jacket, and circled the words *The Lake Shore Limited,* and its arrival time: *Ar 1:20 P (Grand Cen-*

tral Terminal). Then he circled the other train's name, and its arrival time: *Ar 4:05 P* (*Penn Sta.*). He studied what he had circled for a few moments, committing the information to memory. Then he placed the train schedule on the table with the picture of Motta and the telegram.

Next, Vaughan took from the attaché case a matchbook from the Charter Arms bar, the one on which Guido Leary had written his number in Singapore. Taking up his pen again, Vaughan transferred the number to the inside of the next object—his Pan Am plane ticket, one-way from JFK to Singapore, July 11, 10:25 A.M., via Los Angeles, Tokyo, Hong Kong.

He put the matchbook on the desk with the other objects.

A piece of hotel stationery was next out of the attaché case, bearing a series of names and telephone numbers, each with the (202) Washington area code. Each had the time and the date called—some he had called several times during the last week—and all bore the same, neatly lettered designation of rejection after them: *WCB*—"Will Call Back." He glowered at the paper, then put it on the pile on the table with the others.

A final manila envelope emerged: Vaughan shook out a batch of papers and cards onto the desk, and began to move quickly through them. There were two passports: one new, one old. The old one he opened and glanced at briefly: a younger photo of him, followed by dozens of stamps. He threw it on the pile. The second passport was new: the picture was the Vaughan of recent weeks, with the crumbling visage. And it bore a new name: *Alexander T. Powers.* Vaughan put it in his inside jacket pocket.

Next came a booklet of American Express traveler's checks, $5,000 worth, all made out in his new name. This went into his pocket with the passport.

The remaining papers were all the documents of his identity as Jennings Vaughan: Social Security card, driver's li-

cense, several credit cards, a small stack of business cards—
Space Dynamics Corporation, New Haven, Connecticut,
and a telephone number—all the symbols of the steadfast, legitimate existence he had maintained for thirty-five years.

Vaughan stood up, gathered the papers he had accumu-
lated on the desk, and walked into the bathroom. Standing
over the toilet in the gloom, using Guido Leary's Charter
Arms matches, he began to burn the papers, one by
one—first the documents of his identity as Jennings
Vaughan; then the photo of Michael Motta and Diane, and
the envelope it had come in; the train schedule; the telegram from Arthur Cross; and finally the matchbook itself—
until nothing was left but swirling ashes disappearing into
the New York city sewer system.

He emerged from the bathroom, divested of all traces of
his former identity or any business he might be engaged
upon; he was simply Alexander T. Powers—a man with a paralysis in the right side of his face, a gun, a passport, some
traveler's checks, and a plane ticket to Singapore.

He went to the window and opened it to let out the
smoke and the fumes. Then he went to the desk, closed his
attaché case, and put it by his bed with the suitcase. He patted the Walther beneath his jacket, pulled back his left
coatsleeve, and glanced quickly at his Timex: July 9, 11:40.

He took the New York *Times* from the table and left the
room.

In the elevator down, the operator, a black man, looked at
him curiously, then shook his head: Vaughan was holding
the *Times* in front of his face.

He walked across the old Gotham lobby, still holding up
the paper. Then, stepping out into the Fifth Avenue crowds,
Jennings Vaughan, once the invisible operative, felt all the
bitter agony of being conspicuous. His disfigurement was
like a magnet, eliciting the curious gaze, the fascination, the
pity of men, women and children. No matter which way he

turned, there were faces—along the thronged streets that had once provided him with the safety of cover—to gape, to mock, to study, to stare.

He ducked quickly into a taxi. The driver, turning, winced uncomfortably at the sight of his face.

"Grand Central," Vaughan said. The words came out sideways, in a muddled George Raft lisp, as if spoken through pebbles.

"Whazzat?" the driver queried.

Vaughan struggled to recompose his mouth, find another way to emit the words comprehensibly. "Grand Central," he repeated. The driver nodded, and took off down Fifth Avenue. Vaughan sat back against the seat, his forehead drenched in sweat, and stared stonily ahead.

The taxi slowed in traffic between Forty-ninth and Fiftieth. Instinctively, Vaughan turned and looked out into Rockefeller Plaza. Tourists milled; street musicians and hawkers, brightly colored banners and balloons flew over a carnival atmosphere—all of it seen by the gray, cold man in the back of a taxi who had once, in his way, secretly possessed it all.

His eyes moved slowly up the side of the great building where men who thought they ruled the world had given license to hunt and to kill, in the name of the Good and the True. They still ruled, perhaps; but they no longer needed him. If the life rushing by outside the taxi was a Technicolor movie, Vaughan's was an old black-and-white newsreel of borders crossed, assassinations by night, covert alliances made and broken, ruses and disguises, insurrections punished, coups and countercoups, secret monies, and precise murders.

Unconsciously, Vaughan patted his gun, then touched his forehead with the rolled New York *Times*—making the sign of the cross, as it were, before the only temple of worship he had ever known.

The taxi lurched and moved on. And Vaughan, the discarded operative, turned and faced forward, his attention narrowing now to focus, through crosshairs, upon his final target.

26

Matt Grossman took a silver vial out of the pocket of his
checkered slacks, held up a tiny gold spoon suspended
from a chain around his neck, and tapped out a line of cocaine. He brought the spoon up to his left nostril, closed his
right one with his other finger, and inhaled quickly. A couple of sneezes followed, then the sudden watering of his
eyes.

Grossman was sitting on a red vinyl couch with Marty
Karp and Jay Kippel in the small backstage waiting room
provided by the network for talk-show guests and their en-
tourages. A large TV console displayed the show hostess
prattling softly with a diet book author. The door was
slightly ajar; across the hall Candy Snow, about to become
the hostess' final guest of the afternoon, sat before a lit mirror, a white bib over her silks, getting fussed over by a
makeup man.

Grossman repeated the ritual of filling the spoon, and held it out to Marty Karp. Marty shook his head and waved it away. Grossman looked at him, surprised.

"Marty Karp? Refusing a snort?"

It was true; Marty seemed sober, distant, shrunk down inside himself. He gazed morosely at the TV, fidgeted with his hands, his small hatchet face drawn, his eyes haunted.

Grossman shrugged, and polished off the spoon himself. He sat back against the vinyl in his silk shirt with the wide collar, the new blazer and the Gucci loafers and the jewelry, his belly spilling over the top of the checkered slacks, his nose running. He picked up his copy of *Billboard* from the glass coffee table in front of him, and rapped it with his knuckles.

"Number one in all three trades, Marty," he said expansively. "Did I make you guys look good? Did I come to you with a great talent? Did I deliver?"

Marty looked sullenly at Jay Kippel, puffing his pipe impassively before the TV, then turned back to Grossman. "First time I've seen you in a jacket in your whole life," he said irritably. "You even got your teeth cleaned. Is this what success does?"

Grossman grinned, undaunted. "So here's what I want, Marty," he said, sitting forward on the couch. "I want to renegotiate her contract. I want a bigger production budget for the next album. Creative control over the cover. More advertising and tour support. I want to put her out on the road, Marty. A concert tour. America wants to see Candy Snow."

"Hey. Back off. Wait awhile," Marty said. "You haven't even got your first royalty statement yet. You spent the whole advance already? On that stuff?" He pointed at Grossman's gold spoon.

"My broad delivered," Grossman said, pressing. "Frankly, we got interest from other labels. You gotta take care of us, Marty."

"Come see me next week. When we get back to the Coast."

"*Matt?*" Candy Snow's whining, scared voice broke into the room from across the hall. "I don't *look* right."

Grossman threw up his hands in mock exasperation. "Broad's so dumb," he said. "Keep her on Quaaludes all day or she'd drive me crazy." He laughed heavily, got up and walked out of the room.

Marty turned to Jay Kippel and shook his head. "Can you believe that? 'America wants to see Candy Snow.' My ass. Guy's an animal. An ingrate."

The dry little lawyer didn't answer, but continued gazing silently at the TV.

"*Get her eyes right, asshole!*" Grossman was ranting across the hall. "We don't need your show, faggot! We're number one! Where the fuck is the producer?"

Marty got up and closed the door. He turned and looked at Kippel miserably. "Was I like that, Jay?"

Kippel gazed carefully up at Marty, trying to gauge the extent of his melancholy.

"When I was coming up," Marty said, "was I like that?"

"He's just hungry, Marty," Kippel said softly. "Sure. You were like that. You'd do anything."

Marty tightened. "Don't ever say that to me, Jay."

Kippel took his pipe out of his mouth. "Okay, Marty," he said quietly.

The door opened suddenly. A young man in hip, flashy clothes burst into the room. "You see the trades?" he said breathlessly. Then, seeing the copy of *Billboard* on the table, he stopped by the door.

"What is it, Joey?" Marty said.

"I just wanted to say . . ." Joey Russo was smiling awkwardly, shaking his head, fishing for words. "You're a genius, Marty," he blurted. He tapped his fingers to the side of his head. "Golden ears. Just like they say."

Marty gazed glumly up into Joey Russo's eager sycophant's face. "Okay, Joey," he said. Joey Russo, as RPM's East Coast Director of Promotion, presently had the job of ushering Candy Snow around New York on her whirlwind promotional tour, capitalizing on the runaway hit and her sudden, orchestrated ascent to stardom.

"So where do you go after this?" Marty asked him.

"Take her to the trades. Photos and interviews. Then the radio stations. Tomorrow morning she signs records at Goody's."

"What about *Newsweek?*"

"We got a story. Same with *Time*. I got a maybe on a cover. *The Rock* story came out today. It's dynamite. Did you see the billboard in Times Square?"

"What do you mean did I see it, schmuck? I'm the one that ordered it."

Joe Russo, chagrined, looked at the floor.

"Did you get the bodyguards?" Marty asked.

"Yeah. Two big black dudes."

"Okay. Go next door, Joey. See how she's doing. Cool Grossman off. Keep him from hitting somebody."

"Sure, Marty."

As Joey Russo started to back out of the room, Marty said, "Hey, Joey."

Joey Russo turned around.

"How's your dad?"

"Okay," Joey Russo said quietly. "He had surgery last week."

"Tell him hello."

"Sure, Marty."

When he had left the room and closed the door, Marty said to Kippel, "Make a note to have Ruffino send his old man a case of scotch."

"He can't have scotch. He just had open-heart surgery."

"So send him some flowers. Send him something. He's the biggest retail chain owner in the Midwest. He's the guy that broke Candy Snow."

"Mob?"

"Yeah."

A still of Candy Snow appeared on the TV monitor, followed by a commercial. Marty began to pace the small room, his head down, his hands jammed in the pockets of his slacks.

"What is it?" Kippel said. "What's the matter?"

"I don't know. I'm nervous about the meeting. I gotta get a haircut. I'm depressed about Eddie. Why did that happen?" Marty said, full of anguish. "Why?"

"Lucchessi says he doesn't know anything about it."

"Eddie and me," he said. "We go back forty years. We were like this." He held up two fingers together.

The talk-show hostess reappeared after the commercial and announced Candy Snow to warm applause. Marty stopped before the console to watch. The curtain parted: Candy Snow stood, microphone in hand, dressed like an expensive hooker, and began to lip-sync "So Hot, So High." Mercifully, the camera hung on a long shot.

Marty reached down and turned the sound off.

"Hear that song one more time," he said edgily, "I think I'll puke." He turned to Kippel. "Look. Candy Snow's a one-shot. She's from hunger. No more money for Grossman. He's an asshole who lucked into something he doesn't understand. Let them go someplace else. We got our numbers from the both of them, didn't we?"

"Yeah. I got the second-quarter printouts for the meeting."

"Good?"

"Very good."

"You sure?"

"Yes, Marty. I'm sure," Kippel said softly. "Did you see Lisa's album went Top Ten?"

Marty glared at him. "I don't want to hear about that."

"Okay. Okay," Kippel said in his dry, soothing voice. "Everything's going to be fine. We're going in tomorrow with a number-one single and album, and acceptable figures."

"The Nazis here?"

"Heller's at the Plaza. Probably watching the show right now."

"Translators?"

"They're bringing them. The meeting starts at ten, goes all day. Around four the press will come in for photos. The press releases are already printed up."

Marty threw up his hands, and his face knitted with pain. "How the hell can we cut a deal, Jay," he said, "when Heller has us by the balls like this? They know everything about us. We have no cards to play."

"They want your company."

"How do we know they won't pull another surprise on us?"

"Because we have something on them."

"What do you mean?"

"You've got a hole card, Marty."

Marty stopped pacing and stood before the TV, facing Kippel, as Candy Snow finished her song.

"I got it from Lucchessi," Kippel said, "that Heller is very nervous about what happened with Lisa. They didn't want bloodshed. This guy Vaughan was hired by them. He exceeded orders, went off on his own. Lucchessi didn't know that Heller didn't want a killing. So Heller's ass is in a sling. We know who killed her. We can make noise. They could even stand for a murder rap. We have something on them. Understand? It's a standoff."

Marty looked at Kippel. A faint smile crossed his lips. "No shit," he said softly.

Kippel went on in his quiet, even voice. "We don't talk about what happened, they don't talk about it. An ordinary, legit meeting. Both sides go through the motions, sign the deal. The same deal we already agreed to in principle. No changes will be suggested. No surprises. It's just a formality."

Candy Snow finished her song and sat down with the talk-show guests. Marty began to pace the room again.

"Jay," he said suddenly. "I need a broad."

Kippel, taken aback, took his pipe out of his mouth.

"Eddie always used to get me broads when we came to New York," Marty went on. "I need one tonight."

Kippel slowly knocked his pipe in the ashtray. "That's a little out of my line, Marty."

Marty sat down and put his head in his hands. "I feel terrible. I don't feel like I thought I'd feel at this moment. I wish I hadn't done it, Jay," he said miserably. "I liked it the way it was. I miss Lisa. I miss Eddie. I built up that company. I was happy there." Marty gazed at Kippel, full of wounded righteousness. "These corporate guys are going to move in with their lawyers and accountants and turn it into a different kind of game. All they care about is the bottom line. They don't give a shit about the music."

Kippel listened dubiously to Marty's lament, but didn't answer.

"Whatever happened to Motta? Is he back?"

Kippel shook his head. "I don't know."

"You heard from him?"

"No."

"He's probably gone too," he said glumly. "Those were my people, Jay. My world." He stared emptily at the TV as final credits appeared over the image of the smiling talk-show hostess waving goodbye. "What the fuck am I going to do?" Marty said. "I don't even know how to play golf. How many times can Hedda get her hair done? I'm going to miss the action," Marty said.

"The action's over, Marty," Kippel replied, relighting his pipe. "But you're going to get the big cheese. The thing you fought for your whole life. Tomorrow you're going to get it. You'll be rich. And you'll have respect."

Kippel watched with relief as Marty slowly began to brighten, and began the steep ascent back up the roller coaster. He saw the hard little flame rekindle in his mercurial eyes, the bantam-cock chest begin to swell beneath the silk shirt and blue blazer. Kippel knew that the mania forming in Marty would last through the meeting the next day; at this point, that was all that mattered.

By the time the door opened and Grossman walked in with his flushed ingenue in tow, Marty's transformation was complete; he was *on*.

"You were dynamite, baby," he said effusively, up on the balls of his feet, rushing forward to greet Candy Snow. He embraced her and kissed her hard on the lips through the pancake makeup. Then, looking to see that Grossman had turned away, he whispered: "Ninth floor. Sherry. Come after ten."

Candy Snow looked at him dumbly, full of surprise. But only for a moment: a cheeky smile broke slowly across her face, and her false eyelashes fluttered.

Marty, wired and intense, his eyes hot and jumpy, looked over at Grossman. He tapped the side of his nose a couple of times—his signal that he was back in action, ready for that snort.

27

Motta climbed out of the taxi that had brought him from Penn Station to the southeast corner of Washington Square, at University Place, and paid the driver. Still swaying from the train, he hurried along the sweltering late-afternoon streets around NYU, looking in windows, anxious to find what he needed before the stores closed.

He found a stationery store with a cardboard sign on the window that said TYPEWRITER RENTALS. DAY OR WEEK. Inside, he rented an old battered Smith-Corona portable on the day rate from an intense, Hasidic man, dressed inexplicably in a sweater, who wouldn't accept an out-of-state check. Motta paid him in cash, purchasing as well several manila envelopes, a ream of cheap twenty-pound erasable bond, and a half-dozen pencils.

He walked back outside through the clamping heat, bought several bottles of beer at a corner market, and stuffed them into his shoulder bag. Then he returned to Washington Square and began to walk across, among the bums and conga players in tank tops and the human jetsam of the breezeless, desperate afternoon. It struck Motta, hauling the typewriter over the steaming, pigeon-stained cement, as the cramped city closed in around him, how he was a stranger here, a tourist, the city's contours and smells indecipherable and alien. On a freeway he controlled his destiny, his speed; here, reality stared back at eye level; motion was finite, escape ultimately impossible.

Halfway across the square, he saw he had guessed well; the Hotel Ervin was still there, just as he had remembered, on the corner of Waverly and MacDougal. One assumes old landmarks remain in reality exactly as in the mind, but it had been ten years, and things change. He sped up, crossed Waverly Place, and brought himself to the entrance of the old building.

The lobby, too, had changed little. The walls, a hospital green, were stained with dirt, grease and unnameable effluvia. Torn carpets, if they had once had pattern, were now only black, filthy, blurred matting. The lobby's barren ambience evoked an afternoon Motta had once spent in the burned-out desolation of East Berlin. Stepping to the registration desk, he heard a roach crackle underfoot.

ROOMS $20–$28 A NIGHT
PAYMENT IN ADVANCE

The desk clerk on duty was a black man with a pocked face, greasy white shirt and a spattered tie who looked at him through yellow eyes, lids half-closed, from behind bulletproof glass inside a grilled, barricaded office.

Motta might once have attached a certain beatnik lyricism to the Ervin; now, it appeared to him merely as what it was—a rotten hellhole, a Village junkie's hotel, a stark abode of ruined dreams—and, at this moment, an oasis of sort, an anonymous refuge from the naked streets and the frightening specter of the man who, in his mind, might own them.

Motta slipped two twenties under the glass.

The clerk took the money, handed him back change and a key the size of his arm, and pointed him silently toward the elevator. Motta traversed the lobby, passing an old white security guard, his face as cracked and torn as the rotted brown leather couch in whose embrace he dozed.

It was a tiny, cramped elevator with broken walls of exposed cables and pulleys, smelling of tobacco, urine and rancid jism. He pushed the button for the fourth floor. After a moment, the door closed; the elevator began a lurching, tentative ascent.

Motta's memory of the Ervin had to do with chasing down a sallow English rock guitarist with amphetamine eyes and fast fingers who had holed up here after being kicked out of the Chelsea, in itself a feat. Motta had come after him, with a girlfriend from *The Rock*, in search of a feature that had been written but had never run, aborted by the guitarist's untimely death—electrocuted in concert by his own amplifier.

All of that seemed so long ago. On recent trips East he had been the record-company hotshot, running on RPM's elastic expense account, his turf the midtown hotels: the Sherry, the Pierre, the Plaza, the Drake, the Navarro. Now, he thought darkly as the elevator door opened, another full circle made.

He traversed a dank hallway with stained linoleum floors lit by a single bare bulb, limp sounds of degenerate life bleeding through the old walls. He came to a room halfway down, and turned the key in the lock.

It was a tiny room, a sweat box, all but dark though it was still afternoon. A narrow dusty window, frozen shut, provided a view of a sooted slit of space between buildings. The bed, an ancient steel frame with a foul mattress, was chained to the floor—as was an old black and white TV. The closet was a metal locker, the kind one sees in gyms, with pornography scrawled over its sides in words and images.

Motta put his typewriter and his shoulder bag onto the bed, and went into the bathroom. There were no towels, no soap. He threw cold water on his face, and dried himself on the bedspread. Then he opened a beer and stood in the middle of the dim room, feeling the sweat pouring down his sides, counting cockroaches.

When he had finished the beer he went out into the hall, locked the door, and walked to a pay telephone at the end of the empty corridor. He picked the phone up off its cradle; to his surprise, he got a dial tone. He called the operator, gave her the Oakland number and charged it to his number in Los Angeles.

"Diane?"

"Michael. God. Where have you been?"

"Jamie okay?"

"Why haven't you called?"

"Is Jamie okay?" he repeated.

"Yes. He's at your mother's. But listen. Something's happened."

"Tell me."

"Somebody broke in here. They didn't take any money. They took . . . they took our *wedding* picture."

Motta's hand tightened around the telephone.

"Who *are* they, Michael? What do they want?"

"Did they take anything else?"

"No. Where are you? You sound far away."

"Listen. Tomorrow afternoon you can take Jamie back. But not before."

"Why tomorrow?"

"Because it will be over."

"*What* will be over?" Her voice was full of pleading, panic.

"The whole thing. Don't ask me any more about it."

"Are you safe?"

"Don't worry."

"What are you doing? Where are you?"

"Diane. I have to go."

"When will I hear from you again?"

"Soon."

"Michael?"

"What?"

"Jamie liked the Eagles watch. I gave it to him even though it's not his birthday yet."

"I'm glad. Give him a kiss for me."

"I love you, Michael."

Motta hadn't said those words to her in years.

"I love you too," he said.

There, it wasn't so bad.

Back in the room he flipped a loose light switch next to the door, its switchplate missing, exposing a greasy little cavern of frayed, ancient wires and mummified insects. A bare sputtering bulb, hanging over the bed, weakly challenged the looming darkness. He set up the Smith-Corona on the bed and plugged the cord into the wall. From his shoulder bag he took his notebook. Out came the Beretta, too, to take its familiar place beside him. He took off his sweat-soaked shirt, threw it on the floor, and opened another beer.

Then as the late summer afternoon drained away somewhere outside where he couldn't see, discernible only in the faint recession of what little light lay in the sooty well outside the crusted window, Motta sat crosslegged on the sagging Hotel Ervin bed, pouring sweat, haunted, intense and unutterably alone, and began to type up his story.

He wrote on through the evening, the banal sounds of the hotel closing around him—murmurs and bangings, the opening and closing of the elevator at the end of the hall to admit ill-controlled footsteps, an idle fornication somewhere upstairs, bottles breaking.

Finally, somewhere around ten, he stood up, his back aching, head throbbing, empty beer bottles scattered about him on the floor, triumphantly holding it up in his hand.

He had his piece.

Jennings Vaughan sat on a cement bench in Washington Square Park in the dark, meticulously folding a wax paper that had moments earlier surrounded a hamburger, and dropped it into a waste can next to him. He pulled back the left sleeve of his coat and looked at his Timex: it was ten minutes after ten. He sat back, his newspaper folded in his lap, and gazed impassively at the entrance to the Hotel Ervin across the street.

The park was quiet, dark, sparse with shadowed, idle night traffic—drunks, muggers, junkies, timorous students—the chronic, unnameable human detritus that fills the Village park's days and nights. To Vaughan, all of it was insignificant, remote—hardly there at all—except for the Hotel Ervin. A wino stumbled by and started to size him up as a mark. But the forbidding visage, lit cruelly by the glare of a passing headlight, caused him to recede silently back into the night, muttering.

It had been a good many years since Vaughan had staked anybody out. Hong Kong, probably, in 1965, a mission of vengeance upon an errant Taiwanese opium dealer—they were all Chinese, except for the Americans—who had violated the delicate balance of trade with the Shan tribesmen in the Laotian hills by undercutting an American interest. The execution, in a foul, narrow alley full of cats, had been swift, silent. As for New York, Vaughan would have had to go back to 1946, and a café in Little Italy, not far from where he now sat, with an old *capo* don who controlled most of Harlem, setting up heroin lines for the Old Boys back in Asia via the Hong Kong refineries. He had introduced a game that had permanently altered the face of the city, a game going on this very minute in another section of the park. But such recollections were only distant traces as Vaughan sat, blank and inert, in the Village darkness. Jennings Vaughan in bohemia: it might just as well have been the Venezuelan jungles, the Kurdish highlands, the Mongolian steppes.

Two young black men came swaggering up the path out of the park's shadows. They were big and bad and stoned. In the dimness, they saw an old man in a suit with a silver crewcut and, as they drew closer, a crippled face. To them, he looked simply like prey, easy prey.

"Hey, man. You got any spare change?"

But Vaughan had suddenly become interested in the emergence of a figure from the Hotel Ervin. He was trying to peer between the two dark, muscular bodies and get a better look at the man who stood hesitantly a hundred yards away, with something under his arm, looking eastward up Waverly Place.

"Hey, look at this dude's face," said the one holding a quart of beer in a brown paper bag.

·They moved closer. Vaughan glanced up at them briefly with cold, indifferent gaze. The two men were irritating him; they were in his way.

"Give us your money, old man."

It was a casual, almost friendly request, an invitation to make it easy, as the one who had spoken took out a switchblade and turned it in the faint light.

Vaughan had little doubt now that the figure starting to move eastward along Waverly Place, parallel to the park, was Michael Motta. He stood up.

The black man with the blade shoved him back down on the bench. He brought the switchblade to Vaughan's neck, and held it.

"Cool it, ugly old man. Give me your wallet."

Vaughan looked up, surprised, as if realizing for the first time that the two men were actually presuming to block his way. For a brief instant he acknowledged their existence.

Then the ugly old man with the slumped, frozen half-face made a swift movement with his left arm. It cleared the black man's arm from his throat, sent the switchblade flying through the air to drop, clattering, on the pavement, and straightened the man up. Vaughan stood quite suddenly, at the same time bringing up a blow with the side of his right hand so swift and hard, and at such an angle to the throat, that it crushed the man's windpipe with a sickening *crack*. The man dropped to the ground like a stone, gurgling. Vaughan delivered a trained, accurate kick to the man's jaw with his brown wing-tipped Brooks Brothers right shoe, practically severing the skull from the spine; it made a terrible dull ripping sound.

The other man, watching his friend dying on the pavement, began to back off. "Keep the money, man," he whispered, his eyes and his voice full of terror. "It's okay, man. Be cool."

Vaughan turned away quickly to watch the figure hurrying east along Waverly. Then he turned back to the man with the beer in the brown bag trying to slip away. He reached inside his coat, slid his Walther from its holster, and aimed it at the back of the fleeing figure. It made a spitting sound, like air being let out of a jet, just once. The man's shoulder blades whipped back, almost touching. He dropped to his knees, fifteen feet away. Then he fell forward on his face.

Vaughan put his gun away, picked his newspaper up off the bench, and rushed diagonally across the park, all his attention now on the figure hurrying along the sidewalk opposite.

Vaughan recognized the tall, lean body, the brown hair—though somewhat shorter than in the wedding picture—the shape of the head, the slightly bent shoulders and long legs. He was wearing the same clothes as when Vaughan had picked him up coming off the train at Penn Station: jeans, tennis shoes and a tweed jacket in spite of the heat, suggest-

ing that he might be carrying a weapon. Several manila envelopes were tucked under his left arm, one of them fat with
papers, the others seemingly empty.

At the foot of Fifth Avenue, across from the old arched
entrance to Washington Square, Motta turned and looked
nervously over his shoulder. Vaughan hadn't counted on
Motta suspecting he was being followed; but the way he
looked directly behind him also told him that he had no fa-
miliarity with the movements of a tail.

Motta began to walk north up Fifth Avenue. It was a hot,
dense summer night, and Vaughan had to move fast to keep
up; Motta's legs were longer than his. He considered doing
it here, among the old brownstones, but there were too
many people. And he wanted to get away from the park,
and the two bodies he had left behind.

Vaughan dropped into his professional gait, an idle manner of walking, gaze unfocused, eyes averted from the target, looking down. Only now, as different from years past,
the face betrayed him. As they neared busy Eighth Street,
scarcely a person passed who did not either stare rudely at
him, or pointedly look away, which had the same effect. It
was not the quality of the attention—curiosity, pity, revul-
sion—that bothered him; he was too much the puritan for
that—but rather the fact that he was an object of attention
at all. For Vaughan, whose entire life had functioned
around a cultivated neutrality, to feel so exposed, so visible,
the object of unremitting gaze, was a humiliation of the first
order. Guido Leary, the veteran mercenary, had he been
there to watch the old operative unravel, would have
smiled.

Motta turned left on Eighth Street, then quickly entered a
drugstore. Vaughan waited just shy of the entrance, across
the street. Motta came out moments later, seemingly carrying nothing more than what he had taken in. He continued
west on Eighth, then repeated the same thing in a stationery
store—went in, and came out quickly.

The crowds were thick, boisterous, young and full of color. Vaughan moved among them—a cold, gray, erect, anomalous figure—burning with chagrin, fighting to maintain control.

Motta turned into a busy bookstore with a large glass front. Vaughan stood waiting across the street and down a few feet, his newspaper half open. Searching for Motta through the glass, he suddenly realized what each of the stores Motta had entered had in common.

Each had a sign in the window that said XEROX.

It was less than twelve hours to the meeting at the Sherry. Vaughan was certain now that Motta was carrying something that would endanger him. Tightening with fury, he reached up behind the newspaper and felt the bulge of the cooling Walther PPK/S beneath his coat.

Motta went directly to the checkout counter.

"Where's your Xerox?" he said to the clerk.

"Upstairs," she said, smiling.

She was pretty.

"Does it work?"

"Should."

"Thanks."

In the unaccountably vivid exchange of words, Motta realized he hadn't really spoken to anyone in four days, not since he had left Amanda at the station in Los Angeles.

He walked up a wide, paperback-lined stairway, pushing through a gaggle of students. The second-level balcony was full of tables piled with discount art books. He found the Xerox machine. It said COPIES 15¢. Muttering, Motta went back down the stairs and gave the girl a ten-dollar bill. She handed him a hundred dimes in a roll.

"Put in two dimes," she said. "It'll give you back a nickel each time."

She was so friendly.

Back upstairs, Motta took from the manila envelope the
piece he had typed in the Hotel Ervin, placed the first page
on the glass, and put in two dimes. He pushed the "Copy"
button and watched with relief as it spit out a nickel
change, and made a copy. Finally, he had found a machine
that worked.

Motta repeated the procedure with each sheet until he
had three copies of each of the original fifteen pages. It took
him about twenty minutes. He collated the pages, recopied
a couple that hadn't come out, then stuffed a set of each into
the unmarked envelopes. He fastened the clips, stuck the
four manilas under his arm, and walked back down the
stairs.

He stood for a moment at the entrance, looking out
through the open glass doors. He was utterly helpless in the
streets; if someone wanted to follow him, do him harm, they
were free to do so. His only advantage lay in the fact that
Vaughan's face, if it were Vaughan, was known to him; and
Vaughan might not expect that. He thought of the square
man in Ferret's newspaper clipping. Eddie Malone had said
he still wore a crewcut, though it was gray now. And he had
a tic in the right side of his face that went off sometimes.
How little that was to go on, he thought.

He shot a last lingering glance at the girl behind the
counter. She was smiling at him again. Like an angel.

He stepped back outside into the night streets, looking
quickly left, then right, then left again, searching for dangers whose shapes he had little hope of recognizing. Then
he turned west and walked up Eighth Street, determined to
keep to the busy streets, cursing himself for not knowing the
city better.

At MacDougal he turned left and began to walk the several dark blocks toward the Ervin. At one point he thought
he heard someone behind him. He stopped, and turned, but
there was only a woman walking a pair of poodles.

At the entrance to the Ervin, the same feeling gripped him. He turned slowly around once more and looked up the street.

It was empty.

He knew he should sleep. He had to be up early, and the streets were not safe. But the fetid, roach-ridden little room awaiting him upstairs hardly beckoned. He gazed at the pair of drunks on the stairs he would have to climb over to enter the lobby.

A swirling blue light drew his attention across the street into the park. An ambulance was idling, not far from the corner, on Waverly. Several cops and a small crowd were clustered. He saw two bodies being loaded in.

"Some bad motherfucker did that," he heard a voice say.

Motta turned away and looked up at the dark Hotel Ervin.

He would chance it with the streets for a while.

He walked on down MacDougal further into the Village.

Vaughan moved carefully through the night, paying no more attention to the ambulance and the little drama occurring in the park than if it had been a thousand miles away. That was then; this was now.

He had almost taken Motta in the block approaching the Ervin. But a woman and her poodles had intruded. Now he had one empty block of quiet brownstones until Bleecker, and the busy heart of the Village. Vaughan decided to commit.

He crossed onto Motta's side of the street a short distance behind him. There was nobody else on the sidewalk, and a half block to the intersection. Motta, his manila envelopes under his arm, seemed to be walking more freely, with less purpose, less paranoia than before. Vaughan was twenty feet behind him; he had a clear target.

He reached inside his coat and gripped the pistol's cold

crosshatched handle. It didn't matter now if Motta turned; Vaughan was into his move.

In a single gesture, he whipped out the Walther and pulled the top back to cock it. He stopped, planted his feet, pointed—and fired.

A kind of elation gripped Vaughan as the gun went off—an exultation, a joy. For, simultaneous with the shot, a surge of life burst through his deadened face in the form of a sudden, immensely pleasurable spasm: the return of the tic. Happily, he reached up with his left hand to feel the place where the sensation had returned. And he did it with unabashed vanity; he could have been a young girl discovering the emergence of a breast. The face had hardened again now; but if it happened once, he knew, it could happen again.

Smiling the half-smile available to him, he looked ahead to study his victim.

But Motta, quite alive, was walking undisturbed down the street, nearing the corner. Vaughan watched him merge into the crowded intersection.

The tic had cost him his kill.

Guido Leary would have laughed; Vaughan didn't.

Motta moved through the sweltering, festive late-night Village streets, past Indian shops, cafés, tacky boutiques, record stores and kabob stands, feeling oddly energized, buoyant, wired—relieved of some burden, it would seem, from having written, then copied, the story.

He paused at the entrance to a small basement jazz and folk club. The intense, wailing sound of a saxophone wound up from below, threading the air like some rich incense of the ear. Motta looked at a sandwich-board marquee propped at the entrance. It said:

DEXTER GREEN
TONIGHT ONLY

He went to the window and bought a ticket from a girl. Then he walked to the door, handed his ticket to a bearded man, and went inside.

The ticket taker dropped the ticket into a cardboard box at his feet. Looking back into the street, his attention was drawn to a man with close-cropped silver hair and a paralysis on one side of his face, moving through the crowd.

Now, there's someone, the ticket taker thought instinctively, who just wouldn't dig this music.

But that only deepened his surprise when the man stepped to the window and bought a ticket.

To Motta, it was as if his world had come to a stop. And into this clear, motionless void, music rushed in—the direct transmittal of human truth, the ancient communion, washing before it artifice and death.

Dexter Green was a saxophonist, a black man. He stood on the small stage, tall and upright behind dark glasses, washed by a yellow spotlight he couldn't see: for he was blind. Although his presence erased considerations of age, he must have been nearing sixty. There was a trio: piano, bass, drums. But Dexter Green was the whole show, the clear center, releasing from a tenor, an alto, a flute, a bass clarinet and a variety of native reeds and woodwinds as fervent, as passionate a music as Motta had ever heard.

There in the damp, warm cavern, Motta began to reoccupy himself, race to the center of his own existence. For Dexter Green was washing his soul clean.

A sudden, wordless elation swept through him, carrying away all the pain and the hurt and anxiety. Like a small flame, his own passions—dimmed into cynicism, finally to die with Lisa—flared and came back to life.

He and Lisa: dreaming, up on the mountain, Truth, Beauty. It was still there. It was always there—the wonder, the fragility, the fullness. It was Motta who'd forgotten how to find it.

And he knew, watching and listening to the message of the blind artist only a few feet from him, that the source of light and of vision, and of power, had nothing to do with Marty Karp, or Klaus Heller, or a business that occupied itself with the buying and selling of "culture," where songs fell silent, where tense men in gray rooms talked with dead voices while outside their doors life flowed, full and rich and unchecked. Motta knew he would no longer lend them power, acquiesce by indifference or fear to their empty dreams of wealth. Not while Dexter Green lived to testify.

The band had stopped. Dexter Green was playing alone—unamplified, unassisted by any electronics, even a microphone—weaving a spiraling, gathering, inventive line, moving from instrument to instrument, tapping out the deep code of the race, performing the elemental leap of energy from soul to soul that admits of no adversity, no lies.

And Motta suddenly felt Amanda's perfect message of simplicity and flesh and pleasure—and he knew that he would reach for her in Jamaica. Whether he made it or not seemed a question that belonged to another domain. What mattered was that he was released, free to run for the future.

Dexter Green, tall and joyous and transported, his head thrown back, fingering his reeds, was looking somewhere out where Motta couldn't quite yet see. Rejoined by his band, he rushed to a furious, ecstatic climax.

And neither Dexter Green nor Motta, sitting near the stage, realized the presence of the man at the darkened rear of the room, stonily watching the musician who had once saved his life, and the stranger who now threatened it.

28

Motta entered the Hotel Ervin lobby just after two in the morning. At the window the night clerk, a sallow man with sunken, tubercular cheeks and a Lucky dangling from his lips, slid the key under the bulletproof glass.

Motta, still carrying his manila envelopes, crossed the dank, hollow lobby. The night security guard, a tall young black man with inert, empty eyes, stood, arms folded, next to the cracked, collapsed couch, his pistol snapped into his side holster.

The elevator door was open. Motta entered the putrid cell and pushed the fourth-floor button. After several noisy vacillations, the door began to close. Motta stared up at the walls' inner workings, and waited.

The door was almost shut when a gloved hand appeared suddenly in the space between the wall and the door. It

pushed hard against the rubber bumper that ran the length
of the door's edge.

The door shuddered and began to retract.

Standing there, his face not more than a few feet away
from Motta's own, was Jennings Vaughan.

In the strobe-like register of detail that urgency confers
upon a moment, Motta took him in thoroughly—as he imagined Vaughan did him. He was much older than in the
newspaper clipping. The reputed errant tic had hardened
into a visage much more stony, more chilling, more terrible.
He wore the dark-blue suit, the striped Ivy League tie. He
was shorter than Motta, but thickly built; he looked fit. His
eyes were gray, cold, empty. The smile in the old news clipping was long gone.

And that Cold War crewcut.

Next Motta noticed his right arm. It was jammed into the
pocket of his jacket. He saw the tip of the gun pressing
through the blue suit material, pointed upward, directly at
Motta's heart.

Motta looked beyond him into the lobby. The security
guard was gone.

Vaughan stepped into the elevator. He turned and stood
just to the left of Motta, their shoulders almost touching. He
reached forward and pushed the fourth-floor button.

Together, they watched the door shut. This time, it closed
all the way.

As the elevator began its churning ascent, Motta tried
furiously to absorb the moment's improbable character, inventory its dangers. Vaughan had found him; it was, in a
way, what he had hoped for. But the conditions of the encounter were all to Vaughan's advantage. In the tiny,
cramped elevator, Vaughan's presence at his shoulder was
like a thunder.

Motta began to move his right hand idly toward his hip.
Vaughan might not know he was armed; he had to find out.
His fingers reached the Beretta and slid around the grip.

"Lower your hand," Vaughan mumbled. "Slowly."

He raised his eyes to meet Vaughan's.

"What?" Motta said. He hadn't understood Vaughan's words. It was ridiculous, asking him to repeat them.

"Lower your hand," Vaughan repeated.

Motta lowered his hand.

As the elevator rattled upward, Motta decided Vaughan wouldn't kill him in the elevator. Someone might be there when the door opened. He would kill him in the hallway of the fourth floor as soon as they got off—if it were empty. No: more likely he would do it in his room. Motta thought of going to the wrong room, in the hope that someone would answer the door. But his room number was written in large black greasepaint on the Lucite key handle in his left hand.

The elevator slowed, lurched, settled, stopped.

Slowly, the door began to open. Motta prayed for people in the hallway. Crowds, carnivals of them.

But there was only the long, narrow fourth-floor corridor, the dim sickly light, the filthy green walls, the linoleum floor, the silver pay telephone on the wall at the far end of the hall.

"Walk to your room," Vaughan said.

Motta stepped forward. He felt Vaughan move quickly behind him. The tip of the revolver pressed hard against the small of his back, just above his own weapon.

It was over. He was dead.

Terrible, bleak thoughts swept him as he walked down the hall. He would never see Amanda again. He wouldn't make it to Jamaica's white beaches. He wouldn't see little Jamie wearing his Eagles watch. He would not complete what he had come to New York to do. Vaughan would win. And Heller. And Marty Karp.

They always win.

And the brief ecstasy he had known in the Village club earlier was but a final illumination before death, a dirge, a requiem, a black mass.

And Vaughan: he would take the manila envelopes and destroy them. He would walk into the meeting in the morning, witness the signing of the deal, collect his money and fly off to Singapore.

And sometime in the afternoon a Puerto Rican maid would enter the room with her passkey and find Motta's spine-shattered body sprawled on the Hotel Ervin floor. Motta felt a rush of bitterness. It just wasn't right.

They came to the door. Turning the key in the lock, Motta tried to imagine a final move, a slip, a turn, a way to spin away from the gun in his back, get to his own weapon.

How terrible it is, he thought, to be an amateur in contention with a professional. All one's ideas are rudimentary; the professional has already taken them into account. When the professional is a killer and the amateur the victim, there is an added finality.

He took a step into the darkened room, his coffin. Vaughan followed him inside, and reached behind to close the door.

"Turn on the light," he said. Motta reached to the wall, feeling for the loose switch. His hand grabbed the exposed wiring behind the missing switchplate, and ripped it free.

The bulb exploded, plunging the room into blackness.

In the sudden blinding flash, the shift, Motta felt the gunshot, felt the bullet enter his spine and explode in a flash of agony. The tape recording of his life sped up, rolled past in a spitting howl, then wound tightly shut, like a carpet. He felt his life scramble, dissipate, ebb, dissolve.

He felt himself die.

But it was only the shadow bullet, the shadow image, the holographic imprint of the near-event. For he was on the floor now, rolling in the pitch blackness, reaching for his own gun. In the hiatus of space, the strobe effect, the tracer dislocation provided by the bulb, Motta had spun away. The bullet had gone off. But not into him. It had thudded into the bed's filthy matting, and lodged somewhere in its depths.

They scrambled in the dark, guns drawn, going only by sound. Motta felt a shift in the equation; sound was an element he could work with. He knew about sound. Sound was something he loved.

And Motta knew the room; Vaughan didn't.

Motta was crouched next to the metal bed, on the side away from the bathroom, the Beretta in his right hand, feeling with his left the degree of clearance under the bed. He thought he could sense Vaughan on the other side of the room, against the wall, by the bathroom. But he couldn't be sure. The room was pitch black. No more than six feet separated them.

He knew Vaughan wouldn't shoot until he had found his target. The walls were too thin. A bad bullet would bring a neighbor's attention, and the security guard from below. Should one of them try to open the door to emit light, or escape, it would expose him to a bullet.

A tiny slit of light bled through the ragged crack at the foot of the door to the hall. Not enough to illuminate the room yet. For now there were just the sounds. But it could only be a matter of a minute, or less, before the eyes would adjust.

Then one, or both, would die.

Motta lowered himself to the floor, striving to breathe soundlessly. He thought he sensed Vaughan moving toward him, along the wall away from the bathroom. Then Motta thought he saw the faintest glint of the gun's steel, searching him out, pointing just to his left. In a brief few seconds, as the pupils widened, the light would come.

If he were to do anything, it would have to be now.

Keeping his eyes on the area where he sensed Vaughan to be, he carefully felt for the metal typewriter case from the old rented Smith-Corona. He found it, felt its handle. He picked it up and slowly moved it a few inches in front of his face. He didn't grip it too hard. Then he stretched himself out flat onto his stomach, to present as narrow a target as possible.

He began to edge under the bed to the other side, crawling past the point where he imagined Vaughan to be against the wall opposite, holding the typewriter case in front of his face with his left hand, the Beretta in his right.

He watched the silvery gun's tip, waving, tracking with him, close to target. He saw it settle as it found him. He ducked behind the case.

It went off.

The bullet smashed into the typewriter case, knocking it into Motta's head. It flew from his hand. Motta heard the "thunk" as the bullet ricocheted into the hall door. The typewriter case clattered across the floor.

Motta, stunned, turned over once, rolling free of the bed. Then he jumped up on the bed and fell flat.

The sound of the squeaking springs gave Vaughan his location. Motta saw the pistol's tip, at the foot of the bed, raising up to find him. It stopped, and leveled.

Checkmate.

He held his gun hard down on the back of Vaughan's skull, pressing against the crewcut, bearing in on the cranium, bringing the point home.

"Drop it," Motta whispered.

The blackness was beginning to lift: Motta could just see the shape of Vaughan's body directly below him, on all fours, at the foot of the old metal bed. He looked like an animal.

Keeping the Beretta's tip pressed hard into his skull, Motta reached down and picked Vaughan's Walther up with his other hand. He gripped it and slipped his finger over the trigger. He pushed it, too, hard into Vaughan's head, right above the ear.

"Turn and crawl over to the corner," Motta said. "By the locker. If you raise your hands up off the floor I'll kill you."

As Vaughan turned around, Motta kept the two guns pressed into his head.

Vaughan began to edge slowly away toward the corner. Motta pulled back, staying free of Vaughan's legs. He sat down on the edge of the bed, keeping his pistols trained upon the back of Vaughan's skull.

Vaughan came to the gym locker.

"Turn around."

As Vaughan did, Motta leveled both guns upon his face.

Someone turned on a light in a room a floor above. A faint glow bled through the narrow window well outside. They could see each other's eyes now.

Vaughan, on all fours, was looking coldly up at him out of his ruined face. Motta tried to read fear, the kind of fear he had just gone through. If it was there, he couldn't find it.

"Sit back against the locker. Facing me," Motta said. "If you move to either side I'll shoot you."

Vaughan slowly adjusted himself into a sitting position against the locker with the pornography scrawled all over it. Motta tracked him carefully, pointing the two pistols straight at his face.

Neither moved nor spoke. There was only the thick sound of exhausted breathing as they measured each other across the six feet of floor separating them.

Then Motta whispered, "I found you, Vaughan."

Vaughan's breath caught short at the sound of his name. Motta's right finger tightened around the Beretta's trigger; his left settled over the unfamiliar contours of the Walther. He could feel the pain in his forehead where the typewriter case had struck. Already his arms were growing heavy from the weight of the pistols.

"You knew my name," Vaughan hissed.

Motta nodded. "You're not invisible anymore."

Through the dimness Motta saw Vaughan's shoulders rise and tighten, his eyes cast about the room for some tool of escape; but there was little in the cheap, barren cell to offer him hope. Vaughan's face settled into a twisted, hardened mask of fury. Motta rested his elbows on his thighs to steady his arms, keeping his aim level with Vaughan's forehead.

"So what are you going to do?" Vaughan said through the gloom.

"Kill you," Motta answered.

Vaughan, struggling to master his rage, took in the room another time. There was only the bed, the typewriter, the locker, and the envelopes he knew now must not leave the hotel. His best hope was the amateur sitting across from him on the bed, training the two pistols upon him. Already the Walther in Motta's left hand had dipped away from Vaughan's face: Vaughan considered moving against him.

Then Motta corrected the Walther's aim.

Vaughan settled back against the locker. He saw he needed time. Time was opportunity; he must make more of it.

He looked at Motta, probing for the thing that would turn him into a reasonable man, soften his resolve to kill. For in that instant, Vaughan would take command.

A door opened at the far end of the hall. Now it was Vaughan whose eyes filled with hope. He listened to the desultory voices and footsteps of a drunken couple approaching.

"Make a sound," Motta whispered, "and I'll kill you."

The Walther had a silencer; the Beretta, no. The silencer wouldn't draw the couple's attention if fired. Vaughan prepared to move across the unbroachable six feet of floor the instant Motta turned the slightest attention toward the door.

The couple passed noisily abreast of the room. But Motta held Vaughan firmly in his gaze, both pistols leveled.

Then they were gone, swallowed by the elevator.

Vaughan sat back again to wait.

"You had Lisa Wilde killed," Motta said through the shadows. "Why?"

Vaughan looked at him and said nothing. It struck him

that perhaps he had the superior force of conviction. This Motta was just a broken-down young man; no doubt he had been in love with Lisa Wilde. Vaughan sensed his position strengthening as he sat in the shadows.

"Why?" Motta repeated.

Vaughan could hear the pain in Motta's voice; it was almost a plea. Vaughan wondered if telling him might diffuse Motta's anger, shift the equation. Perhaps that's all he really wanted: an explanation; an answer; a release from the cross he bore. Vaughan, feeling Motta's growing intensity, saw he had little to lose by telling.

"I had no choice," he said.

Motta stiffened.

"I followed her the day she came back from Morocco. She went to Marty Karp's house to see him. While he was in the pool she went to his room. She found papers spelling out the whole arrangement with Lucchessi, to use her publishing as collateral to buy the hit for Candy Snow."

"So she knew," Motta whispered.

Vaughan nodded. "She took the papers. Marty found out. He tried to persuade her not to do anything. But she wouldn't change her mind. She made an appointment to see her lawyers."

"But she never went."

"No. I destroyed the papers before she could go. She thought Marty had stolen them back."

"That's why she wanted to meet with me. To tell me all this."

"Yes."

Vaughan felt new danger, as Motta's anger rose and peaked; quickly, he continued.

"My job was to protect Heller's interests. If she had spoken out, the acquisition would have been jeopardized."

"Did Heller authorize you to have her killed?"

"Not officially. But they didn't fire me when they found

out." He gazed impassively at Motta. "They never do. After all," he said, "it solved their problem."

"But she was innocent," Motta said. "She was not the one who had created the situation."

"That has nothing to do with it."

Vaughan could feel the rush of hatred directed at him. But it was ebbing, losing force in the face of his explanations. He was growing quite certain that Motta would not, could not kill him.

Motta felt the soreness in his hand and the heaviness of the weapons. His eyes, clouded with rage, had begun to drift. Vaughan's icy rationale, his terrible, empty pragmatism, was a narcotic, numbing him, eroding his will.

"It was an operation," Vaughan was saying, "like any other, with an objective. My job was to see that objective was met."

Motta stared wearily at Vaughan, despising him.

"What are you going to do?" Vaughan said coolly. "Nobody will listen to you. You have no proof. You will get none. Killing me won't change anything."

His eyes were shining in the dark with cold amusement.

"You are naive," he said. "You imagine the world as it should be. Not as it is. You, and Dexter Green, and Lisa Wilde."

Vaughan moved—sudden and swift: sagging onto his back, ducking the pistol's line, sliding forward across the floor, extending a coiled, trained foot for Motta's, which had raised off the floor as Vaughan had anticipated, to resist the rush of his own, heel to heel, Vaughan's momentum giving him the superior force, upending Motta, throwing him back on the bed, legs splayed, arms akimbo, broken by surprise.

Motta, through spread legs, saw Vaughan's hideous visage at the foot of the bed, rising, swelling toward him, bearing down. Twisting away to his right, off the bed, twisting to avoid Vaughan's belly leap, feeling Vaughan's steel hand rake agony across his back, falling to the floor, rolling over, all the way over, a holy roll that, in the same motion, carried him back up onto his own feet, he was miraculously facing the bed, his guns leveled once more at Vaughan: a crouched, glowering Vaughan, chest heaving, eyes burning.

And then Motta saw the blood drain from Vaughan's face, the fear enter, silent and pure and final, and possess him.

Motta's fingers had closed over the Beretta's trigger. He brought it up to his face and sighted it levelly at Vaughan's forehead, directly between the mismatched halves of the face. His eyes locked into focus.

Looking down the barrel, he knew he had arrived at the moment he had sought since that afternoon on Mulholland.

Two different philosophies, Lisa had said. *To yourself, you're making life-bringing visions. To them, you're just another digit in the power equation.*

Then she had said: *You could exercise the art of power on your own behalf* . . .

Motta's finger tightened on the trigger.

Vaughan's eyes were wide and frozen, his terror unmasked.

Don't you desire vengeance? Motta had asked Dexter Green.

I wouldn't honor him, Dexter Green had said, *by letting him in my heart. He will die of his own dream. I will live by mine.*

Motta let up on the trigger.

A wave of relief passed through him: He was through it.

Vaughan was huddled on the bed, his face bathed in cold sweat, his lips white, overtaken by terror. And Motta saw now that it was over for Vaughan too; something in him had snapped, forever.

"Take off your clothes," Motta said.

Vaughan stared back at him, empty and confused.

"Take them off. Sitting down."

Motta watched his quivering left hand remove the glove from his right. He took off the coat and the striped tie. Next came the shoulder holster. Then the shirt with the button-down collar. And the wing-tipped shoes. Then the pants.

He laid them in a neat pile on the bed.

He sat, in his socks and underwear, gazing at the floor, still trembling from his look into the eye of death. His skin was pale, gray-hued, silver hairs matting his chest.

"The underwear too," Motta said. "And the socks."

Vaughan took off the socks first, one at a time. As he was slipping out of his shorts, Motta could feel his abject humiliation.

When he was naked, Motta said, "Get down off the bed and crawl into the bathroom."

Vaughan put his feet on the floor on the far side of the bed, dropped to his knees, and crawled to the small bathroom. Motta moved behind him and stood. He could see Vaughan's gray, flaccid testicles swaying as he went.

"Get into the bathtub."

Vaughan climbed over the edge into the cracked, yellowed tub. Then he turned, sat and faced Motta out of the shadows. Motta watched his eyes dart hopelessly around the empty bathroom.

"Run yourself a bath."

As Vaughan did, Motta crouched down in front of the door. He lay the Walther in front of him on the floor where he could reach it quickly. The Beretta he kept trained on Vaughan. With his left hand he grabbed Vaughan's clothes from the bed and began to go through them.

He took out the new passport, the traveler's checks, the plane ticket to Singapore.

"Alexander T. Powers," he called out to Vaughan over the running water. "Off on a one-way business trip to Singapore."

He stuck the papers in his own inside coat pocket.

In Vaughan's pants he found a wallet with nothing in it but several hundred dollar bills. He left it on the floor.

Motta flipped open the Walther handle and took out the

seven-shot clip inside. There were three bullets gone. Wondering who had been the unhappy recipient of the first one, he closed the pistol handle.

The clip had a pair of feeder locks, or prongs, that stuck up at the top, through which the bullets were guided into the gun's chamber. With the butt end of the Walther, holding the clip down with his shoe, he began to hammer the feeder locks shut, trapping the bullets in the magazine. It was soft tin, and bent easily. Vaughan watched him miserably from the bath.

The clip could be bent out again, but that would take time. And Motta wasn't trying to take Vaughan's weapon away. On the contrary. He wanted him armed.

But not now. Not yet.

Motta stood up and walked to the bathroom door.

"Turn off the bath."

Vaughan sat in the tub of steaming water, watching Motta dazedly.

"You had a son once," Motta said. "Your wife killed him, before she killed herself."

He threw the clip in the tub.

"He would have been about my age."

Motta picked up the Walther and threw it in the bath. It made a small *plop* and sank.

He backed away from the bathroom, keeping Vaughan in his sights with the Beretta. Vaughan sat helplessly in the tub. Motta picked up his manila envelopes from the floor where they had fallen. Then he stepped to the door.

"Your son," he said, opening the door, "would have liked her music."

Motta slipped the clip out of the Beretta, then threw the empty pistol at Vaughan. Vaughan reached out to catch it, but it hit the wall and slid into the bathtub.

The door closed; Motta was gone.

Vaughan lurched to his feet and stood, bare and trembling, dripping water, looking for something with which to dry himself. But there was nothing.

No towels, no soap.

Emitting a low moan, he sat back down in the bath and began trying to bend out the Walther clip with his fingers.

It took Motta about fifteen seconds to get down the stairs, another few seconds to walk across the lobby at a walk and hand the key to the desk clerk.

Then he was out on the street, running west on Waverly.

A heady euphoria, the sort that a near brush with death will unleash, overtook him as he ran. Suppressing the urge to shout, to scream, he flew up the street, chuckling wildly, patting the envelopes tucked safely under his arm.

Just before Sixth Avenue he took out Vaughan's false passport, plane ticket and traveler's checks. He tore them up and cast the bits to the wind. Into a brimming trash can he threw the Beretta clips.

A taxi was waiting at Sixth Avenue, door open, facing uptown.

How perfect, Motta thought.

How goddamn perfect.

29

Marty Karp emerged from the bathroom of the Sherry Netherland suite in his underwear, a towel over his shoulders, patting his face with cologne. His small, hard eyes glittered. He was up—way, way up—for the biggest day of his life.

Candy Snow was sitting at the bedroom dressing table in a slip, teasing out her hair. Marty came behind her, bent down and kissed her neck. He reached in and felt her breasts; she turned and smiled up at him.

He walked to the window and looked down. It was a hot summer morning. Central Park's treetops were a thick yellow-green. The hansoms were lined up at the corner. Traffic inched along Fifth Avenue below. Sun glinted off the Plaza Hotel windows across the street.

Marty looked at his watch; it was nine-thirty.

Candy Snow had picked up her dress from the floor by the bed where it had fallen the night before, and was slipping it over her head. Marty watched her take from her purse a plastic vial, fish out a couple of Valium with shaking fingers, and step into the bathroom.

Marty went to the closet and began to dress. First came a silk shirt; then an expensive new dark-blue suit he had bought in Beverly Hills. Finally, he stepped into a pair of brown Gucci loafers.

Candy Snow came back out into the bedroom, grabbed her purse and walked distractedly to the mirror where Marty stood, tying his tie.

"You look nice," she said in a small, timorous voice.

Marty, seeing her in the glass, turned to her. They were about the same height. She was looking at him, trembling and unsure.

"Am I good, Marty?" she whispered.

"You were good, baby," he said.

"No," she said, shaking her head slowly. "I mean . . . am I a good singer?"

Marty looked at her for a moment without expression.

"You're great," he said, deadpanning. "The best."

She smiled sadly, and waited expectantly for a kiss.

But Marty just reached down and patted her on the ass. "Work time, baby," he said. He took her arm and led her, pouting, through the sitting room.

"'Bye, Marty," she whispered at the door, dabbing at her eyes with a Kleenex. She reached forward and kissed him quickly, then took off unsteadily down the hall.

As she left, a team of uniformed hotel attendants emerged from an elevator, swept down the hall and entered the suite. They went to the long oval conference table in the sitting room and began to clean up the remnants of breakfast and set up for the meeting.

Following them in was Jay Kippel, leading three stone-faced young RPM lawyers from Los Angeles carrying briefcases.

"Jay," Marty said, greeting him effusively. "We got everything?"

"All set." He looked at Marty curiously. "Was that Candy? At the elevator?"

"Yeah." Marty winced, and twisted a finger at the side of his head. "Broad's lulu." Then he brightened suddenly, and grinned. "How do I look?"

The little lawyer quickly appraised him. "Never seen you in a suit before," he said.

"Do I look legit?"

Kippel smiled faintly. "Yeah. You look great."

The attendants had cleared the conference table, placed twelve chairs around it, and set it up with pitchers of coffee and water, cups and glasses, ashtrays, yellow notepads and pencils. RPM's lawyers quickly sat down along one side and opened their briefcases. The attendants left.

Kippel stood watching Marty pace the floor hungrily, trying to decide if he was watching cocaine mania, or simply adrenalin—or if indeed it even mattered any more. Kippel was worried, very worried; he would be glad when the day was over.

"I wish Eddie was here," Marty muttered twice.

"It's okay, Marty," Kippel whispered soothingly. "It's okay."

Marty was standing in the middle of the floor looking fixedly at his watch when the knock came.

"It's them, Jay," he said, his eyes filling with panic.

"Relax," Kippel said helplessly to Marty's back; for Marty, running the heel of his hand along the side of his fresh razor trim, had sprung, like a cat, for the door.

He threw it open.

A tall, fair, neatly attired man of about fifty gazed down at Marty's uptilted head out of cold, blue eyes. Five spectral men in dark suits stood behind him in the shadows of the hallway.

"Mr. Karp?" he said in a thick accent, extending his hand. "I am Klaus Heller."

Marty, pumping Klaus Heller's hand vigorously, backed into the room. Heller's lawyers and translators walked across to the conference table, shook hands with their counterparts opposite, and sat down.

Heller introduced himself to Kippel, as did Heller's aide, a pale, bespectacled man with no discernible accent. Then the two Germans walked to the table to put down their brief-cases.

"They've got one more lawyer than we have," Marty, near hysteria, whispered to Kippel.

"Don't worry about it," Kippel muttered back. "The whole thing's just a formality."

"He's slick," Marty whispered. "Very slick." Kippel could feel Marty's defensiveness, his admiration, his fear.

Heller and his aide returned to the center of the room. For a moment, the four of them stood in silence, smiling un-comfortably.

"You have a good room at the Plaza?" Marty asked.

"Oh, yes," Heller answered. "Very nice."

"Good. Good." Marty nodded emphatically.

"I stay there often," Heller said. "We've become so much more active in the American market the last few years. Our film ventures, and our publishing." He smiled pleasantly down at Marty. "And now RPM."

Marty was brimming with tension; like a hot, sizzling wire, Kippel thought uneasily.

"I saw your singer," Heller was saying. "On the television. That Candy Snow girl. She's quite good, isn't she?"

"Number one with a bullet in all three trades," Marty shot back.

Heller looked quizzically at him, then turned and said something to his aide in German.

Marty, realizing he hadn't understood, added, "She's number one. In America. Right now."

"Ah. Very good," Klaus Heller said, nodding. "I must admit I don't follow the pop music . . ."

"What kind of music do you like?" Marty asked amiably, working to make conversation.

Heller, a head taller than Marty, gazed down at him with quiet condescension. "Oh. Well. Sometimes I listen to the . . . opera. Or Mozart."

Kippel, watching the dialogue with growing alarm, decided it was time to get the whole charade started.

"Frankfurt," Marty said suddenly. "Nice place. I was there at the end of the war."

Kippel winced. He saw Heller's eyes harden and narrow—then settle back into cool, blue impassivity. "Gentlemen?" he said quickly, gesturing toward the table.

As the four men walked to the table and took their places —Heller and his aide at one end of the oval, Marty and Kippel at the other—a brisk, almost celebratory air took over. There was every reason to be pleased; the deal was locked in, and it was expected that everyone would make out handsomely. Heller would turn the acquisition into profits; Marty Karp would make his fortune; and Jay Kippel had his own, private reasons to be happy. The fact that the acquisition had come about by murder, as well as a peculiar form of mutual blackmail, Kippel considered to be the best possible guarantee of quick, smooth negotiations.

Marty Karp sat stiffly in his new suit, keyed up, waiting to begin, watching the table like a hawk. Kippel had to be amused; Marty's stock negotiating style was somewhat different: shirt open, feet up on the table in his office at RPM, surrounded by a pleasant ambience of dope and profanity, spraying five- and six-figure numbers around like buckshot. But today—today was legit. And the numbers had a lot more zeroes at the end.

The scenario called for both parties to spend the day going through the motions, ironing out smaller details: questions of accounting procedures; lines of payment; currency

exchanges; warehousing; returns. Kippel would work to keep
it light, level, avoid contention, keep Marty on an even keel.

The big points had already been agreed to. The Heller
Group was buying into RPM, Inc., for $50 million. Owner-
ship would be fifty-fifty. Either had the right to buy the
other out at some future date; but the terms were such that
it would be Heller, not Marty, who would be able to swing
it. And that, indeed, is just what would happen—something
which Kippel, but not Marty, knew. Heller planned, in one
year's time, to squeeze Marty out.

And Jay Kippel would stay on—just as he and Lucchessi
and Martoni had planned—as Vice President, Operations, re-
porting directly to Heller in Frankfurt. He had written the
option into the contract himself. A snug arrangement: Heller
and Vegas—peddling music and drugs.

Later that afternoon the press would come; the official
signing would take place; statements would be released.
There would be champagne, and the new logo would be un-
furled: *RPM Records, a Division of the Heller Group.*

The lawyers faced each other, fingering piles of contracts
and notes. Coffee was poured. Klaus Heller was looking at
the one vacant chair next to his aide.

"Where's Vaughan?" he asked in German. The aide shook
his head. Heller shrugged, and turned to look down the
table.

"Shall we begin?" he said.

Everyone nodded.

"You have the second-quarter figures with you?" Heller
asked Marty.

Marty nodded, with a touch of triumph; he turned to
Kippel, who took a sheaf of computer printouts from the
young lawyer at his arm and handed them down the table to
Klaus Heller. Heller gave them to his aide. The aide looked
quickly at them, then said a few words in German, pointing
out the bottom-line figures to his boss.

"Very nice," Heller said to Marty. He smiled stiffly.

"We shipped six million units of Candy Snow," Marty said, nodding vigorously.

"So I see. And *Lisa Wilde's Greatest Hits* did very well," Heller said.

Why is he saying that? Kippel thought, tightening. *Why is he even mentioning her name?* He looked anxiously at Marty, then back at Heller.

Heller was smiling tightly, with what Kippel could only read as a sadistic twinkle in his pale eyes.

But then the computer figures were folded away; attention turned to the contracts. Kippel felt Marty relax.

"There was a question about aligning our accounting procedures on Far East sales . . ." said one of Heller's lawyers, in a light accent. He had one of the contracts open before him, his notes beside it. "Contract Three, Worldwide, Page 11, Paragraph Four . . ."

Papers shuffled, and everyone turned to the item in question.

Thank God, Kippel thought, *it has begun.*

And so it went, quickly and smoothly, clauses queried, revisions suggested, both sides amiably conceding points, until a little after ten-thirty, when a knock came at the door. The young lawyer next to Kippel rose to answer it.

While the lawyers pored over their contracts, the four principals watched the lawyer cross the carpet, reach the door, open it.

It was a hotel bellboy, bearing two manila envelopes.

The lawyer took them, closed the door and, gazing down at the identical envelopes in his hand, walked back to the table.

One was marked: KLAUS HELLER. URGENT.

The other bore the same message to Marty.

The lawyer soberly handed each his envelope, and sat back down.

"What the fuck is this?" Marty whispered to Kippel. At the

other end of the table, Heller was looking curiously at his package. Marty, seeing Heller hand his copy to his aide to open, aped him; he handed his to Kippel.

One of RPM's lawyers had raised a point about inventory procedures on returns. As papers shuffled and the lawyer began to read quietly from his notes, Kippel opened the manila envelope. At the other end of the table, Heller's aide did the same.

"If we figure acceptable returns, less damaged units," the lawyer was muttering, "based upon the same ninety-day accounting period . . ."

But the words were lost on Kippel. Marty, sensing something was wrong, turned to him. Kippel had paled. Marty quickly looked over his shoulder.

It was Marty's turn to blanch. His eyes widened with terror.

"Motta," he whispered.

Kippel looked fearfully into Marty's eyes and nodded.

"How much?"

"Everything, Marty," Kippel whispered, sickening. "He found out everything."

Marty's hands began to tremble; sweat flooded his forehead.

Kippel glanced up the table. Heller's aide was desperately trying to get his boss's attention.

The RPM lawyer, sensing something was occurring, stopped speaking; the room lapsed into a terrible silence.

Klaus Heller's face began to redden as his aide whispered to him. He grabbed the document and perused it quickly.

Marty had grabbed Kippel's arm. He was staring at him in terror, shaking his head. "How?" he whispered. "How did he find out?"

Kippel's eyes wavered; he looked back down at the document. Finally, he said it: "Eddie."

Marty turned to stone. "Eddie," he whispered. He put his hand to his face. "Eddie," he said again. "My best fuckin' friend." He looked at Kippel, panicked. "We gotta get out of here, Jay."

"You crazy?"

An angry Klaus Heller was staring down the table at Marty Karp. "Who is this Michael Motta?" he asked, his voice trembling.

"Guy who worked for us," Marty replied woodenly, swallowing.

"He saw the . . . accident," Kippel added.

Heller glared at Marty. He hit the pages in his hand with his knuckles. "Why did he write this?"

Marty stared helplessly back at him.

"Where is this Motta?" Heller said, swelling with rage.

Kippel had just finished reading the whole article. He was ashen. He looked up.

"He says he's releasing it to the papers."

"*Which* papers?" Marty and Heller asked in unison.

"He doesn't say," he replied weakly.

"This will ruin us," Heller said, choking with fury.

"*You?* What about *us?*" Marty retorted.

Up to this point, nothing had been said which would reveal the content of the problem to the lawyers; they merely sat, looking at their hands, in fear and confusion. But now, as the full meaning of what was in the article spread among the four men, like some terrible dark tide, the last remains of civility began to crumble.

"Where the hell is Vaughan?" Heller spat out in German to his aide. "He was supposed to have handled anything like this."

But the aide just shook his head.

Marty, hearing Vaughan's name, shouted out angrily, "Vaughan! That's the guy. The killer. You hired him. You turned him loose. He put out the contract on my best singer!"

"Eddie too," Kippel whispered miserably to Marty.

"*Eddie?*" Marty said incredulously. He turned and gazed

furiously down the table at Heller. "He had Eddie offed?"

"It is all because you got involved with your American criminals!" Heller shouted back. "You brought this on yourself!"

Marty jumped up. "How I finance my company is my own fuckin' business!" he screamed. "I did nothing wrong. I made an arrangement that is made all the time in my business. I am delivering my company in good shape." He pointed at the computer readouts on the table. "*That's* all you should care about."

"You lied to us about your financial condition!" Heller yelled, rising to his feet.

Marty began to wave his fists. "What do you know about my business? What do you know about music? Dope! *That's* what you know about! *That's* your business!"

Kippel, cowering beneath Marty's hysterical eruption, ducking his flailing arms, felt like weeping. He knew now that it was all over, all of it—finished, ruined.

"Motherfucker!" Marty yelled at Heller.

"Swine!"

"Nazi!"

"Jew!" Heller screamed, hurling the epithet at Marty, banging his fist on the table.

The lawyers, pinned hopelessly in the crossfire, sweated and squirmed, praying for deliverance from the terrible turn of events.

"So where is he? Where's your killer?" Marty shouted.

Heller, livid, clenched his fists and turned to gaze where Marty was pointing—at the empty chair where Jennings Vaughan was supposed to be.

The unraveling: it was just like Guido Leary had said—as inevitable, as orderly as the decay of an unstable element; irreversible once it started; speeding up with a pure Newtonian velocity; the inadmissible burden of consequence, cleaving the spirit, opening a breach as wide as the universe, as deep as time, into which the world, in reverse, simply poured, down a black hole; a condition of infinite culpability —beyond blame, shame, or regret.

Jennings Vaughan stood in front of the Sherry Netherland Hotel, sleepless and mussed and haggard, his face as crumpled as his suit, blinking in the sunlight—no longer aware of the stares of the crowd that a day earlier had raised in him a rage; the rigid, erect bearing, once breasted against the elements, collapsed into a haunted slouch; the laser mind and steel warrior hand a mad, harrowing mix of disordered stimuli. He was simply another piece of the street's nameless flotsam now, unheard messages playing electrically across his thin, dry lips, the world outside him a cracked mirror.

Vaughan would have been hard put to describe how he had gotten from the Hotel Ervin to where he now stood; how, sitting in the bath, it had taken him an hour to bend out the Walther's feeder clip; how he had stood firing naked into the bedroom mattress to test the clip, wasting a bullet, leaving three remaining; how he had put his rumpled suit back on over the holster and stumbled down through the hotel and out into the night; how he had stalked the Village streets and alleys, in the hope Motta was still downtown somewhere; how a pair of cops had found him on Waverly, picking up bits of paper off the sidewalk, seemingly trying to put them back together, and had taken him for another demented, face-ravaged bum, not worth running in.

Vaughan had spent the dawn hours trying to form coherent words into a telephone in a booth; for his face had slumped another degree, and his mind seemed to be disintegrating. The forger had said it would take two days to make up new papers, a new passport. Vaughan had agreed, though he had no way of paying without the money from Heller—which meant he must go to the meeting.

But the envelopes: *What was in them? Where were they? What damage had they done?*

"The creature from the black lagoon," the cabbie had

whispered into his phone to the dispatcher, rushing uptown, relieved to deposit the grotesque stranger in front of the Sherry at ten minutes to eleven.

Vaughan's eyes ran up the ornate hotel facade to the spired tip twenty-nine stories above, split by the sun. He was afraid to go in; and he was afraid not to. He was deeply, deeply afraid.

Then the revolving door spun him into the lobby, the gilt walls and red carpet sucked him forward and hurled him toward the middle elevator, which opened to admit him.

On the way up he thought about different things: Singapore, and how Guido's native doctors would fix his face; the good days, the opium days back in the Burmese hills; his wife's corpse in the New Haven morgue; shrapnel; napalm; burning huts; and the enemies, the endless, inexhaustible parade of enemies down through the years. *It's a new age down there*, Guido had said. *Wide open. Just like the old days. I need an advisor.*

He lurched down the ninth-floor hall to the door, and knocked. Someone let him in; the door closed behind him. *All the broads you want.*

In an instant, he saw them coming toward him: two flushed, raging men in dark suits, eyes burning with menace. *The Good and the True . . .*

Three rounds left in the clip . . .

As Vaughan reached inside his jacket, some sort of light exploded in his head. And as the Walther came out he felt his face come alive—and form into a smile.

Once.

And then again.

And then for the last time ever.

30

Michael Motta sat with Tim Duggan in the darkened rear of
the mirrored Sherry Netherland bar, where breakfast is
served before the bar opens. It was eleven o'clock. Their
table faced the glass door leading into the lobby hallway.

"So that was the rogue's gallery," Duggan said mischie-
vously. "The big Aryan with the stoolies in tow. And
Vaughan. With the crewcut and the Frankenstein face.
What a heavy."

Motta nodded.

"It's all over, Michael," Duggan said, shaking his head.
"The nail is in the coffin."

"So you'll print it?" Motta said.

Duggan held up his manila envelope. "If I have to typeset
it myself."

Motta looked at him and smiled. "You crossed over, Tim,"
he said.

"I did, didn't I?" Duggan said quietly. He looked around the room. "I wish the bar was open. We could do this up righteous."

They toasted coffee cups.

"To swift justice," Duggan said.

The waiter came with the check. Motta reached for his wallet, but Duggan stayed his hand.

"On *The Rock*," he said.

Motta stood up. They shook hands.

"Thanks for bed and breakfast," Motta said.

Duggan laughed. "It was a cheap tradeoff."

As Motta walked out of the Sherry bar and onto the sunlit street he heard a couple of sirens approaching. A cop car and an ambulance pulled up in front of the Sherry.

But Motta kept on walking. He was going the other way.

Coda

Baby baby we've got a date
Come on baby now don't be late . . .

BOB MARLEY AND THE WAILERS

31

Malcolm Dickens stood in his robe at the window, peering out through the plastic curtains at the boats bobbing in Avalon Harbor. He usually slept until noon. But this morning something had stirred him quite abruptly out of sleep.

Now, as he watched beads of sunlight dance off the surface of the sea, a tremulous smile began to creep across his face. It was entirely unexpected, and he had no clue to its source. But there it was: a little rivulet of a grin, widening into a smile, now breaking into a torrent of chuckles, to spread finally into a big oceanic laugh—until a sudden cough sent him rummaging in the pocket of his robe for his throat spray.

But the satisfaction, nameless and inexplicable, lingered like a sweet perfume—and would for days to come.

"I'll be goddamned," Dickens muttered with happy surprise. Then, shaking his head, he shuffled off to the can to take a very welcome and magnanimous morning pee.

32

Monk Purcell sat hunched over the wheel of his van, driving east across the steaming desert. His wife sat next to him. In back were his unfinished paintings, and their belongings. A golden retriever, its tongue lolling out, snoozed at his shoulder.

"Any regrets?" his wife said, looking over at him.

"About leaving RPM?"

She nodded. "You going to miss having all that media at your fingertips?"

Ahead, the early-evening sky spread before him, suffused with an unearthly desert glow.

Monk Purcell turned to her and smiled. "No," he said.

"We be in Taos soon?"

"Soon," he said quietly.

33

By all rights, it was a moment—in RPM's fairly brief annals—to be relished.

Joe Ruffino, Marketing, was sitting on one side of the conference table in his toupee and his gold jewelry, a party hat on, stone drunk. Darrell Johns, Sales—that thin-lipped, corn-fed, bone-dry Puritan—sat across from him in his plaid Sears wash-and-wear jacket, fast approaching Ruffino's sotted state of slobbery. Unable to wait until the grand moment, they had consumed the first of the three bottles of chilled Moët sitting in buckets on the conference table. Adding to the festive air were the hefty second-quarter bonus checks each had just removed from envelopes and now held up to the ceiling light with flushed rapture.

"Sight for sore eyes," Darrell Johns said unsteadily.

"Fuckin' right," Ruffino agreed. "We busted balls for this."

The frizzy, titted blonde who always attended to the

Monday morning Product Meetings—including today's gutted facsimile—was busy setting up a small black conference phone speaker at the head of the table, where Marty usually sat, for the big call from New York, due in momentarily. Behind her was the green blackboard, empty today, and a turntable, spinning silently with nothing on it.

And then there was the cake: a square, gooey job with green-and-pink icing that said: RPM/MULTIGRAM RECORDS. A DIVISION OF THE HELLER GROUP. And below it, the new logo: a disc, bent into the shape of a globe of planet Earth, with the hole in the center poised—if one looked closely—somewhere over Germany.

"Where the hell is everybody?" slurred Ruffino, looking around the empty room.

"Motta's on leave," Darrell Johns said, still staring at his bonus check. "Or gone. Nobody seems to know. Monk Purcell quit. And Len Woolf, he retired."

"See?" Ruffino said knowingly. "Your classic losers. Those guys left just when it was about to happen. They could've caught the brass ring. Like you and me."

Darrell Johns nodded blearily at Ruffino's profundity.

"Hey," said Ruffino. "Where's Tiny Braun?"

As if in answer, the frizzy blonde, drunk herself by now, weaved to the door and opened it. And into the room swept fat, bearded, earringed Al "Tiny" Braun, Promotion—in full Nazi drag.

Boots, riding crop, the whole shot.

At the sight of him, Ruffino and Darrel Johns's mouths dropped open like a pair of falling bricks.

"*Sieg Heil!*" Tiny Braun bellowed. The costume was much too small for him, and clumps of hairy gut bled between the buttons of his sweatstained shirt.

But when he began goosestepping around the table, crying "*Eins, zwei, drei, vier . . . ,*" it sent Ruffino and Darrell Johns into hysterical howls.

Tears came to Joe Ruffino's eyes. "Oh, fuck. I can't stand

it," he moaned, grabbing his gut and doubling over with pained laughter. "That's even better than the bear outfit he wore to WBKR in Detroit in seventy-seven."

The blonde, caught up in the general madness, ran back to the turntable and put on the single of Candy Snow's "So Hot, So High." At the pulsing sounds of the song that had sweetened all their lives with bonuses, a true mania swept the room, and Joe Ruffino and Darrell Johns came up out of their seats.

The three of them—Ruffino, Johns and the blonde—funny hats and all, fell into a bunny-hop line behind Tiny Braun in his Nazi outfit, and began goosestepping around the conference table.

Old goateed Len Woolf, recently retired Vice President, A&R, had he been there at that moment, might well have been inspired to hasten his already imminent demise.

After four times around the table, the record went into its fade, and Tiny Braun, pouring sweat, slumped down in a chair. Ruffino and the blonde followed suit.

But Darrell Johns just stood in front of the blackboard, possessed by uncontrollable laughter—something which left the others somewhat dumbstruck, for nobody had ever seen RPM's Vice President of Sales laugh before.

The surprise mounted as Darrell Johns suddenly reached forward, picked up a fresh bottle of champagne from a bucket, and popped the cork. Then, giggling hysterically, he sprayed everyone in the room.

Ruffino's response to the dousing was to dig his fingers into the big cake, gouge out a piece, and rub it slowly into Tiny Braun's florid, bearded face.

Tiny Braun, not to be outdone, grabbed a fistful of cake himself and did something he'd been wanting to do all year: he rubbed it all over the blonde's big, bra-less, bouncing breasts.

She giggled, she shook as she tried to fend off Tiny Braun's hammy, insistent hands. And only the sudden ringing of the phone in the outer office on the private line—signaling the call from New York—rescued her. She quickly fled the room.

The remaining three sat, covered in champagne and cake, chests heaving, staring expectantly at the hissing, crackling little black box in front of them on the table.

"This is it," Ruffino whispered, leaning forward.

"Marty? Marty? Is that you?" Al Braun called out, taking off his Nazi hat. "Hullo? Marty?"

"Marty?" tried Darrell Johns, Sales. "Marty?"

Then Al Braun, Promotion, turned and looked perplexedly at the other two.

The speaker had gone dead.

Joe Ruffino, Marketing, was the first to turn and see the disheveled blonde in the doorway, eyes wide with horror, hand over her mouth, the message clutched in her trembling hand.

34

Ferret was standing over his table in the back of the Windward Café, piling the last of his papers into a cardboard box, when the man came in with the telegram.

Ferret took it and opened it quickly. He held it up to the white beachfront light pouring in through the window.

Then the girl behind the counter saw him break into an expression so sweet, so angelic that it reminded her of the little postcards of the baby Jesus her mother sold on the streets of Mazatlán.

Exultant, Ferret rushed back to his table and grabbed a couple of cardboard boxes under his arms.

"*Donde va?*" said the girl behind the counter, alarmed.

"Mexico," he said happily, smiling at her. "Finish my book. I'm done here." He stopped, looked at her and cocked his head to one side.

"Hey," he said suddenly. "Want to get married?"

She didn't understand.

He put his two forefingers together.

"You. Me. *Esposa.*"

She blushed, and broke into a shy smile.

"*Por qué no?*"

"Precisely," Ferret said, his eyes shining with a luminous intensity. "*Por qué no?*"

35

Two monks were sitting in the rectory dining hall, eating their rice and seaweed and drinking iced *cha*, green tea. They looked up as old Klaus Heller, the one they called Gaijin-san, came in and sat down. He looked tired, drawn, disturbed.

"His meditation doesn't go well," whispered the first monk to the other.

"He had an interview with the roshi this morning," the second replied under his breath.

"He made a nice donation to the temple," the first muttered.

"Money can get you an interview with the roshi," the second one said. "But it can't buy your way into heaven."

The two monks giggled behind their hands.

36

Amanda shielded her eyes with her hand as she watched the silver plane drop from the sky and circle into its descent. It swept onto the Kingston runway and braked to a stop.

She stood worriedly at the passenger terminal entrance in a brightly colored sun dress. She kept her eyes on the cabin door as it opened and the passengers began to pour down the ladder.

Then she broke into a smile as wide as the sky.

DISCARD

W24
ADD2009
LC2013
#C10

9-18-81

F   Cohan, Tony
        Canary